THIS IS MY FAITH

This Is My Faith

The Convictions of Representative Americans Today

EDITED BY

STEWART G. COLE

HARPER & BROTHERS   NEW YORK

Library of Congress catalog card number: 55-11403

CONTENTS

v

25,768

PREFACE

Suppose you were asked to state the fundamental convictions that support your life, which you may think of as the basis of your religious faith. What would you say? You might answer in one of the more or less conventional patterns of religious belief. But if you were a thoughtful person, it is unlikely that you would have a quick reply.

Most of us are cautious in answering such a question. We may hedge because we are unwilling to reveal the gist of our faith, believing that it serves best when nurtured in private. Or we may keep silent because we are uncertain where we stand on the deepest issues of the human adventure. Intellectual confusion and skepticism have caught many of us short-visioned. Others have never given the subject persistent thought. They have assumed that it remains a problem for the sophisticate. Yet every person has the right and the responsibility to make up his mind for himself about the meaning and purpose of human life.

The individuals whose essays appear in the volume have recorded the foundations of their faith. Theirs has been a dedicated service. They were no doubt prompted by mingled feelings in committing themselves to this assignment. Probably each of them accepted the invitation believing that he should share such light as he has with those who, like himself, belong to a bewildered generation.

The exchange of ideas and heart-searchings in an extensive correspondence with the essayists has been an enriching experience for me. My warm appreciation goes to these men on my own behalf as well as for the readers who will find challenge in their essays.

The contributors join me in the hope that clarifying their own convictions will encourage others to do likewise. Those who attempt it will also find the effort rewarding. Within themselves they will discover, beyond the glamor of our material accomplishments and beneath the veneer of our traditional confessions of creed, a profound yearning for the truth that set man free. They will also realize that, rather than arresting the process, bringing their deepest convictions to the surface and comparing them with others will strengthen their faith, and thus aid the cause of the good, full life to which every individual has an important contribution to make.

I record my thanks to Mildred Wiese Cole for her unfailing loyalty and help in the preparation of this book, and to Ann Shalmony for her painstaking secretarial work.

STEWART G. COLE

I

A SEARCH FOR

RELIGIOUS CONVICTIONS

A SEARCH FOR

RELIGIOUS CONVICTIONS

A<small>N INESCAPABLE</small> question haunts every thinking person today: Where can man turn to discover those spiritual values which social experience has shown do contribute to human well-being? Such a challenge prompted the present inquiry. In these pages the reader will find the personal viewpoints and convictions of twenty-five representative men in contemporary life.

This is essentially a religious inquiry, a quest for profound values to sustain human beings in adverse times. The dedication and the method of the search may be more significant than the convictions concerning spiritual values that result as a consequence of the search.

The frontiers of a living faith always remain mobile. They move as people refocus their understanding of the world they live in and as the individual rediscovers his sense of the fundamental meaning and purpose of human life. For those of us who inherited Western civilization, these frontiers have shifted several times. They were reconstructed (1) at the Hebraic-Roman meeting of cultures in the Eastern Mediterranean world as a result of the quality of human living that Jesus of Nazareth introduced; (2) during the challenge of Greek thought upon the early Christian ethos; (3) when the Church of Rome emerged as the formative force in Western society; (4) as a consequence of the impact of the awakening spirit of human freedom and self-initiative upon the peoples of England and the Continent, and later upon America; and (5) by reason of the influence of scientific thinking upon modern man's ideas of the self, society, and the cosmos.

We are living in the latest of this succession of revolutionary epochs. The names of Gandhi, Marx, Freud, and Einstein symbolize profound changes occurring in the orientation of human life, thought, and values. Likewise, the discovery of thermonuclear energy, the intermingling of peoples on a global scale, the awakening of world-mindedness, and the projection of United Nations' activities for the mutual benefit of all peoples in "one world," are affecting the meaning of life for mankind.

Thoughtful persons are reformulating their religious values. Many of the milestones of faith by which our forebears charted their course are now doubtfully adequate. Traditional orthodoxies, political, economic, social, and religious, are too rigid to explain the complexity of conditions and to provide a meaningful rationale for living in a world in ferment. Novel issues stir the mind and heart of every thinking person. To resolve his quandaries, shall man choose the rugged ways of war or of peace? of naked power or of social responsibility? of despair or of hope? of mammon or of God? Whence can he command the wisdom to determine essential next steps? Has he the will, the patience, the insight to take one step at a time in the painstaking process of rebuilding the structure of "peace on earth, goodwill among men" on the foundations of a new world civilization?

The individual and society alike are currently involved in what Thoreau characterized as an age of "quiet desperation." At the turn of the twentieth century most Western people still clung to an optimistic faith: they affirmed the principle of inevitable progress. This was the best of all possible worlds. Today not a few of our generation are inclined to accept Spengler's thesis of inescapable collapse. For them the horizons of human society have darkened. Blind change is in the saddle. The end is a doomed world.

Many people regard the social confusion of the times as too profound for individual understanding. They hold tenaciously to a convenient tradition for protective purposes. Some turn to their government to ease them through trying times, however long the strain may continue; others believe the church holds the key to a redemptive kingdom and makes it available to those who conform to its rules; still others put their faith in science as the new messiah, and therefore yield their confidence to it to pave the way ahead. In all of these people, faith centers in strengthening the power of the state, the church, or modern science to redeem both the individual and society.

Such persons resort to borrowed capital to meet the current crisis. They grasp for a formula that one tradition or another has hallowed. It may signalize an enshrined constitution, creed, or some other symbol of security. It may be a firm answer to life's enigma that a favorite prophet, poet, or sage has wrested from the proving grounds at his crossroads of life. In any case these people take their values by proxy, turning to some readymade support to steady their course.

An increasing number of persons cannot accept any of these measures. They question the idea that a set of uncriticized inherited values is adequate to sustain individuals in process of becoming mature and responsible human beings. Furthermore, they doubt the validity of every axiom of the good life that is presented as an authoritarian key to human redemption. They believe that man *as man* must "work out his own salvation" in terms of the moral and spiritual capital which becomes available to him in the course of his own essential quest. If, by choice, he embraces certain traditional values, he makes them his own by a process of testing and rediscovery in meeting the contemporary issues that arise in the stress and strain of living. Thus he arrives at them on his own initiative by fulfilling the conditions that make them purposeful and meaningful.

Whatever values a mature man is discovering, he finds it necessary to conceive them in a relatively new frame of reference. He is reworking his philosophy of life, changing his social and cosmic worldview, and redefining his own role in relation to ultimate reality. The concepts of human personality and mankind are emerging in a clearer perspective. They are being interpreted in the light of the better understanding of the universe, which embraces personality and mankind, affording them high purpose and promise.

The implications of the problems arising in the current world situation have been challenging the editor of this anthology for many years. An opportunity to secure significant comment on them came when the Conference on Science, Philosophy and Religion in Relation to the Democratic Way of Life announced its 1952 theme, "Foundations for World Organization: A Political and Cultural Appraisal." On invitation, a paper was prepared for the occasion dealing with

the subject, "The World Faith of a Secularist."[1] A broad orientation
of the central issue being raised in these introductory pages was
set forth in that paper and some pivotal questions were highlighted.
The paper became the springboard for this book. Its substance is
condensed in the following paragraphs.

There are two broad trends in man's search for a faith to sustain himself
in our times. One stresses the viewpoint of organized religion. The church,
of whatsoever faith or sect, presents a familiar position. Its testimony
rests upon allegedly supernatural truths which God has revealed to man
and made available for his salvation. Man embraces the values inherent
in this redemption through the ministry of the divinely appointed church.

   The other search for spiritual reality springs from sources beyond the
range of organized religion. They have been called "secular" in character, and include the potent values of secular idealism. Not a few serious-
minded persons are attempting to untangle the discordant skeins of life
and are discovering nourishment of mind and heart by recourse to (1)
the values intrinsic to the democratic way of living, (2) the inspiration
afforded by science for the improvement of the human lot, and (3) personal satisfactions resulting from the pursuit of the good, the true, and
the beautiful. From this point of view a person achieves life's meaning
and purpose as he dedicates himself to the unfinished tasks facing mankind. He is convinced that spiritual reality undergirds him as he meets the
conditions of such commitments.

   These two quests for basic values, the church-centered and the secular-
oriented, are competitive in America. Advocates of the one tend to dis-
count the fitness of the other. As a consequence the conflict is splitting
the loyalty of many persons and bifurcating the value-structure of our
culture. Rather than endeavoring to accommodate both of these approaches to the good life, thus affording the individual and society access
to a more inclusive value system, spokesmen for each viewpoint tend to
remain adamant, pleading the sufficiency of their own particular cause.
Church leaders freely attack secularism as though it were an abortive
movement attempting to wean individuals away from primary spiritual
moorings, whereas secularists charge that the church is resorting to

[1] Lyman Bryson, Louis Finkelstein, Harold D. Lasswell and R. M. MacIver,
Eds., *Foundations of World Organization: A Political and Cultural Appraisal*
(New York: Harper & Brothers, 1952), Chap. XXXVIII. The title of the
paper was later rephrased for its current use and called, "Man's Quest for
Spiritual Reality."

authoritarian claims to defend its assumed priority in matters pertaining to the things of the spirit.

The hour has arrived in this impasse when Americans can no longer persevere in such callous half-truths without doing irreparable harm to the fountainheads of their historic faith. They need to soberly equate all the resources available to the inner life of man, including the finest values of both the Judaeo-Christian tradition and secular idealism, if they are to counter the devastating conditions of inhumanity that threaten our people no less than the rest of the world. Otherwise, they will barter away their birthright of religious *and* secular values.

The comments that were made with respect to this paper during the Conference, and later in correspondence, indicated the vitality of the theme and the need for further development of it. In 1954 a letter was addressed to a number of important persons, of which the following excerpts are pertinent:

In view of the confusion in our thinking about the validity of any dependable source of moral and spiritual values, I am undertaking an inquiry into the religious foundations of faith of representative leaders in contemporary life.[2]

The purposes of this study are:

a. to provide a challenge for re-thinking the foundations of human purpose and values in the mid-twentieth century;

b. to assess the impacts of the Judaeo-Christian religions, the worldview of modern science, and the value-structure of democracy, upon man in his search for a valid faith; and

c. to publish a symposium setting forth the viewpoints of these recognized and dedicated men and women.

The response I received to a paper in a symposium on "Foundations of World Organization" presented at the Conference on Science, Philosophy and Religion in Relation to the Democratic Way of Life, stimulated me to undertake the inquiry. Attached you will find a reprint of this

[2] Included in the list were individuals from the fields of the physical and social sciences, the humanities, public affairs, psychology, and philosophy, as well as leaders in the Protestant, Catholic, and Jewish faiths. Each in his own way and from his own viewpoint was invited to present his testimony to a living faith.

The editor regrets that he was unsuccessful in his efforts to secure the cooperation of representative women as well as of the clergy of the three historic faiths of Western civilization. He made an extended endeavor to have a sampling of their viewpoints included in this study.

article with editorial abbreviations.[3] Using this paper as a springboard, would you be willing to contribute your personal testimony in terms of the five questions that are appended?

The questions were:

• 1. In *the Judaeo-Christian religions,* stripped of their divergent ethnic, doctrinal, and structural factors, what religious values, *as you use the term religion,* do you think should be emphasized in contemporary thought and practice?

• 2. In the light of *the worldview that modern science is unfolding,* what grounds have you for religious convictions about cosmic reality? Do you think that it cares for man's well-being? If you think that it does, how do you reconcile your convictions with such evidence as Nature's apparent indifference to the highest interests of man and its occasional destructive treatment of him?

• 3. Are the human values expressing *the genius of the democratic movement and of personal moral character* intrinsic elements of your religious faith? If not, what relative place do you accord them in religion? If so, are they the sole grounds of your religious faith? And, if so, why?

• 4. Do you assume that *the supreme values available to moral man, of whatsoever source,* are aspects of *one* spiritual reality? If so, how do you relate in your faith the survival values of the Judaeo-Christian religions (question one), the dynamic values inherent in the activity of the cosmos (question two), and the creative values emerging in man's struggle to build a society of free men (question three)? If not, how do you relate these various value-structures in your conception of spiritual reality?

• 5. Does *the concept "God"* serve an essential purpose in your rationale of religion? If so, what is the particular content of your inference when you use this concept? If not, what is your source for knowledge and guidance with respect to the highest type of human life?

A second letter addressed to those who accepted the invitation to share in this study helped further to structure the pattern of the inquiry. It read:

It may add to the clarity of the procedure in the preparation of the essays and to the strength of the finished anthology if I share with you some of the results of my recent conferences with a number of the contributors. We should bear in mind that:

[3] A resume appears above.

1. The inquiry is conceived in terms of these questions to provide the reader of the book with a close parallel in structure of materials, so that he can more easily recognize the elements of similarity and difference in the various contributions. Some of you may, by virtue of your special interest, give more consideration to one question than to another, although it is hoped that each of you will treat all five of the related subjects.

2. The five questions are predicated on the assumption that the three major forces contributing to the making of Western civilization, and more particularly to American culture, are the Judaeo-Christian tradition, the field and worldview of science, and the democratic movement. For this reason questions 1, 2, and 3 in the inquiry deal with them respectively. Question 4 raises the issue as to the possibility of an integration of human values; and question 5 is in the nature of a footnote to the others, though by no means unimportant.

3. Countless men and women, in search of guidance with respect to the basic values of human life and a sense of direction in these confused times, need the kind of stimulation that mature and dedicated leaders can offer them. They will respond more to your frank and personal convictions, distilled out of a lifetime of disciplined commitment to the challenges of the modern world, than to abstract essays interpreting the theme. I hope that you will write, therefore, what is deepest in your mind and heart concerning your own personal faith.

The men whose essays appear in these pages have met the challenge with candor and forthrightness. They wrote under difficulty in an endeavor to keep their essays within the prescribed limitations of space. For this reason one could charge most of them with expressing views here and there that sound dogmatic, when opportunity for further clarification of the theme would have made their positions appear less arbitrary. This problem was inescapable. The reader will bear in mind the handicap under which the contributors labored. The authors appear in alphabetical order.

S. G. C.

II

THE PERSONAL FAITH

OF TWENTY-FIVE

REPRESENTATIVE AMERICANS

Each of the following essays is subdivided into sections I, II, III, IV, and V, with the exception of four essays. They are those of Albert Einstein, Philipp G. Frank, Hudson Hoagland, and Robert Ulich, each of whom chose his own method of presenting his views. The first method of subdivision was selected to suggest the juncture at which the writer shifts from one topic to the next in meeting the five questions as they were submitted to him and served to structure this inquiry. The reader will want to refer frequently to the questions, which are listed on page 8, in order to recapture the implications of the particular subject under discussion and to follow step by step the development of the essayist's viewpoint.

The reader may note that Adolph Keller is of Swiss nationality. However, he is as much at home in America as he is in Europe, has been for decades a friendly interpreter of one continent to the other, and is at present living in this country.

WILLIAM CLAYTON BOWER

For a generation William Clayton Bower has taken a leading role in rethinking the concepts of religion and education and relating them in a philosophy of religious education. Educated at Tri-State College, Butler College, and Columbia University, ordained to the Ministry, Disciples of Christ, in 1923, he served in pastorates in Indiana, New York and California. He taught religious education for thirteen years at Transylvania College and the College of the Bible at Lexington, Kentucky, and for seventeen years at the University of Chicago. Dr. Bower has been a member of the Educational Commission and Executive Committee of the International Council of Religious Education, the White House Conference on Children in a Democracy, the American Association for the Advancement of Science, and the Religious Education Association. His books include The Curriculum of Religious Education *(1925);* Character through Creative Experience *(1931);* Church and State in Education *(1944); and* Moral and Spiritual Values in Education *(1952).*

I

VIEWED in their historical development, in my judgment the Judaeo-Christian religions contribute six fundamental religious values to contemporary thought and practice.

1. A profound sense of human brotherhood. Though in its primitive form this concept was based upon the blood kinship of the clan, including Jahweh as an integral member, through the interaction of the ancient Hebrews with other races and cultures the concept of brotherhood evolved into a conception of the oneness of mankind that transcended race, nation, and culture.

2. Social justice. This was the direct outgrowth of the sense of

13

brotherhood and the fatherhood of God. As interpreted by the eighth-century prophets, social justice was not an abstract idea, but was conceived in terms of concrete and specific economic, social, and political conditions.

3. Universalism. Though, as suggested above, the concepts of brotherhood, social justice, and Jahweh as a tribal father were in their original forms conceived in terms of tribalism and later narrow nationalism, through the interaction of the primitive Hebrews with other peoples and cultures particularly during the period of international conflict, these concepts became ethicized, spiritualized, and universalized. In later Judaism, Jahweh became the God of all races and cultures, and concomitantly the idea of brotherhood and justice was extended to all mankind.

4. Ethical monotheism. The crowning achievement of Judaism and its greatest contribution to the thought and life of mankind in any age was ethical monotheism. This noble achievement gathers up into itself and heightens all the other moral and spiritual values that emerged out of the historical experience of the ancient Hebrews.

5. Dynamic rather than static values. It is of the greatest importance to note that all these values were highly dynamic. They not only grew out of the social and historical experience of the Hebrew people, but were subject to continuous change as their experience changed. Thus these values were not given and static absolutes invading their life from some supposedly supernatural realm, but emergent within and integral to their experience growing out of their interaction with their natural and social world, growing and changing as the experience changed.

6. The Messianic hope. Notwithstanding its origin in national crises and tragedy and its apocalyptic and utopian elements, this hope envisioned a better world as the goal for human hopes and striving, a hope that burned ever brighter as frustration and tragedy deepened. This hope lives on in Christianity as the social gospel.

It was upon the level of ethical monotheism with its universal, ethical, and spiritual conception of life and the world that Christianity emerged upon the field of history. Jesus, its founder, himself a Jew whose thought and life were in the tradition of the eighth-century prophets, in his teaching added nothing new to the substantive content of that tradition. According to the earliest Gospels, he interpreted man's relation to God and the world in terms of the commonplace experiences of everyday life illumined and controlled by two simple principles—supreme devotion to God and love of one's neighbor as one's self, without metaphysical or theological interpretation; the age-old Hebrew conception of the fatherhood of God and the brotherhood of man. It was not until the interaction of primitive Christianity as a way of life with the mystery religions and Oriental-Greek philosophy that Christianity became theologized and was transformed into a redemptive religion, embroidered with an elaborate system of authoritative dogma and cultus.

These fundamental values—the brotherhood of man under the fatherhood of God (however interpreted), social justice, universalism, hope for an improved society, and dynamic values in a world of change—seem to me to be relevant to the conditions and demands of life in the modern world with its widened contacts of cultures, its growing tension between the white and colored races throughout the world, its hazardous international relations with the ever-present threat of the destruction of civilized life on this planet, and its greatly accelerated tempo of change affecting the deepest foundations of our life.

II

In my opinion, we are deeply indebted to modern science for religiously significant insights and achievements. Modern science more than any other preceding mode of thought has made possible a realistic and sustaining concept of a universe as man's home. Its emphasis upon natural law in terms of dependable and predictable antecedents and consequents has for the first time revealed a structure of reality that is satisfying to man's reason and offers a foundation upon which he can depend for purposeful effort in the setting up of valued ends and the devising of means for attaining them. At the same time that it has given him an ordered universe, it has vastly extended its time and space dimensions beyond the limits of his imagination.

Science has given man a new role in his relation to reality. Through increasing understanding of the processes of nature he has ceased to be merely a passive subject of the operation of these forces but, within limits, has achieved an increasing measure of control over them, even to the awesome penetration of the structure of the atom and control over its behavior. His relation to nature has become one not merely of reaction to, but of interaction with, its operations. If with his initial successes in this direction he has developed a heady overconfidence in himself and an undisciplined optimism, he has, with deeper penetration into the massive operation of these forces, begun to develop a humility in keeping with his human limitations. Nevertheless, he has increasingly become purposive and creative in his participation in the operations of his natural and social world.

At the same time he has achieved some understanding of himself as regards his biological origin and the constituent elements of his nature, together with his associated life in society. Meanwhile, he has become culturally self-conscious, with some insight into the nature of culture and the ways in which it develops. Perhaps it is not too much to expect that in time through knowledge of himself and of society he will be able to order his associated life toward social goals in a way comparable with his technical knowledge and control of nature.

Perhaps the most important religious result of these advances through modern science is the establishment of man as an integral part of nature. In its more mature forms, this awareness leads to a wholehearted acceptance of life and a trust in it. But such an identification with the life process casts out the fears induced in man by a more primitive type of theological thinking and tends to lessen the tensions created by the sense of being an alien in a world set over against him and for the most part indifferent if not hostile to him. Instead of a degraded natural world and a supernatural world inhabited by capricious benevolent or malevolent spirits or arbitrary and vengeful deities which must be placated by gifts and adulation, the universe has become his home.

Such considerations as these render somewhat irrelevant the question as to whether the cosmos cares for man's well-being, which is based upon the assumption that man is something not only apart from nature but opposed to it. The crises and tragedies of his own personal life are one with the crises and tragedies in nature in its evolutionary thrust toward new and emergent forms. Notwithstanding its uniformities, conflict and tragedy are phases of a universe that is still in the process of creation, with the collision of planets and the birth and death of worlds. The death of the eighteen upon whom the Tower of Siloam fell was not the result of an act of vengence on the part of a supernatural deity but an event in the course of nature. This acceptance of life as a wholehearted participant in its processes is far different from a fatalistic resignation to the decrees of a hostile universe. This way lies peace to the troubled soul that accepts its oneness with total reality, even in the experience of death.

III

For me, most assuredly, democracy, with its emphasis upon the supreme value of persons, freedom, and equal opportunity for self-realization for all, irrespective of race, color, or economic status, is not far removed from the integration of economic, social, political, intellectual, aesthetic, and moral values which I hold, as set forth under the fourth question, to be the fundamental and universal basis of the creative and vital aspects of all historical religions.

To me, the final criterion of religion is ethical. I hold that religion is as amenable to ethical criticism as any other form of human behavior. It is a noteworthy fact to anyone acquainted with the history of religion that many forms of religion, including contemporary forms, have not only been primitive and pre-scientific in their beliefs and practices but have ruthlessly violated ethical values. This means that the ultimate sanction of moral behavior is not religion, as is generally affirmed, but the ethical demands of associated living in the kind of world our empirical experience reveals. The Judaeo-Christian religion offers a striking proof of this fact. The most scathing criticism of the eighth-century prophets and of Jesus was directed against traditional, official, and orthodox religion.

Historically, ethical monotheism was achieved in spite of the continuous and often violent opposition of traditional and authoritative religion. Moreover, it is equally true that the transformation of the primitive, anthropomorphic, racial, and national religion of the Hebrews into the lofty ethical monotheism of later Judaism was the outgrowth of empirical resolution of economic, political, and national issues in the successive cultural periods of the conquest of Canaan, settlement upon the land, international conflict, and the collapse of the Hebrew state.

It is common knowledge that many of the contemporary movements of social reform have been strenuously opposed by the vested interests of organized religion. On the other hand, it is equally true that the most significant of these movements have sprung from the profound religious convictions of the vital and ethically sensitive sections of the religious community. These two attitudes have always existed side by side in the religious community, and always in conflict.

It should be noted, however, that democracy is a highly dynamic idea and has undergone and is now undergoing fundamental change. Originally, it assumed the form of political democracy. But more recently it is being extended to include industrial and race relations. Democracy as we know it still has many defects, though it seems to us to be the latest and highest form of associated living yet achieved. For one thing, with its emphasis upon individual freedom, democracy has yet to achieve an effective corporateness that is compatible with the worth of persons and individual freedom. Neither freedom nor corporateness in isolation from the other is a valid social concept. Democracy has yet to achieve a creative corporateness that integrates these two sets of values. For this reason I should not identify religion with any given historical form of democracy, however closely related their fundamental values may be.

Similarly, morality is a dynamic concept. Contrary to the general assumption as to their given and absolute character, each of the moral values has its natural history. What is moral in any given behavior situation depends upon the concrete factors in the situation. What is judged to be moral in one cultural milieu is judged to be immoral in another. Similarly, what is judged to be moral in one period of a people's history is revised or discarded in a later period in the light of growing experience, as in the case of *lex talionis* or the tribal law of blood revenge.

Moral values have changed throughout history as the result of new insights into human relations, and it may be assumed that they will change with a widening and deepening social experience, since the history of the development of moral values seems to indicate that they are inherent in the life process. Such an insight seems to have led the Founder of Christianity explicitly to repudiate traditional moral precepts in his religious tradition in favor of more mature and spiritual moral-ethical demands. It also seems to have led him to refrain from formulating rules of conduct, but instead to rely upon two basic inner principles of conduct, the love of God and love for one's neighbor, or the still more simple principle of doing to others as one would have them do to him. For this reason, primary as they are in religion, I should not be willing to identify religion with the changing moral standards of any given historic period of culture.

IV

Unquestionably, the trend in the scientific, as distinguished from the theological, study of religion during the last three-quarters of a century by the use of historical, psychological, and sociological methods has been toward a valuational concept of religion in its functional relation to the life process.

In keeping with this trend, I hold that religion is not only a valuational type of personal and social experience, but a particular form of valuational experience—to use the late Dr. George A. Coe's pregnant term, the *revaluation* of all the specialized values of man's experience. This process is more than the sum of all other values— economic, political, social, intellectual, aesthetic, and ethical. It is a *revaluation* of all these more or less specialized values from which, through integration and transformation, emerges a total meaning and worth of life in responsible relation to total reality as man has experienced it.

In this process of revaluation, the functional relation of religion to the practical interests and activities of the common life is twofold and reciprocal. On the one hand, as the history of religion shows, the substantive content of religious beliefs and practices is derived from the practical interests and activities of the group. This explains why the beliefs and practices of one religious group in one cultural milieu differ from those of another group in a different cultural milieu, as in the cases of Egypt, Assyria, Palestine, Greece, India, and

Western Europe. It also explains why these beliefs and practices change within a given group, as in the case of the development of the idea of Jahweh among the ancient Hebrews, the doctrine of the Atonement in European Christianity, and the reconstruction of religious thinking in the contemporary scientific period.

On the other hand, once the revaluation of all particular values involved in all the practical interests and activities of the common life has taken place, religion re-enters the several areas of experience as a factor of cross-criticism and reconstruction, as when political activity is not only subjected to the cross-criticism of intellectual, social, aesthetic, and moral values, but is judged in the light of the powerful impact of the total meaning and worth of life in its widest social and cosmic setting. Through this two-way process vital religion that is functionally related to experience is always creating tensions between actual and ideal intentions and action on the one hand, and the resolution of them on the other.

For this reason it is impossible to speak of the religion of a given people except in the most general terms. Instead, one must speak of their religion during different periods of their cultural evolution. Thus, for example, one must speak of the religion of the Hebrews in successive historical periods—the primitive period of migration and the conquest of Canaan, settlement upon the land, international conflict, and the collapse of the Hebrew state. In like manner, one must speak of the Christianity of the Palestinian period, of the transition to European soil, of the Patristic period, of the Middle Ages, of the Reformation and the Counter Reformation, and of the contemporary period.

From these considerations it follows that religion is a *quality* that potentially attaches to any and every experience of the common life arising out of man's interaction with his natural, social, and cosmic world. Thus, religion does not enter human experience from some supposedly "supernatural" realm in a dualistic universe split into the "natural" (with which God and the spiritual have little or nothing to do) and the "supernatural" (with which God and the spiritual are especially identified). Rather, religion is a quality that is potentially inherent in every phase of man's interaction with an objective world in which the unknown is continuous with the known. In such a view, the so-called "natural" and "supernatural" become meaningless terms and yield to a conception in which the material and the spiritual become undifferentiated aspects of a process with the whole of which God is involved, as much in the "material" as in the "spiritual."

Neither is religion something which one "gets" or "loses." He *is* religious if and to the extent that every act and relationship in living is judged and carried through in the light of this summation and transformation of all values into a total meaning and worth of life in its responsible relation to the whole of reality which the historical religions have identified with God. He *is* nonreligious or irreligious if and to the extent that his acts and decisions in everyday living are carried on without reference or in opposition to these fundamental and comprehending values.

It also follows that religion is primarily a social phenomenon and a phase of a people's changing culture. Even if one conceives of religion as what one does with his solitude, to use Whitehead's phrase, his religious ideas, attitudes, and practices are conditioned by the social milieu in which he lives.

In this connection, it is interesting to note that traditional and official religion has often been hostile to the significant religious insights that have arisen in the so-called "secular" world outside ecclesiastical and orthodox organized religion. Such was the case of the Copernican concept of the universe, the doctrine of evolution, and the nature of man as brought to light by modern psychology. This process follows a fairly well-defined cycle—initial opposition (often accompanied by persecution), reluctant coming to terms with the new idea, and final acceptance and incorporation into the official body of belief.

From the point of view outlined above, no reconciliation is required between the survival values of the Judaeo-Christian religions, the dynamic values inherent in the activity of the cosmos, and the creative values emerging in man's struggle to build a society of free men, since in their functional relation to the life process no conflict exists.

V

I should say that throughout the history of religion the term "God," however interpreted, has been used to represent that aspect of reality which comes to light when all the values inherent in man's interaction with his objective world are integrated and heightened into a comprehending meaning and worth of life in relation to total reality. The term has often carried crass animistic, anthropomorphic, racial, and narrow nationalistic connotations. On the other hand, it has carried the loftiest and most spiritual connotations of ethical monotheism— "God is a spirit, and they who worship him must worship in spirit and truth."

Notwithstanding the fact that the term "God" has carried meanings that are no longer acceptable to mature religious persons in a scientific age, some symbol would seem to be necessary to render manageable intellectually and emotionally what persists as a reality in the experience of mankind. It seems not too much to say that, if the term "God" were dispensed with, some other symbol would be invented to express what the word has historically stood for, such as "Humanity," or "The All," as some have proposed. To say that this historic term should be abolished because it means so many different things to different people seems to me beside the point, since differences of interpretation of any symbol by people with different backgrounds and interests is inevitable, except perhaps in the case of precise, reproducible scientific formulas.

Moreover, it should be recognized that the meaning of symbols changes with changing personal and social experience. The term "democracy" is a case in point. As was pointed out above, the earliest meaning of democracy was political—"government directly by the people collectively," as the dictionary has it. But in a growing social experience democracy has been extended to industry—as in collective bargaining, the participation of workers in management— and to race relations. The term "democracy," like "God," has been grossly distorted and recently made a means of the enslavement of whole peoples "liberated" by a ruthless Communist regime which denies both God and the rights of individual persons. Yet it is not seriously proposed that the free peoples of the world should abolish the term "democracy." The term "freedom" is likewise undergoing a change in its connotation, especially with reference to its social implications. Freedom, too, has been distorted and suborned to serve selfish purposes, as in laissez-faire economics, license, and anarchy.

In the light of these considerations, I should hold that the source of knowledge and guidance with respect to the highest type of human life inheres in the nature of reality as it is disclosed in the empirical experience of the race, over long periods of time and under widely varying conditions of living. God, who in mature religious thought may be conceived of as a creator and conserver of values, becomes the impelling and creative aspect of that *process* which Whitehead affirms to be *reality*. To one who holds this view, God is continuously and creatively at work in the processes of history.

This may or may not involve a personal concept of God in terms of human personality as we know it. There are those who feel that a personal conception of God does not add to the validity of religious experience, aside from the intellectual difficulties involved. On the other hand, there are those who are convinced that a personality-producing universe must have personal qualities, as the late Shailer Mathews affirmed. Others who find it impossible intellectually to conceive the nature of God nevertheless find that that which is represented by this universal and ancient term is to them objectively and overwhelmingly real.

From this point of view, "revelation" takes on a new and vaster dimension. To the understanding mind and sensitive spirit, reality is disclosing itself in every scientific discovery and social experience. Revelation so conceived becomes one aspect of an undifferentiated process that is inquiry and discovery on the part of man and response and disclosure on the part of reality. Truth as we know it emerges at the point where the inquiring, experimenting, and endlessly searching human spirit encounters reality in its interaction with nature, society, and the cosmic order by which man's mortal life is enveloped and supported. Like the dynamic world in which he lives, truth itself is dynamic—a process, a becoming in which change and continuity are inseparably united.

HOWARD H. BRINTON

Howard H. Brinton, educator and lecturer, is possibly the best known interpreter of American Quakerism today. A graduate of Haverford College, Harvard, and the University of California, he began his teaching career at Friends' Boarding School in Ohio in 1906. After teaching at Guilford College, Earlham College, and Mills College, Dr. Brinton became Director of Pendle Hill, a Quaker Graduate School for religious and social study. Long affiliated with the American Friends' Service Committee, both here and abroad, he served as a delegate to the World Council of Churches in Amsterdam, in 1948, and is a member of the American Theological Society and the American Philosophical Association. He has written several books including The Mystic Will *(1930);* Creative Worship *(1931);* Quaker Education *(1940); and* Friends for 300 Years *(1952).*

I

I HAVE just returned from two years in the Orient where I was in close contact with several Oriental religions, particularly Japanese Buddhism. Since these religions have met the needs of hundreds of millions of people, they contain important methods and truths from which Christianity can learn. That in recent years their power has weakened, particularly because of the overwhelming prestige of Western science, is not to their discredit as compared to the Judaeo-Christian religions.

The same thing has happened to religion in the West. Nevertheless, on returning to the United States, I feel that the Western religions, with some exceptions, retain a power which Oriental religions do not generally have today. This power is directed toward the social betterment of mankind and seems to operate in spite of theological systems which emphasize different elements.

If we divide the principal current religions into two groups, one group originating in western Asia—Judaism, Christianity and Islam— the other originating in India—Hinduism, Buddhism and their derivatives—we find in the first group the conception of God as creator and man as cooperating with him through obedience to His will in the process of creation. The emphasis in this first group is on action rather than on contemplation; on doing, rather than solely on being. There are many exceptions to any generalization when large numbers of heterogeneous people are involved.

The teachings of the Jewish prophets and of Jesus of Nazareth present a code of ethics which has a dynamic and religious base in the conception of God as Father whose love encompasses his justice. In contrast, many forms of Hinduism and Buddhism do not think of ultimate Being as personal and concerned with ethical behavior, but rather as the impersonal ground of all existence to be "known" by an experience transcending this phenomenal transitory world. The ethical code of Buddhism is a lofty one centered in compassion and a sense of the unity of all life, but this code exists only as a preparation for an experience which goes beyond ethics and is possible only for a few.

Christianity, in its earliest form, had as its goal an ideal social order, the Kingdom of Heaven, a conception developed out of Judaism. The preaching of Jesus was largely confined to the kind of behavior calculated to provide admittance to this Kingdom, however this Kingdom might come into being, whether suddenly or gradually. Many Christian missionaries to Asia proclaim, instead of this communal Kingdom of Heaven, an individual future salvation based on a mysterious divine process incomprehensible to the average Oriental. In contrast to this individual emphasis we see the growing success of communism, promising like early Christianity to provide an ideal type of human society. Communism has been described as a Christian heresy because it has taken over the Christian doctrine of the ideal social order but has substituted violence as a means for its achievement instead of dependence on spiritual forces which come from God.

But this social emphasis is only one side of the coin. The reverse side is inward religious experience. Christianity, as a religious movement, began with an outpouring of the Spirit at Pentecost and it was the continued sense of the Spirit in the worshiping group which gave early Christianity its power and propagating capacity. Such inward experiences do not differ greatly in the various religions of the world. Mysticism is much the same everywhere. "The Spirit bloweth where it listeth." It is confined to no one religion or religious form. Often it is in evidence outside of any organized religion, in fact the very organization of religion may be its greatest obstacle. Yet even in its mysticism Christianity may possess its own peculiar value. If the Christian believes that the Divine Spirit which comes out from God to create the world and to bring men to new birth is the same Spirit that became incarnate in Jesus in the highest degree possible to man, then communion with that spirit is not communion with a formless unknown. The life and teachings of Jesus form an objective standard by which the subjective revelation may be checked and aided. That the Spirit within all men which gives intuitive religious knowledge, spiritual power, and the sense of unity with all men everywhere, is also the Inward Christ and at one with the Christ of history, is a doctrine which is not contrary to liberal Christianity.

Accordingly, there are two unique religious values which I think should be emphasized in contemporary thought and practice in the Judaeo-Christian religions. The first is the ethical code revealed in the teachings of the prophets and of Jesus, which presents the condition for bringing about an ideal social order. The second is an inward religious experience of the Divine Spirit which is more than a vague mysticism because of the revelation of the character of that Spirit in the life of Jesus of Nazareth.

II

I believe that the history of life on this planet, and particularly the history of mankind, indicates a kind and degree of progress which can only be explained by the belief, to use the words of the question presented by the editor of this inquiry, that "cosmic reality . . . cares for man's well-being." Man, however, appears to be endowed with freedom to help or hinder his own progress. To secure this "care" he must cooperate with those forces in the universe which promote his well-being, but the evidence indicates that, on the whole, he gets more than he might be thought to deserve. Though the whole evolutionary process from the earliest beginnings of life to the present has exhibited many retrogressions and mistakes, yet in general, progress or development is evident though not inevitable. It is difficult to account for this progress except by the hypothesis that there is a Mind immanent in nature.

If progress has been due to the elimination of the weak by the strong, then the so-called "care" of the "cosmic reality" would not perhaps be evident. Many biologists today do not accept this theory of evolutionary progress. They believe that the basis of progress is cooperation, not competition. That which destroys its environment destroys itself. Those forms of life which can cooperate with other forms and which are so generalized that they are adaptable to changes in environment have the highest survival value. The belligerent, destructive forms are eventually eliminated. History shows that both among animals and among men, militarism in all its forms is eventually a fatal disease. This indicates the character of the cosmic reality which cares for man provided man himself cares for his fellow man. Our trespasses are forgiven insofar as we forgive others their trespasses.

The problem of Job, "Why should the righteous suffer," is not so difficult to answer when we are dealing with man-made calamities. The suffering of one man for the sins of another is not justified on the basis of an extremely individualistic conception of human society. But such individualism is an illusion. All life is fundamentally one and human society is in varying degrees an organic whole in which one part suffers for the other parts, as happens, for example, in a human body. The suffering of Christ on the cross for the sins of mankind, as interpreted by Christianity, reveals that God Himself shares in this vicarious suffering. But all suffering is not redemptive. There is suffering which is destructive.

In dealing with calamities which are the result of the forces of nature the problem is more difficult. But suffering of any kind, whether due to natural or man-made disasters, need not be evil unless man makes it so. It can and often has been a source of good without which the development of human character and capacity would be impossible. For example, in the temperate zones where life is in some respects more difficult than in the tropics there has been greater progress than in torrid zones where life is easier. That life in the arctic zone has not exhibited progress indicates that progress is not promoted when difficulties are increased beyond a certain point.

The extraordinary and surprising combination of physical conditions and events on this planet which has made life possible (such as the expansion of water on freezing) has seemed to some first-rate scientists more than simply fortuitous. The physical sciences, being the most advanced, have gone furthest in relieving us of the conception that the universe is a soulless mechanism, indifferent to life. The top ranking physical scientists are among those who are most aware of the limits of their science, which are confined only to the metrical aspects of reality. They recognize what all men instinctively know, the existence of a spiritual reality which is not subject to scientific experiment and measurement and which is the basis of our ultimate values. The universe is now more mysterious than it ever was, in spite of the progress made by man in his mastery over nature. The main cause of suffering today is not nature but man himself, who has turned constructive natural forces into the channel of destruction.

III

The "human values expressing the genius of the democratic movement and of personal moral character" are "intrinsic elements" of my religious faith, but they are secondary elements, being derived from what are more fundamental elements. The democratic movement has a spiritual origin in the doctrine of the supreme worth of the individual in the sight of God. Democracy in the Anglo-Saxon world evolved out of the English Reformation in the seventeenth century, which saw salvation as dependent on the direct relationship between man and God rather than on the relationship between man and the Church. But Protestant individualism, if carried too far, cannot be a basis for democracy. To be successful, democracy must draw on the spirit of disinterested service in some individuals who put the interest of society above their own individual interests. Such unselfish service is a product of religion—not of any religion, but of a religion which creates unity among men by recognizing fundamental unity in which all share. This sense of unity may be derived from the doctrine of the Fatherhood of God and the brotherhood of man expressed by Jesus in the two great commandments "thou shalt love the Lord thy God . . . and thy neighbor as thyself." Or it may be derived from such a feeling of unity as is expressed in John's gospel in the figure "I am the vine and ye are the branches." This figure, which may be used to express the unity of all life, is more characteristic of the Eastern than of the Western religions, but it did not result in democracy in the East for it was not balanced there by the belief in the supreme worth of the individual. Christianity, being both Hellenic and Hebraic in its origins, contains both a sense of the importance of individual human personality which is largely Hebraic in origin, and a sense of a deep underlying metaphysical unity derived from Greek thought. Democracy is an intrinsic element in a fully matured Christianity.

What has been said regarding democracy applies also to personal moral character. Moral behavior, insofar as it is not blind obedience to rules and traditions, is a derivative of religion even though it may not be recognized as such. In a genuine moral act man, consciously or unconsciously, recognizes his unity with a life larger than his own and this, in my view, is religion. This larger life may be the life of his tribe or nation, in which case his religion is primitive and immature. In the more highly developed religions this larger life is the life of God or the life which comes out from God, whether He be thought of as personal or impersonal. In my religion this larger life recognized in every moral act is not only greater than the individual in the sense of being more inclusive, but it is also superhuman and comes down from "above" in order to create unity among men. This belief in a power, grace, or light coming down from some order of existence higher than human is not due to a logical deduction based on a philosophical or theological system but to inward, mystical experience.

IV

I believe "that the supreme values available to moral man from whatsoever source are aspects of one spiritual reality." For the word

"supreme" I would substitute the word "absolute" to distinguish
these values from values that are relative and pragmatic and that
are concerned with means rather than with ends. Supreme values
are therefore intrinsic rather than extrinsic. Thus the Platonic triad
of beauty, truth, and goodness are valuable for what they are in
themselves rather than for any use they may have for carrying out
some human interest beyond themselves. By the words "one spiritual
reality" I mean God. Thus I would say that all absolute values are
aspects of God who is the one absolute who includes all other absolutes.
The one human experience which is absolutely valuable in the sense
that it is not a means to an end is an experience of communion with
God which in its more self-conscious and deliberate form may be
called prayer, worship, meditation, or contemplation. All absolute
values are aspects of this one whether recognized as such or not.
Truth, beauty, and goodness are aspects of communion with God,
for they are not in their highest form derived from man's self-
centered interests. When man listens to the voice of God and obeys it,
he does so regardless of apparent consequences. The consequences of
any good action are ultimately good, but man does not know what
these ultimate consequences are. He must, accordingly, depend on
that which appears to be good in itself because it is an aspect of the
one spiritual reality.

The three parts of Question IV may be considered as referring to
the superhuman, the human, and the subhuman. The Judaeo-Christian
religions are directed toward man's relations with the superhuman;
man's efforts to build a free society are on the human level; while the
"activity of the cosmos" is concerned with nature which can be considered subhuman. All are aspects of one spiritual reality, but they
represent different degrees of man's apprehension of this reality. In
nature this spiritual reality is seen dimly, in man's activities more
clearly, and in the highest forms of religion most clearly, but seldom
with complete clarity. Man has often thought of himself as inhabiting
a twilight zone of human reason between a light world above and a
dark world beneath. The dark world of nature, being the basis of
physical life, is not evil in itself but evil only if life is centered in it
through sensual indulgence. Man may attempt to center his life in
human reason, but many have found even this inadequate. Reason in

seeking ultimate meanings becomes lost in a maze of paradoxes. Accordingly, many have sought and some have succeeded in centering their lives in the light world above where knowledge of the ultimate meaning of life comes through Divine Revelation.

This oversimplified picture, based too much on a figure of speech, seems to correspond to much that is in human experience. In nature, "red in tooth and claw," the one spiritual reality is obscured; in human activity, particularly when that activity is directed toward the creation of a free society, there is a clearer revelation of the One Spiritual Source; and in the higher religions man sees more clearly and discerns that the character of this Source is Love. Through Love the creative process rises up from the first level to the second and from the second to the third.

These three levels can be related by considering them as stages in man's religious growth, though this is too large a subject to be developed here. Primitive man worships aspects of nature, including the biological ties of kinship in his tribal community. With the growth of self-consciousness and individuality comes the struggle to build a free society where man is not dominated by human individuals or by natural forces. Nature, ceasing to be an object of worship, comes more and more under human control. Finally man, lonely and isolated by an overdevelopment of individualism and divided within himself by detachment from the roots of his being in the life of nature, seeks communion with a spiritual Reality higher than himself and more universal than his tribal deity, who can inspire and unify him from within and make him a part of an inspired and unified spiritual community.

V

The concept "God" has an essential place in my religion, though there are religions such as Buddhism in which this concept does not have a place. However, if the concept be sufficiently broadened, even Buddhism might be included.

But neither "God" nor "religion" are discovered through conceptual thinking, but ultimately only through an ineffable mystical experience. We are here concerned not with thinking but with feeling, for feeling is as much an organ of knowledge as thinking. Definitions, however, are useful and can be used to deal with at least one aspect of God. On this basis I would accept most of the definitions found in the various philosophies of religion. For example, to say with Whitehead that God is the "principle of concretion" is true, but this comes very far from exhausting the concept. One cannot pray to or sing hymns to a "principle of concretion." James' concept of the divine More has important elements of truth, but his pragmatic theory that God exists because he is successfully used does not go far enough. God is also contemplated and enjoyed for what He is in Himself. Similar comments might be made on the Idea of the Good of Plato, the Substance of Spinoza, and the Absolute Idea of Hegel. All see some aspect of God.

Particularly illuminating and instructive are some modern theories of Evolution. According to them God is a creative, integrating, and perfecting power in the world, working for unity and cooperation in nature, in human society, and in the human individual. There is, in the evolutionary process, evidence of an upward pull toward the ideal which comes from a higher level than that on which the process is taking place. We are ignorant of how this upward pull operates on the lower levels but we find in ourselves such a pull which creates and draws us toward our religious and moral ideals. The experience of this Power which lifts us upward is an experience of God.

LEONARD CARMICHAEL

Leonard Carmichael has been Secretary (administrative head) of the Smithsonian Institution, the nation's largest museum and oldest research organization with a full-time staff of investigators, since 1953. Before this he was for fourteen years President of Tufts College. A graduate of Tufts, he has a Ph.D. degree and an honorary LL.D. from Harvard. He taught biology at Tufts and psychology at Princeton, Brown, and Rochester. He established the National Roster of Scientific and Specialized Personnel during the Second World War. He has been adviser to several Federal agencies. He is a past President of the American Psychological Association and a member of the American Philosophical Society and the National Academy of Sciences. He is author or joint author of books and articles including Elements of Human Psychology *(1930);* Manual of Child Psychology *(1946); and* Reading and Visual Fatigue *(1947).*

I

IT IS difficult for me to answer Question I exactly as it is phrased. My parents were members of the Episcopal Church which is the American branch of the worldwide Anglican Communion. I was thus born an Episcopalian, I was raised as an Episcopalian, and I am an Episcopalian by conviction.

The Anglican churches of the world think of themselves as sharing with the Greek Orthodox Church, the Roman Catholic Church, certain Lutheran churches, and a number of other Communions a traditional and ever-growing body of religious teaching which has been guarded and advanced ever since the Old and New Testaments came into being. These bodies consider the church to be a living organiza-

33

tion of truth which is maintained in each generation by bishops whose authority goes back in unbroken succession to the Apostles.

It is difficult for me to believe that this point of view can be stripped of its "ethnic," "doctrinal," and "structural" factors and still be fully effective in regard to religious or other values. The teachings of the Anglican Church, for example, constitute a well organized intellectual system which includes theology, ethics, and a great body of canon law. It would be rash for a layman to try to single out any series of statements from this closely knit and consistent system for emphasis. Nevertheless, it does seem to me that, so far as contemporary thought and practice are concerned, the emphasis given in the teachings of the Anglican Church to the individual person's responsibility for his own moral and ethical life as he lives in society is of especial importance.

It may well be that certain forms of organized society make it easier for individuals to be good in a social and ethical sense than do other forms of government. It seems to me, however, that our age especially needs an emphasis on the fact that the self-directed but religiously inspired regeneration of individuals is the surest road to the regeneration of society, and not vice versa. History demonstrates that good, and indeed saintly, men can live under a wide variety of social, economic, and political organizations. This observation, therefore, counteracts the erroneous (or "more bathtubs") view advocated by communism and other types of utopian socialism that if the physical and social environments are changed, the individuals who make up society will automatically become good in one or two generations. Human nature in certain respects is essentially limited and has changed little in historic times. This means that men and women are now, as in the past, prone to what theologians call sin. It may be that only by participation in a sound religious system can weak and frail human beings be sufficiently strengthened as individuals to strive for what they themselves know is good and to try hard to overcome as far as possible ever-present temptations to do what they know is evil.

In my opinion a good society may be defined as a society made up of individuals who, to the maximum degree possible, try to resist those thoughts, words, and deeds that a good religion recognizes as evil and to approach as nearly as they can that state of goodness for which they have learned to strive in the religious system that they accept. Of such societies those seem best in which individuals not only negatively try to avoid evil but also, alone and through organized social effort, positively try to achieve lasting accomplishments. It seems to me to be important that a society strive to be so constituted that individuals in it will produce great works of literature, art, music, architecture, coherent philosophical systems, true advances in pure and applied science, successful business and industrial organizations, and other physical, intellectual, and spiritual achievements. It seems more important to do everything possible to make such achievements a reality than to produce an ephemeral state called happiness in a certain number of the members of a given society. Happiness itself is more apt to come as a by-product of achievement than when it is itself made a goal or objective.

It has not been demonstrated that the value system, which is basic to a society of men who are trying to be good, diligent, and achieving, can be long maintained in the absence of the acceptance by many such men of an inspiring religious system which makes each person feel accountable in a more than human sense for all of his public and private actions.

A church of the sort named in the first paragraphs above is thus not just a set of intellectual beliefs. Through ceremonies and sacraments, through the music and art of its services and its beautiful buildings, as well as through its rules of everyday conduct, the church elevates the emotions and gives continuing instruction which imparts true ambition to the free lives of many of its members. Such a church also recognizes that all individuals are not the same and that all are not equally able to use abstractions and that some people, at any rate, learn best by parables and symbols. Required acts of devotion, special dietary rules, and the repeated cycles of the church year keep alive the message of religion in the daily lives of its members.

The hundreds of millions of individuals now living who, in varying degrees and with different educational and intellectual backgrounds, participate in the life of the organized churches mentioned in the first paragraphs above form a great bulwark of free men who abhor totalitarian communism. They recognize communism as the greatest of heresies that the world has known since the beginning of the Christian Era. Totalitarian communism attempts to use an unreal day-dream-like picture of a humanly impossible collectivist Utopia as an opiate to rob its adherents of their will to individual achievement and their belief in truth itself. Communism also destroys the human belief that an individual by his own effort and by his own free choice may influence his life for good or ill. Communism thus tries to teach the individual that his personal life has no lasting or cosmic meaning. Socially the end product of this view is bound to be a police state in which men and women must be governed by fear because they have lost the inner desire to govern themselves by the love of those things which a good organized religion teaches them to work for and to hold dear. Men who strive to live according to the teachings of a good religious system of the sort described above can be free in any social or economic system which does not physically destroy them or prohibit them from learning about religion itself.

II

Question II is also difficult; one which might require a book and not a few words for its complete answer. In general I believe that man physically is as much an object of nature as is a tree or a star or a starfish, and his make-up and actions are subject to he same laws or ones comparable to those which govern these nonhuman objects. Man shares with the other higher mammals the possession of good sense organs, a highly elaborated living calculating device called a brain and well-balanced muscles. Man's living body is also maintained as a physiological unity by the products of its own glands. The great difference between man and all other living organisms, however, lies in the human individual's ability to use tools effectively to make other complex tools, and to use language and symbols in involved and precise ways. The use of language and symbols both in overt speech and in thought is basic to human action. As Plato said, "The soul when thinking appears to me to be just talking—asking questions of herself and answering them. . . ."

Because of memory and the development of written language and mathematics, each new generation of men can profit by the successes and failures of previous generations. This ability has allowed man in the relatively few thousand years that his race has existed upon the globe to develop science and art and to have a highly structured religion. In this evolution ideas, ideals, values, and general concepts have been developed, revealed, or discovered. Some of these concepts, like that of "infinity," are in a sense absolute and may be wholly independent of a particular time or place or of the experience of any individual human being. Naturally a highly developed religion makes use of many such "eternal" and "absolute" intellectual concepts.

Through invention and science man has also tremendously increased his power over the rest of nature. For example, he has substituted other energy sources for the old, hard, painful work of weak human muscles, and through medicine and public health techniques he has increased his likelihood of survival and of comfort during life. By developing music and art he has learned to give a variety of meanings and pleasures to a new side of life which is uniquely human. Language, for example, has become not only a method of communication but, in literature and especially in poetry, a source of aesthetic enjoyment.

Through progressive and cumulative experience or revelation, religion has also developed so that today most men, because of ease of communication, may learn about a course of individual and social living called "good" in such religions and also have their efforts to live according to this knowledge emotionally reinforced. This religious knowledge thus provides a basis for the sane and constructive coexistence of individuals in groups and societies made up of other free individuals who are also striving to live according to a religiously reinforced code of civil and religious law.

III

I believe that democracy is the best system of government so far formulated by man. I am convinced that this system, especially as outlined by such great political thinkers and men of action as Benjamin Franklin, George Washington, John Adams, Alexander Hamilton, and Abraham Lincoln, has provided the world with a form of government better than any other ever known before. I further believe that many of the ideas which are best in this system are but an application of the teachings of the type of organized religion to which reference is given in the first paragraphs of this paper. It may be repeated here, however, that history shows that men who have proper religious attitudes may lead good and indeed saintly lives under a wide variety of political, social, and economic organizations.

In the long run a democracy which depends upon the will of the majority can only be sound and morally good if the individuals who make up the majority are able, on the basis of individually held value systems, to make judgments which are in a moral and ethical sense valid and good. As noted above, it has not been demonstrated that a complex modern society, made up as it is and must be of individuals of varying intellectual capacities, can maintain such a value system in the absence of ardently held personal religious beliefs. A purely relativistic theory of ethics which recognizes nothing as absolutely good or evil, and which is thought of as independent of religious or legal sanctions, is no better guide for an individual than is a compass that swings at random for a mariner.

IV

It is difficult to answer Question IV briefly. As I have attempted to point out, I believe that an organized religious system and a proper and fixed value system are closely related. There are those who wish to think of religious teachings as an assembling or a codification of the moral and social wisdom of the ages derived by trial and error through countless human generations. Others prefer to think of religion and religious teachings as resulting from a long series of Divine revelations. It does not seem to me that a study of religion itself or of ethical systems alone can decide which of these two answers is the correct one. Some scientifically minded individuals may prefer to think of the Commandments and codes of morals which are recognized, for example, in modern organized Christianity as a mere product of human social evolution. Such individuals wish to apply to the study of these concepts the same techniques that are used in the study of paleontology as it considers the evolution of the horse's hoof from one of the digits of a five-toed ancestor. A naturalistic study of this sort will demonstrate, I think, that the teachings of religion are indeed instructions which give meaning to human life and also assist individual men, women, and children in the difficult job of trying to live together in a harmonious and achieving way in family groups and in organized society. The possibility that some social values are so fundamental that they are "discovered" rather than "constructed" should not be forgotten. Some of those who wish to consider that the moral law has truly a Divine origin will not necessarily differ from naturalistic thinkers in accepting a chronology of its development. But they will assert that the teachings of the religion which they acknowledge are correct because these teachings are an exemplification of fixed Divine Laws as they have been gradually but explicitly revealed to man.

The great difference between the naturalistic and the Divine theory of the development of ethics and of values may not necessarily be in the nature of the teachings themselves, but rather in the demand the systems make on the individual that such teachings be accepted and acted on at all times in every day life. Here it seems to the present writer that the Divine theory has a great advantage. According to this view individual men strive to be good and charitable, that is, to obey the teachings of their religion not only because it is socially and individually expedient to do so but also because it is absolutely and eternally right to do so. They believe that "honesty is the best policy," and also that it is fundamentally right to try to be honest.

In a religious system such as that described in the first paragraphs of this paper the adherent accepts the view that his own personal destiny, not only in time but also in eternity, depends upon the success that he has in his own life struggle and his effort to live out his existence in this world in harmony with the highest teachings of his religion. He is convinced that his beliefs themselves as well as his good works are important. The fact that man may lead a better life if he accepts this religious view of his destiny is a naturalistic argument for what may be the necessity of a belief in a Divine Providence in the ordering of a satisfactory modern human society. The value of this view can be expanded and made specific by many examples. It should be pointed out that this is not the only, or even necessarily the best, argument for religion to those who deeply and personally accept the postulates of an organized religious system of the sort described in the first paragraphs of this paper. The naturalistic argument for the acceptance of the Divinity-inspired theory of the nature of religion is here proposed primarily for those who now live outside a system of a self-accepted formal religion.

To return to Question Four, therefore, it seems to me that a strong argument may be made for the view that the maintenance of the highest value structures recognized by modern man in his individual and social living may well be dependent upon his absolute acceptance of the reality of a Divinely revealed religion in which values are fixed and established and are not thought of as subjective or as merely relative to particular times or places.

V

If the preceding arguments have been clear, it is obvious that the best and clearest meanings of such words as "God," "Trinity," or "Incarnation" may well be those which have been developed and are accepted by the individuals who are the official interpreters of a continuing and coherent religious system and organization. In the Anglican churches such interpretations are made by official convocations of living bishops, other clergy, and lay people who are guided in their conclusions by the Scriptures, the pronouncements of the early Church Councils, theology, and canon law. A mechanism thus exists for the definition of the concepts of religion which is above the whim of any individual, just as our American system of law provides for the interpretation of the meaning of our Constitution.

Certainly in the formulation of the definition of words such as "God" the interpretations of the medieval mind at its best are important. The nineteenth and twentieth centuries are the centuries in which quantitative science has seen its greatest flowering. In the same way it may be that the Scholastic Fathers such as Duns Scotus and above all St. Thomas Aquinas lived in a time that fostered those who had a genius for the subtle interpretation of concepts such as that of "God." It may be that our age needs to discipline itself so that it can again learn to listen to the wisdom of St. Thomas as it considers such definitions.

In conclusion then, my opinion is that if one accepts religion as exemplified in the Anglican churches one should turn to those who have, through study and above all through practice, come to be experts in its official doctrines and teachings, if one wishes a definition of terms or an explanation of the many and detailed relationships that exist between religion and life. Few modern men can be experts in more than one field. The biologist does not try to rewrite chemistry when he attempts to work out the chemical basis of the physiological actions of the body. The astronomer does not reformulate physics when he deals with solar phenomena. It is often foolish for the layman to assume that he knows enough medicine to prescribe his own treatment when he is ill or enough law to defend himself in a lawsuit. In the same way it may be valuable to remember that there are experts in the correct use of concepts such as those which are basic in ethics and theology.

I do not believe that modern man can exist *as well as he now knows how to exist* without the sincere self-acceptance of an organized and positive system of concepts and beliefs. I am therefore convinced that such a coherent and fixed value system, especially as it relates to man's life in society, is best given him by active membership in churches such as those described in the first two paragraphs of this paper.

STEWART G. COLE

For seventeen years Stewart G. Cole has been an educational consultant and lecturer in the field of intercultural relations. Born in Canada, a graduate of McMaster University and the University of Chicago, he has taught religion at Carleton College, Crozer Theological Seminary, the University of Pennsylvania, and the University of Chicago. He became the executive director of the Bureau for Intercultural Education (1939) and has taught in this field at Teachers College (Columbia), University of California, Stanford, Arizona, and the University of New Mexico. He is a Fellow of the American Association for the Advancement of Science; formerly vice-president, he is now a Fellow of the Conference on Science, Philosophy and Religion; and a member of the board of the Religious Education Association. Dr. Cole's publications include The History of Fundamentalism *(1930);* Christian and Character Education *(1936);* Liberal Education In a Democracy *(1940); and* Minorities and the American Promise *co-author (1954).*

I

THE Judaeo-Christian tradition, stripped of its secondary and extraneous elements, affirms three values of paramount importance to our generation: the creatureness of man, ethical sensitivity, and personal dedication to the good life.

First: The Creatureness of Man. Man knows himself as a child of a benign cosmic world. Out of it he has emerged a human being, upon it he remains singularly dependent, and toward it in his better moments he acquires a profound sense of identification, affinity, and reverence. These spiritual discoveries reinforce human faith and introduce man to God, as we shall later suggest.[1]

This view of man stamps Judaism and Christianity with striking individuality. In contrast with the other factors shaping Western civilization, religion has taken seriously the sobering significance of the creatureness of mankind. Man discovers himself as a creature not only born of human stock and subject to a social milieu but man, *qua* man, as the offspring of the cosmos. The forces of the universe produced, pervade, and sustain him, and they make it necessary for him to reckon with them in arriving at his sense of the ultimate meaning and value of human existence.

Conventional Judaism and Christianity have interpreted this interest in supernaturalistic terms. They resort to otherworldly references and the idea of divine intervention into the natural world to account for the meaning of man. In my judgment such a viewpoint is not essential to a reasonable faith; nor is it warranted in the light of what we know about the rise and development of human life on this planet. I believe that man is an integral part of an amazingly creative natural world, of a cosmic order of reality which, although it transcends the human plane, is "closer [to man] than breathing, nearer than hands and feet." The sources of every man's salvation lie within his immediate reach and his own available orbit of life. In brief, God is "natural."

The basic insight of human creatureness, cherished by the Judaeo-Christian tradition, remains sound. Its orientation requires rethinking. Can Christians and Jews recover the distilled dynamics of this religious impulse from the accumulated encrustations which have all but snuffed out its vitality? If they succeed, they will discard the anthropomorphic and transcendental aspects of historic religion. These center about the biblical stories of creation, the "fall" of man, favoritistic deities issuing rewards and punishments to human subjects, "chosen" peoples, theistic incarnations, miracles, and otherworldly apocalypticism. Furthermore, these inquirers will challenge the authoritarian claims of religious spokesmen and institutions, question the ethical propriety of their vested powers in society, and disclaim

---

[1] The concept "spiritual" in this essay refers to those aspects of reality, whether human or cosmic, to which sensitive man imputes values that are of transcendent worth and in terms of which he nurtures his inner life.

the aristocratic defense they make of their favored role. All such phenomena are ephemeral in the historic religions, not essential nor germaine to a viable faith for our times.

On the other hand, consider the warm, filial, imaginative, and self-abandoning faith that has marked the finest expressions of the Judaic and Christian religions. Does not the pearl of matchless price shine forth? Stemming from the deepest reaches of the human heart and directed to profound sources of personal kinship with the environing universe, there persists a vital sense of human sharing in a structure of reality sustaining both man and cosmos. This sensitivity, blossoming through cultivation into the spirit of love, has always activated Jews and Christians in their better moments. It has kindled the lives of the immortal prophets, sages, martyrs, saviors, and the faithful throughout the centuries. The same attitude remains the key to a virile faith for their spiritual lineage today.

Man, a favored child of the cosmic reality that nestles him, may with confidence enlist his lot with the spiritual energies inherent in it and find personal fellowship with them to reinforce the human spirit for high purposes and to inspire in it a faith in a God of love.

Second: Ethical Sensitivity. At its historic best the Judaeo-Christian movement has blazed a trail of ethical insight and social betterment. It has accomplished these purposes not so much through the speculative medium of philosophy as in the mainstream of human life, where social issues are stubborn and inescapable and where they must be met and mastered, or they will deteriorate the moral fiber of man.

There is a distinction between men of philosophic disposition and the trail-blazing representatives of a religious faith. A philosopher contemplates upon the source, nature, and purpose of ethical principles and how they may be implemented to improve human society. A religious person is constrained to identify himself with the grave problems facing his people, to reach decisions as to what courses of action are right and good to resolve them, and then to commit himself to these courses with others to better their common way of life. A philosopher is primarily a man of sincere thought; a religionist a man of responsible action. The latter often turns to the former for light; his thinking, however, is tempered by a sense of social oughtness, self-commitment to remedy the situation, and the practical consequences that follow. Both types of individuals render meritorious service. We are concerned here with the capacity for ethical insight and the commitment to social action which have marked Judaism and Christianity at their best, and which Jews and Christians may well foster today.

The ethical progress of Western civilization, stimulated by the Judaeo-Christian religions, has been intermittent. Many are the conventional historic occasions when Jews and Christians perpetuated a dull devotion to the folkways, creeds, and ceremonials which their social institutions sanctioned. Sometimes they abetted events which lowered their ethical stature and contributed to the moral letdown of society. There is evidence that the contemporary world is suffering somewhat from such religious sterility today. It always happens when men and women attempt to live on the borrowed spiritual capital of their forebears. Now and then, however, a moral upswing of Judaism and Christianity has occurred. Outmoded ways of living, valuing, and thinking are repudiated and higher social frontiers of faith and action are projected.

When such occasions occur, the early stages of ethical change owe their inception to the work of prophets and reformers. These seers, reject the fruitless modes of living which for them, with their rare insight, have become "evil." Out of their daring self-commitment, they painfully articulate new social standards which become spiritual mandates for the times. Eventually, some of these leaders are accepted and enshrined by the religious group as the sages and saviors of a civilization; others remain banned indeterminately from church approval, albeit their service to mankind may be considerable; while still others, despite their distinguished contributions to the cause of the good life, are never known to history. They remain the unsung heroes of modest homes, remote countrysides, and "dark" times and places who in every germinative generation leave their indelible mark upon the upward march of man.

Such noble men and women, within or without the church, are the prime movers in sensitizing social conscience. They pave the hazardous highway for the ethical advance of a people. The kindling light of the better life spreads from those who originally become possessed of it to those who hunger for it. In due time the warmth and value of the illumination reaches out to involve the many in changes of attitude, standard of living, loyalty, and social conduct. In due time the emergent ideals are symbolized for purposes of general communication in ethical precepts, ceremonials, institutions, and creeds.

Thus the decalog traditionally accredited to Moses evolved, the Sermon on the Mount became immortalized, the canon of the Bible was singled out, the synagogue and church arose acquiring their powerful roles, and the principles of the Era of Enlightenment were enshrined in Western civilization. The perennial danger during the process of moral and spiritual growth of a people, even in periods of social ferment, is that individuals may confuse deference to a symbol and loyalty to a value, thus interchanging means and ends of the good life, and substituting the palliative of moral conformity for the yeast of ethical commitment.

Third: Personal Dedication to the Good Life. The Judaeo-Christian movement has produced a succession of men and women who have excelled in moral insight, in the quest of a fellowship with spiritual forces which transcend man and society, and in the championing of a way of life for mankind which springs from these qualities of personal dedication.

The prime fruits of religion are self-dedicated persons. The most significant element in their personalities is the impulse to seek and to live cooperatively the good, full life of man. In the pursuit of this purpose they learn to cultivate the stern discipline of social justice, the gentle spirit of human love, and the reinforcing strength that springs from a trial-by-fire faith in the spiritual purposes of the universe. Such men and women discover that what is really good for creature-man should acquire a universal approval in human society and, furthermore, does have the divine sanction of forces transcending man and society.[2]

Hence, the significance of such persons as Abraham, Moses, David, Hosea, Isaiah, Maimonides, and Spinoza in the Judean faith; and of Jesus, Luke, Paul, Augustine, Ignatius, Aquinas, Hus, Luther, and Fox in the Christian faith; as well as of the great seers of other religions. The Jews focus their loyalty upon a long line of devout patriarchs, whereas Christians single out the sublime personality of

[2] Cp. Walter Lippmann's principle of "the mandate of heaven" in *The Public Philosophy* (Boston: Atlantic-Little, Brown, 1955).

Jesus for special recognition. A personal dedication to the good, full life for all people that distinguished these immortals is the identical trait that can make individual Jews and Christians redemptive forces in contemporary life. Such persons fuse the three dimensions of religion into a triumphant faith. The hunger of their creature impulses reaches out to the responsive forces of cosmic meaning and value, and results in a self-commitment to so live as to raise the ethical level of mankind.

These values of the Judaeo-Christian tradition—the manifestations of the creatureness of man, ethical sensitivity, and personal dedication to the good life—have weathered the test of centuries of acute trial and may well remain abiding incentives to sustain man in the forward march of the human spirit.

II

Modern science projects three basic principles bearing upon man's place in the cosmic world.

First: Evolution. The scientist has introduced the idea of evolution to account for the genesis and development of the cosmic world, including the super galaxies, our solar system, the earth planet, life, man, and human society. It suggests the process by which various aspects of reality—cosmic, mundane, subhuman, and human—are subject to interaction, change, growth, and decline or advance.

Second: Empiricism. The scientist is advancing an empirical method of fact-finding and a consequent fund of verifiable knowledge about every aspect of the knowable world. By means of this kind of information man is learning how to control certain ranges of the human ego, society, and the natural world for the common good.

Third: Worldview. Following three centuries of scientific inquiry, man is beginning to construct a worldview, a cosmology, which suggests what is conceivably his primary role in the natural world and how he can chart his life to fulfill his highest hopes.

What are the implications of these contributions of modern science for human values? Does the cosmos show signs of caring for man, or does it operate without a basic concern for its human offspring?

A preponderance of the American people assume that man is a spiritual orphan, so far as the operation of the natural world is concerned. Conventional religious people attribute this belief to the alleged truth of the "fall" of man as recorded in the story of the Garden of Eden. The sons of Adam must turn to supernatural sources of divine intervention in the natural order for their well-being. Others, including many sophisticated persons, base their doctrine of the universe's indifference to man's highest interests upon the assumptions of Darwinianism. They believe that the individual approaches the fullness of his stature by disregarding the forces of the physical world and concentrating upon the cultivation of fraternal relations with his own kin. Although spokesmen for each of these viewpoints believe that man can and does make reasonably satisfactory biological and psychological adjustments to the physical world, his inner life must look elsewhere for its nurture. That is, spiritually speaking, the worldview suggested by the findings of science leaves all these people —the conventional Jew and Christian of the first group, and the philosophical humanist, the rationalistic skeptic, and the Marxian materialist of the second group—"cold." In their opinions the cosmos does not care for man. It is indifferent to his highest well-being.

It is my firm belief that the cosmos does provide man the means of spiritual support which he requires to live the good, full life. In my judgment an increasing number of people are being inspired by such a nascent faith. They repudiate the claims of supernaturalism, regarding them as religious props without justification in modern thought. They also reject the deterministic assumptions implicit in neo-Darwinianism as inconclusive and inadequate. On the contrary, they affirm that the universe takes a profound interest in its human progeny, and that it can be depended on, when persons establish friendly and meaningful relations with it, to help meet the deepest needs of their inner life.

For is not man an indigenous and functional element in the scheme of cosmic reality? Did not the cosmos conceive him as a mother her child? Does it not sustain him as a devout parent his growing children? And is it not making available to him the potentials of imagination, intelligence, love, and a sense of his high worth, the wherewithal for achieving the goals of the good life?

This is the orientation of faith I implied above when I stressed the idea of the creatureness of man. I believe that the dauntless inquirer has empirical grounds for affirming that the metaphysical and moral potentialities of human life are rooted in the creative processes of the natural world. This discovery permits a cultivation of the highest quality of human-cosmic comaraderie. Thus the psalmist sings, "I will look unto the hills from whence cometh my help"; the Galilean informs us, "Ye are the salt of the earth . . . the light of the world . . . the branches [of the grapevine]"; the lyric poet symbolizes the sublime significance of the "flower in the crannied wall"; the missionary of Lambarene advances the principle of "reverence for life"; and the astrophysicist dignifies the position of his fellowmen by addressing them as "we, the universe."[3]

As a distinguished son possessing this terrestrial birthright, mature man can learn to think the "thoughts" that sustain cosmic reality, to emulate the "morality" that it practices, and to develop fellowship with its "spirit" in high causes. The sensitive person extracts strength from contemplating the boundless dynamics of law and order and of process and design, and from considering the evidences of the good, the true, and the beautiful, all of which characterize the activity of microcosm and macrocosm alike. He discovers that the universe is on the side of the humane man and the good society, and that it visits judgment upon all manner of rash, misdirected, and evil acts of human kind.

This latter observation leads to the question: What about those aspects of cosmic activity which run counter to creative processes, and which sometimes visit tragedy upon its human offspring? For instance, what place do earthquake, famine, disease, and drought have in the pattern of "morality" of the natural world? How do they affect faith respecting cosmic providence? I believe that such events are hazards which necessarily arise in any developmental system of reality involving a measure of autonomous behavior of its constituent parts. Is there not an inherent ambivalence in the natural world as there is in society's structure, providing for the actuality of "good" and "evil" conditions? Be that as it may, empirical evidence substantiates the belief that the forces of good maintain a strong edge over the

[3] Harlow Shapley, "Galaxies and Their Human Worth," fourteenth annual proceedings of the Conference on Science, Philosophy and Religion (New York: Harper & Brothers, 1955), pp. 511-528.

forces of evil, else the destructive factors in the natural world long since have neutralized creative processes and demoralized man.

In summary, modern science is introducing us to a universe which is boundless and beautiful, creative and conservational. This cosmic world is man's inseparable other, his parent, and his providential ally in the good life. In cooperation with its conditions and its laws he learns to satisfy his physical needs. In fellowship with its purposive spirit he may strengthen his personal character and build the foundation of a priceless religious faith.

III

The democratic movement is focusing three values that free man esteems in the modern world. First, it affirms the dignity of the human individual. That is, every man, woman, and child, of whatsoever people, culture, nation, creed, color, status group, job, age, or sex, is a bona fide member of the family of mankind. As such, he represents the highest native value in the manifold ramifications of human society. Wherever the chastening spirit of democracy prevails the individual is thus regarded and respected by his peers.

Second, the democratic movement inspires a people to desire to improve their way of life. It affords them reason to believe that they have the intrinsic capacities of intelligence and moral character to work together, to evaluate the lot of individual members, and to enrich their collective well-being beyond any achievements in their historic past.

And third, democracy acclaims the priority of the bifocal principles of freedom *and* responsibility as binding forces in human relations. They remain prerequisites of the good life not only in interpersonal behavior but also in all aspects of political, economic, religious, cultural, and international living. When these ideals are enlisted in a balanced manner, on the one hand they ensure the integrity of desirable human differences, and on the other hand they build the ties of social unity.

These three working ideals—the dignity of man, the self-improvement of society, and the complementary principles of freedom and responsibility—insofar as they are honored as the *sine qua non* of a vibrant democracy, can and do build in the individual the sinews of moral character and in society the ethical foundations of an enduring social order.

What relations do these basic values of democracy bear to my religious faith? They are intrinsic elements of it. For the qualitative enlistment of a person, when he acts democratically, eventuates in a spiritual experience. Nothing that is sacred to the well-being of an individual or society can remain foreign to modern man's religion, else he becomes a divided self. Take moral freedom, for example. When a person senses it as the exercise of his own individuality in a socal climate in which members respect each other for their inherent dignity, the resulting bond of fraternity that is generated is not unlike the experience of love which religion extols. And what is the act of being democratically responsible in human relations if it does not approximate what religion terms the discipline of social justice?

Many persons identify the prime values of religion with those of democracy. They are the classical humanists who declare that the scope of religion is the inclusive range of human relationships and that its motif is the ethics of universal brotherhood. Their concept of religion is homocentric, as is that of democracy.

From my personal viewpoint such an identification, noble as its impulses and highly consistent as its scale of values are, represents only one sector of the religious man's quest. The humanist dedicates himself to meeting the profound trials and enjoying the rewarding triumphs of democracy. He is, wittingly or unwittingly, disregarding the significance of the cosmic matrix of the human family as well as a primary ground of its spiritual undergirding. He overlooks the inescapable impact of the cosmos upon sensitive man, and the necessity of an alert person coming to terms with the resulting imponderables and imperishables that visit human experience.

IV

Do I assume that the supreme values available to modern man, of whatsoever source, are aspects of one spiritual reality? I do. The historical movements shaping man's value-structure in the Western world are threefold: religion in the Judaeo-Christian pattern, an unfolding scientific inquiry and worldview, and the democratic cause. A constellation of values emanates from each of them. If a single inclusive galaxy of values in which modern man can have firm confidence is to be conceived, then a first step is to identify the principles interpreting the particular values of democracy, scientific worldview, and religion.

Does not the democratic cause concentrate upon human-centered interests and values? the worldview suggested by science upon nonhuman or cosmic-centered interests and values? and the Judaeo-Christian tradition upon human-cosmic-centered interests and values? A comment about each of these areas of human concern is in order.

In the pursuit of democracy man is interested in the improvement of interhuman affairs. He addresses himself to the problems and opportunities affecting for good or ill the well-being of society and its individual members. This is just as true if one looks at the social, economic, technological, or international aspects of the democratic movement as it is if one considers its political role. What contributes to the highest good of all the members of a particular people in their manifold range of human relations: that is the province of democracy.

In contrast, modern science centers its interest in matters pertaining to the physical nature of the cosmic world. This includes the interrogation of all forms of life and all manner of time-space-matter-energy phenomena, and of the widest representation of segmental elements as well as the total structure of the natural world. The scientist works on the assumptions that cause-effect relations operate universally in every aspect of cosmic behavior, and that mechanistic equations, such as $E = Mc^2$,[4] can represent the laws of the physical world. Insofar as man and society come within the scope of the scientist's inquiry, similar descriptive viewpoints are adopted as the basis for experimental study. For our immediate purpose the most significant service of science is its contribution to the making of a modern cosmology, a worldview resting upon certain assumptions and values.

On the other hand, the Judaeo-Christian tradition in its finest expression suggests the circumstances under which man can rise to his highest stature as a socio-cosmic being. This involves his personal reaction not only to the searching issues he faces in human society

[4] This is Albert Einstein's basic formula. A mass (m) of one gram of matter is equivalent in ergs (e) to the square of the velocity of light (c^2) in centimeters per second.

but also to the mystery and the creativity of the cosmic world. That is, creature-man seeks to compass in religion the meaning and purpose of socio-cosmic reality as a functioning whole, and to make his own peace with it. It is assumed that man and society belong to the natural world as children to their parents, and that through their courageous encounter with it such values of the mind and heart become available as are necessary to fulfill man's deepest spiritual needs.

Here are three converging value structures of signal importance to this generation: the democratic frame pertaining to man in his social relations (an ethical orientation); the scientific frame pertaining to man and nature as interacting elements of cosmic activity (a rational orientation); and the religious frame pertaining to man as an interrogator of socio-cosmic reality, bent upon establishing a basis of fellowship with it, and thus projecting a meaningful and purposeful way of life (a mystical and metaphysical approach the counterpart of man's ethical and rational considerations). The three structures are considered here as aspects of maturing man's experience in order to recognize the various constellations of values, the need for the reevaluation of these values, and the responsibility for equating them.

As a matter of fact, the religious person, as defined in this essay, does attempt by his intuitive touch to fuse the value-structures of democracy and applied science into a synthesis of values of transcendent importance. He approaches the challenge as one who is endeavoring to compass the most inclusive bearings of human experience and to meet them as his ally and his other. Such an individual advances a bold, but not unreasoning, affirmation of religious faith, based on what he discovers about the interrelation of himself, his social kin, and the resourceful universe.

In the process of resolving these component value-structures into a working philosophy of life fit for the strains of living in the mid-twentieth century, contemporary man faces three difficult areas of inquiry. They include the problems incidental to reconciling the values of a) democracy and scientific worldview, b) democracy and religion, and c) scientific worldview and religion.

The democratic focus of values contrasts with the scientific approach to sense phenomena at the point of the latter's indifference to human values. While the scientist *as a person* may be socially motivated, *as a scientific inquirer* he remains scrupulously detached so that the empirical method of work to which he is committed can have free play and thus advance the cause of verifiable truth. Science does not deny the validity of democratic values; it must necessarily disregard them within its own framework of operation.

On the other hand, the worldview afforded by the findings of science does involve value judgments. It suggests the limited scope of the democratic scale of values, for the philosophy of democracy treats man as a cosmic orphan, separate from the sustaining forces of the natural world. Thus a democratic society, bent upon improving human relations, tends to contribute to the widening of the breach between the self-sufficient endeavors of man and the spiritual resources available to him that are rooted in the cosmic matrix. This viewpoint lends support to the schism between the so-called "secular" and the "sacred" in man's scale of values.

What of man's relative concern with democracy and religion? Democracy, avowing its confidence in the ability of free men to build the good society, challenges the conventional outlook of Judaism and Christianity at several points. For instance, it questions any assumption about an inherently evil human nature attributable to "fallen" man. It doubts the claim that an individual can redeem his inner life apart from changing the ethical character of the society that conditions him. It is dubious that a religious person possesses absolute truth about the nature of man, human society, and their eschatological destiny. Democracy further charges that the multiple sects of the Judaeo-Christian religions contribute to excessive parochialism and to competitive ecclesiastical power systems. Consequently, they tend to break down the democratic spirit in community, national, and international life.

On the other hand, religion suggests that democracy tends to breed an ethnocentric society when its viewpoint prevails. This makes for provincialism in human thought and practice, discouraging individuals from interrogating the superhuman ranges of reality upon which creature-man is dependent, and by means of which he can enhance immeasurably his own meaning and sense of worth. The values of high religion are in no sense inimical to those of real democracy; although the two sets are identifiable in many particulars, religion is more inclusive of man's outreach to embrace the good, the true, and the beautiful, and more courageous in claiming their essential significance.[5]

In the third place, compare the value-structures of applied science and religion. Much has been written about this intriguing theme. A few observations must suffice here. The cosmic frame of thinking afforded by modern science issues a sharp challenge both to the dualistic worldview entertained by the Judaeo-Christian religions (naturalism and supernaturalism), and to the consequent dual sets of secular and sacred values which they espouse. The universe which science is introducing to modern man dwarfs into insignificance on every relevant count the cosmology of conventional religion. It leaves no need or place in a rationale of values for the supernatural framework which Jews and Christians projected in the pre-scientific era and to which so many of them still cling. As all truth is one, so, we believe, all values are one, and the universe in which man is seeking truth and values to shape a high-minded destiny is also one. Moreover, the scientific worldview, rather than necessarily belittling man's cosmic habitat, as the conventional religionist often charges, may actually enhance it with beauty, mystery, "livingness," and creativity beyond the imagination of creature-man to conjure. At the same time it can afford him ample evidence for believing that the cosmos cares for every reasonable need of its human offspring.

This encounter between the claims of applied science and religion is not a one-way street. Judaism and Christianity question the ultimate adequacy of certain scientific assumptions. For instance, the mechanistic principle that underlies all scientific explorations unquestionably serves a precise purpose within the context of these inquiries, but is it sufficient to compass those wider ranges of reality such as the human mind, the democratic quality of life, or "the mysterious universe" as affirmed by many scientists? A similar case can be made for the concept "material." The religious interpreter deepens his inquiry into the nature of reality and proposes the idea of the spiritual, not in contradistinction to the material but to imply values inherent in physical phenomena and of paramount significance to sensitive

[5] This viewpoint is developed by Stewart G. Cole, *Liberal Education in a Democracy* (New York: Harper & Brothers, 1940), pp. 223-37.

man. Religious faith ranges beyond the scope of science and resorts to more inclusive concepts to compass the imponderables and the invaluables arising in human experience. In brief, it affirms the principles of vitalism and the spiritual, outreaching determinism and the material in its approach to the nature of man, society, and the cosmic world.

A scientist may imply the relative inconsequence of man in contrast with the incomprehensible forces of the physical world. Man may be pictured, for instance, as a recent emergent in the eons of cosmic evolution and a chance mutation from animal ancestry, whose short span of life is being spent on a minor planet in a multi-galaxy universe. "What is man that Thou art mindful of him?" This claim does contain a measure of truth. However, it is equally convincing to note that man is a question-raising offspring of the cosmos, qualified to discover his lowly genesis and gifted to use his insights and ingenuity to become the master of astrophysics and of his mundane destiny.

In conclusion, I believe that modern man can forge the sinews of a religious faith capable of sustaining his ethical, rational, and spiritual integrity. If and as he builds it, he will learn to reconcile the value constellations inherent in the Judaeo-Christian tradition at its best, the worldview that the architects of science are tracing, and the democratic testimony to the enrichment of human relations among all peoples, and to fuse these multiple value systems into a single galaxy of transcendent worth. This supreme venture is one of the human heart in which personal modesty is essential; one of the mind, in which self-confidence and relentless inquiry must prevail; and one of the human will, in which personal commitment to the pursuit of the good, the true, and the beautiful at every crossroad of contemporary life is never relinquished. From my viewpoint this kind of human faith is always in-the-making for the sensitive individual and society.

V

The claims of a man's faith outdistance the horizons of his knowledge. Although somewhat conditioned by the latter, his religious attitudes take due account of the not-fully-known but the believed-in elements of significant reality with which the whole range of human experience has taught him to reckon. Thus such a person keeps his integrity and steers life's course by adequately grounded purposes. For example, an individual sensitive to the insights suggested in this essay *may* exercise religious faith when he plants his corn, drives his automobile, fellowships with a neighbor, works for the achievement of "one world," or senses a sublime personal kinship with the cosmos. Such a person may discover intrinsic values in the dynamics of such situations which can sustain his faith. Insofar as he bets his life on such an inclusive gamut of potential values and attempts to diffuse them throughout human society, he is a religious person.

Therefore, I end this essay on the note that opened it: the sense of human creatureness is the core of high religion. It characterizes all the historic faiths at their best, although it constantly requires recovery from the more doctrinaire and the secondary and inconsequential considerations that tend to stifle it. Like an eternal light it points man to the source of his supreme worth and the wellspring of his life purpose. Man is neither an end nor a *summum bonum* in himself. He remains a mundane creature, nonetheless a creature of paramount importance. He is subject to creative forces of transcendent worth. These reside in the productive, sustaining, and reinforcing processes of the universe. Man "belongs" to this ageless order of reality which sired him and which affords him the capacity to rise in social, moral, and intellectual stature. For this reason these forces are spiritual in character and the reality to which man must give his unswerving allegiance. In league with these forces, he can have a profound feeling of fellowship with God and from them he can draw inspiration and strength to meet the challenge of the good life.

I believe that such a faith needs to undergird man in this age of acute change, confusion, and skepticism. It will help him to abstain from sheer pessimism (Nietzsche), for the high cause to which he is dedicated is shared by other "hands" beyond those of embattled human beings; it will save him from self-worship for he must needs sense his basic dependence (Schleiermacher) upon superhuman help; and it will temper his faith to avoid absolute optimism (William James), for the pursuit of the good life is an interdependent cause in which the highest and the best in man and the cosmos must cooperate to win the better day.

The question remains whether the pluralistic forces in the cosmos to which I have been pointing as the sustaining structure of human faith can be conceived as "God." Are they necessarily many or do they focus in one? Who knows? We do know that man possesses various *persona* by which he makes himself known to his kind. On second thought, how consequential is the question? The essential fact upon which we need to focus our interest in that creature-man is confronted by a spiritual Otherness which is rooted in the physical universe, with which he must come to terms in his pursuit of the ultimate purpose and values of life. He may move forward with confidence using this postulate to reformulate a resurgent religious faith in an age of beneficent science, emancipative democracy, and one potential humanity.

Consequently, the concept "God" serves an essential purpose in my approach to life's meaning and value. It symbolizes the value-reality of transcendent worth to man, even though it remains in the twilight of his verifiable knowledge. "We know in part," wrote the Apostle Paul. This concept is the priceless key to man's hierarchy of values. For is not God the ultimate source and sustainer of all values, human and cosmic, whom man may and does prehend as he meets the conditions of becoming a mature human being? As a person senses Him, does he not find God revealed in all manner of processes of creative activity, countering the forces of disintegration and evil and reinforcing the good, the true, and the beautiful, throughout His boundless socio-cosmic economy? And does not every man, whether he believes it or not, share in the activity of God to the degree that he dares to live the good, full life of an individual among his peers and as a creature-child of a spiritually inspiring universe?

MONROE E. DEUTSCH

Monroe E. Deutsch, who climaxed a long career at the University of California by becoming Vice-President and Provost (1931-37) was also known as a friendly counselor of collegiate youth. A trustee of Mills College, he began his teaching career as a classicist at San Francisco High School, following graduation from the University of California and postgraduate studies abroad. Holder of the Chevalier of the Legion of Honor (France) and other foreign decorations for his international service to students, the late Dr. Deutsch's affiliations included the World Students Service Fund and the American Association for the United Nations. He was president of the Western College Association and the World Affairs Council of Northern California. His books include: The Abundant Life *(1926);* Our Legacy of Religious Freedom *(1941); and* The College from Within *(1952).*

I

THE religious values which should be stressed today are the very ones set forth as fundamental in both the Old and the New Testament. They are those declared by Jesus to be the supreme commandments. Matthew 22.36–40 reads as follows:

Master, which is the great commandment in the law?
Jesus said unto him, Thou shalt love the Lord thy God with all thy heart, and with all thy soul, and with all thy mind.
This is the first and great commandment.
And the second is like unto it, Thou shalt love thy neighbor as thyself.
On these two commandments hang all the law and the prophets.

Both of these commandments had previously been set forth in the Old Testament. Deuteronomy 6:5 reads: "Thou shalt love the Lord thy God with all thy heart, and with all thy soul, and with all thy might." And in Leviticus 19:18 appears the charge: "Thou shalt love thy neighbor as thyself."

Human brotherhood is indeed one of the basic injunctions of the Judaeo-Christian religion, and toward its realization mankind must assuredly press forward. Thomas Jefferson declared: "The truth of the matter is that Nature has implanted in our breasts a love of others, a sense of duty to them, a moral instinct, in short, which prompts us irresistibly to feel and succor their distresses" (June 13, 1814).

To these I should add a third—a belief in the immortality of the soul. About the exact form in which this takes place, I find myself in total darkness. But I cannot believe that the spirit of man with all its achievements and capacities is blotted out completely when the breath leaves the body. It must have been created and developed for more than this.

In short, I find myself in close accord with that great American, Benjamin Franklin. In his famous letter to Ezra Stiles, president of Yale University, he wrote: "Here is my creed. I believe in one God, Creator of the Universe. That he governs it by His providence. That He ought to be worshipped. That the most acceptable service we render Him is doing good to His other children. That the soul of man is immortal, and will be treated with justice in another life respecting its conduct in this. These I take to be the fundamental principles of all sound religion, and I regard them as you do in whatever sect I meet with them. . . ."

II

The recognition of a power greater than human, one that in some manner set this universe into being, lifts man's eyes from the material to the spiritual and gives greater meaning to life itself. What form this power has (certainly not anthropomorphic), we do not know, but its very existence is an inspiration to nobler living. I do believe that the power which was responsible for the beginning of this universe has continued its existence. That its aim is for good and that it seeks the well-being of the world, I am firmly convinced. That at times it results in destruction is due not to any failure of the Deity to seek man's good, but to man's failure or inability to adjust to nature's laws, laws which are beneficial in purpose. Wars, for example, manifest man's weakness. If through tornadoes or earthquakes or fires human life is lost, it is due to the operation of physical laws which are constant and are not altered or checked by any miraculous interposition. Fire burns—that is its nature—and if for any reason fire is kindled, it will fulfill its destiny and serve to benefit mankind or destroy, whether it be property or human life.

Significant are the words of Jefferson written in a letter to John Adams (April 11, 1820): "When we take a view of the universe, in its parts, general or particular, it is impossible for the human mind not to perceive and feel a conviction of design, consummate skill, and indefinite power in every atom of its composition. So irresistible are these evidences of an intelligent and powerful agent, that of the infinite numbers of men who have existed through all time, they have believed, in the proportion of a million at least to a unit, in the hypothesis of an eternal pre-existence of a Creator, rather than that of a self-existing universe."

III

Assuredly the basis for the acceptance of the democratic ideal is belief in the dignity and worth of the individual, of the human spirit —every human spirit—and this in turn springs inevitably from the conception of the brotherhood of man, one of the great commandments. And I cannot conceive of a religion of real significance to mankind that does not call for a moral life: certainly I feel that this is an intrinsic element of any faith worthy to be termed religion.

IV

It is possible for individuals to live a moral life without the aid of any particular creed or indeed of religion at all—but I am convinced that for the vast majority of humanity there is no stronger support for a good life than the aid of religion. And in reliance on God men are strengthened and heartened in the tasks that fall to them. When Lincoln was en route to Washington to assume the presidency, he paused in Springfield, Illinois and delivered an address of which these are the concluding words: "Without the assistance

of that Divine Being who ever attended him [George Washington]
I cannot succeed. With that assistance I cannot fail. Trusting in Him
who can go with me and remains with you, and be everywhere for
good, let us confidently hope that all will yet be well. To His care
commending you, as I hope in your prayers you will commend me,
I bid you an affectionate farewell."

V

The concept of God is fundamental in my religious belief. It is
the power that, whether we understand its workings or not, steadily
moves toward the establishment of a better and a better world. I
admit that I have no clear conception of God—but this does not
lessen my belief in His existence. To make a commonplace comparison, I have no clear conception of electricity, but I know it exists
and know its power. I do not believe that He punishes or rewards
in a future life—heaven and hell are creations of minds that believe
men only do good through hope of reward or fear of punishment.
This is conceiving of God as a taskmaster, a judge (if you will) keeping a record of every human's deeds, good and bad. In my notion this
is demeaning God and regarding Him as a being like us feeble
humans instead of a power infinitely greater and nobler than ourselves.

ALBERT EINSTEIN*

Albert Einstein: mathematical physicist, distinguished philosopher, friend of man. Discoverer of the theory of relativity, and a Nobel Prize winner, the late Mr. Einstein came to the United States from his native Germany in 1933, when he was appointed a life member of the Institute for Advanced Study at Princeton. Prior to this he held teaching positions at Universitat Zurich, Deutsche University, Prague, Technische Hochschule (Zurich), Preuss, and Akademie d. Wissenschaft (Berlin). Einstein, who became a naturalized American citizen in 1940, was awarded the Franklin Institute Medal, membership in the Institute de France, *and honorary degrees from Princeton and Harvard and from thirteen European institutions. In addition to his internationally famous scientific studies he was the author of the following books:* "Living Philosophers" *(with others) (1931); (with Sigmund Freud)* Why War? *(1933);* The World as I See It *(1934); and* Out of My Later Years *(1950).*

I T IS difficult to make a statement on the subject of "religion" because people conceive of it as various matters which have little relationship one to another.

Religion may be understood as a type of *belief* concerning the origin and meaning of the universe. A being (or beings), thought analogous to man, created the universe and guides all events in accordance with his will. This is—in short—the animistic content of most of the traditionally organized religions, including the Judaeo-Christian branch.

* The reader will note that the late Albert Einstein decided not to subdivide his essay following the proposed plan of the inquiry.

On the other hand, religion is often conceived as the totality of convictions concerning the values of all human action and striving. This is the moral content of religion. The reason for including this in the concept of religion lies in the fact that moral evaluation is based on convictions and principles fixed by tradition, hence also a type of *belief* with emphasis on emotions.

Judging psychologically, I believe that the animistic aspect of religion is not in consonance with the causal attitude due to the development of science during the last few centuries.

I consider it of greatest importance that the moral content of religion should become independent from animistic beliefs. This moral content has always been the essence of religion. It was, however, natural that in early times this moral content should be closely linked to the dominant animistic world concept.

It is of greatest importance for humanity that—with the disappearance of the animistic concept—moral tradition should be dissolved from this liaison. The Chinese and Hindus anticipated us substantially in this respect even though they were far from a purely causal concept of nature in the sense of modern science.

Anyone who has freed himself from the animistic concept will consider the drive for improvement and beautification of human relationships a purely human problem—yet the most important of all human problems. Therefore, he would refrain from applying any moral standards to the universe outside of the human realm.

Apart from the deep satisfaction afforded by clear thought and the understanding of objective relationships, the striving for scientific knowledge creates means for the improvement of the human lot. Scientific striving also makes it easier for us to restrain those animalistic instincts which are hampering the improvement of human conditions. The striving for an understanding of nature shows us the sublime lawfulness of existence in the modest framework of our potentialities. It leads him who earnestly seeks to that *humility* which we need so urgently also in the human sphere. I consider it, however, erroneous to believe that scientific knowledge by itself will lead to an improvement of human conditions. The passionate will to contribute to the improvement of these conditions must come from an independent source.

PHILIPP G. FRANK*

In 1910 Philipp G. Frank succeeded Albert Einstein as an instructor in physics at the University of Prague. In 1938 he entered the United States and became a lecturer in mathematics and physics at Harvard. Dr. Frank is chairman of a research project in the philosophy of science sponsored by The National Science Foundation, a Councillor of the American Academy of Arts and Sciences, a past president of the American Association for the Philosophy of Science, and a Fellow of the Conference on Science, Philosophy and Religion. His books include The End of Mechanistic Physics *(1937);* Between Physics and Philosophy *(1940);* Einstein, his Life and Times *(1947); and* Relativity: A Richer Truth *(1951).*

WHILE the picture of the physical world that has been developed by physical science has undergone radical changes since the time of Plato, Aristotle, and St. Thomas, the picture outlined by Thomistic philosophy has not changed. The foundations of the Thomistic doctrine have been and are today: first, the doctrine that every material body in the commonsense meaning of this word, consists actually of "prime matter" and "substantial form," and, second, the doctrine that the laws of nature are not only uniformities but "genuine laws" which are imposed by a lawgiver.

In close connection with these doctrines is the general feature

* Mr. Frank's essay, which was prepared for the fourteenth meeting of the Conference on Science, Philosophy and Religion and entitled, "The Physical Universe as a Symbol," is reproduced here by permission of the author, the Conference, and Harper & Brothers, who have published the proceedings of the Conference under the title, *Symbols and Society* (1955).

of Thomistic philosophy that has been described by a representative of this school as an "analogy of being in the vertical dimension," according to which all physical phenomena are analogous to the phenomena exhibited by living organisms. This is also an analogy to commonsense experience, for the main constituents of our commonsense experience are the behavior of simple mechanisms and the familiar rules about the behavior of our fellow men. All this amounts to the doctrine that our physical universe that can be understood according to physical science by a search for physical laws, causal or statistical ones, is, from the viewpoint of the philosopher, operated for certain purposes "for a common good," as Thomistic philosophers say. The universe is not regarded as a dead machine but as a society of living beings which is somehow similar to human society and can be used as an ideal of how human society should operate. This means that all physical phenomena can be interpreted not only by the traditional laws of physics, but also moral laws.

This interpretation of the physical universe as a moral universe started in antiquity in the writings of Plato and was continued strongly in medieval philosophy, with particular lucidity in the work of St. Thomas. It is easy to understand that in medieval poetry this moral interpretation of the physical universe was a favorite topic. The most famous example of this physico-moral world picture is Dante's *Divine Comedy*, where the physical universe is interpreted as consisting of Hell, Purgatory, and Paradise, or, in other words, as a place where rewards and punishments are dished out according to the moral merits of human beings. The great American philosopher, George Santayana, in his "Essay on Dante," provided a particularly lucid and instructive presentation of the medieval idea about the physical universe. Santayana directs our attention to the fact that the mere distinction between "prime matter" and "substantial form" introduces a moral element into the physical world. The natural lines of cleavage were obliterated, and as Santayana writes "moral lines of cleavage" were substituted for them. "Nature was a compound of ideal purposes and inert matter, or a compound of evil matter and perfect form. . . . Evil was identified with matter."

This doctrine has infiltrated a great many philosophical interpretations of science. Even in our twentieth century, quite a few philos-

ophers and philosophically inclined scientists have extolled Ruther-
ford's "Theory of the Atom," because the largest part of the atom
is empty and only very tiny pieces of matter (nucleus and electrons)
have remained. Like the followers of the medieval philosophers,
these contemporary authors believe that by reducing the quantity of
matter in the physical universe the world has been purged from evil.
For Dante, as Santayana writes, "moral distinctions are displayed
in the order of creation. The creator himself was a poet producing
allegories. The material world was a parable which he built out in
space in order to be enacted." The idea of medieval philosophy,
Christian as well as Jewish and Moslem, was that the purpose of
nature was to produce "the good," and the physical laws were
symbols by which the moral laws are revealed to man.

In order to put all this in the right perspective, we must not forget
that this conception of physical laws was by no means originated in
medieval Scholastics but had its origin far back in antiquity. Santayana pointed out that this moral interpretation of physical phenomena was with particular lucidity presented by Plato in his dialogue
Phaedo. Socrates, the spokesman of Plato in the dialogue, complains
about the way in which some philosophers (in our language, the
scientists) claim to have explained the features of our physical universe, whether the earth is round or flat, how the earth is supported
at its place, etc. These philosophers disappointed him because they
tried to explain everything by what we would call today causal or
physical laws, while he expected them to prove that the actual physical
universe is "the best" in the moral sense of the word. According to
Santayana, this Platonic philosophy that later became the basis of
medieval thought, said bluntly: "The world is a work of reason. It
must be interpreted as we interpret the actions of a man, by its
motives." In order to learn how precisely Plato rejected what we
today call causal or physical explanations, we may quote some sentences from the Platonic dialogue *Phaedo*.

Socrates says:

I imagined that he (the philosopher Anaxogoras) would tell me whether
the earth is flat or round; and whichever was true he would proceed to
show the nature of the best and show that this was best; and if he said
that the earth was in the center of the universe he would further explain

that this position was the best, and I should be satisfied with the explanation given and not want other sort of cause. . . . What expectations I had
formed and how grievously was I disappointed As I proceeded, I found
my philosopher altogether forsaking reason. . . . but having recourse to
air and ether and water and other eccentricities.

It is illuminating to note that the Platonic Socrates calls all
physical causes "eccentricities" in contrast to the explanation by
purposes.

However, we can go back much further if we want to find examples
for the symbolic role of the physical universe. We are all accustomed
to relax every seventh day of the week, and a great many of us
every sixth and seventh day. The root of this habit is a theory of
the Old Testament about the way our physical universe originated.
The Hebrew cosmology has been interpreted through the ages as a
rule of human conduct that has not outlived its validity today.

Among liberal theologians it has become a habit to say that the
Bible is not a textbook of physical science but a guide to moral
behavior. However, it would be more nearly correct to say that the
Bible is a textbook of physical science which teaches science in a
form which has lost greatly its technological value but kept, to a high
degree, its social value. From a careful study of the Book of Genesis,
we can easily learn that even the Law of Causality itself was interpreted by the writers of the Old Testament as an incentive for
moral conduct. After the great Flood, God says to Noah: "I established my Covenant with you and the waters shall never again become
a flood to destroy all flesh . . . while the earth remains, seedtime and
harvest, cold, heat, summer and winter, day and night shall not
cease."

If we remember the scientific meaning of the Law of Causality, we
can say that God pledged after the Flood that the Law of Causality
will remain valid eternally, unless man behaves in such an immoral
way that God would punish him by abolishing causality. God behaves like a constitutional king who proclaims a constitution and
promises not to violate it except in the case of emergency.

The fact that in the Bible the Law of Causality is regarded as a
reward for the good conduct of man becomes completely clear from
some passages in the Talmud, a commentary to the Old Testament

which contains the oral tradition among the Jewish people: "When the Holy One, blessed be He, created the first man, He made him lord above everything, the cow obeyed the plowman and the furrow obeyed the plowman. Adam having sinned, they rose up against him: the cow no longer obeyed the plowman, nor did the furrow obey the plowman. With Noah, they quieted down." It is instructive to note that the reaction of the cow to man, a law of animal psychology, is treated on an equal footing with the reaction of the furrow to the plow, a physical law. In the same way, the laws that governed the motion of liquids served moral purposes. The Talmud continues: "Before Noah, the waters used to rise twice a day, once at morning prayer, and once at evening prayer, and they used to flood the dead in their graves. With Noah, the waters quieted down."

If we consider instead of the ancient Hebrew world picture Copernicus's picture of the physical world, we read in his main book: "The sun is sitting on a royal throne, rules the family of stars moving around it." The planetary system is described by the analogy with the system of government in the monarchy. We have to remember that this analogy was used by Copernicus for the purpose of bolstering his heliocentric system. "The condition of immobility," wrote Copernicus, "is considered more noble and divine than the condition of change and instability, which therefore is more fitting to the earth than the universe."

All these examples lead up to the general conception of the physical universe as analogous to a human society by which this universe becomes a useful symbol for encouraging a desirable way of life. E. Topitsch gave to this conception the name of "socio-cosmic" universe. He collected from a great many sources material from which we learn that this conception did not prevail only among Hebrews and Greeks but also in China, India, and Mesopotamia. "The whole world," Topitsch sums up these examples, "is conceived as a state, a city or a well-ordered household, and the regularities of nature correspond to the rules that govern civil life."[1]

From this conception it became possible to derive what should be regarded as a "natural" or "ideal" structure of human society: the

[1] E. Topitsch, "Society, Technology, and Philosophical Reasoning," *Philosophy of Science,* October 1954, page 275 ff.

structure that corresponded to the structure of the physical universe. By the same argument, the history of mankind was also regarded as determined by the motions of the stars. According to the original idea of astrology, the stars did not determine the life of individual persons but only historic events. Obviously the life of kings belongs in this sphere; but the sale of "horoscopes" to indiscriminate individuals belongs in a decayed phase of astrology.

Werner Jaeger, in his book on *Aristotle,* stresses the close correspondence between the Greek ideas in astronomy and their ideas about the moral order in the city-state. "The human laws should be obeyed," as Topitsch summarizes Jaeger, "because, and insofar as they were a part of the rules governing the cosmos which became, by this reflection, the pattern of the right order in society, the metaphysical foundation of the city-state morality."

However, it would be a great mistake to believe that this symbolic use of the physical universe has been abandoned in our scientific century. When atomic physics abandoned strict determinism as the supreme law for the motions of the smallest particles, this has been used as a symbol for the freedom of human actions. We have only to look into the book of one of the most prominent American lawyers and philosophers of law, *Fate and Freedom* by Jerome N. Frank,[2] in order to learn the moral conclusions which have been drawn from the "nondeterministic" character of the physical world picture that has prevailed in the twentieth century.

The philosophy of Dialectical Materialism which has become the official doctrine of all Marxist groups, has made continuous efforts to shape the picture of the physical world in such a way that the laws of human behavior would be derived from physical laws by way of "dialectics." The laws of "dialectics" have been construed as the most general principles which are equally valid for physical and social phenomena. The most palpable of these principles is the "transition from quantity into quality." If a property increases quantitatively more and more, a point will come when the property undergoes a change in quality. The most famous example in physics is the heating of water. As its temperature increases more and more, the water remains unchanged in quality; it remains water. But at the boiling point water is converted into a body of changed quality, the vapor of

[2] (New York: Simon & Schuster, Inc., 1954).

water. The physicist would not see in this presentation of the boiling process a great help to advancement in the theory of heat. But Friedrich Engels, the main collaborator of Karl Marx, already has pointed out that this presentation shows clearly the analogy between the physical universe and social behavior. If, in a human society, the accumulation of the means of production (capital, machinery, etc.) increases, the character of the society changes only quantitatively; the society remains qualitatively a society of private owners. But if we apply the physical theory in its dialectical presentation, we can expect that after great quantitative changes, great accumulations of capital in few private hands, there will be a qualitative change by which the means of production will be taken out of private hands and will become property of the community.

The prediction of the coming collectivization of private property gets, in the Marxist philosophy, its strength and reliability from the fact that it is derived from a good understanding of the laws governing the physical universe. If we look "understandingly" at physical phenomena such as evaporation, we immediately feel, according to Dialectical Materialism, how properties like temperature are increasing quantitatively more and more without experiencing any qualitative change, until the accumulated drive toward a qualitative change becomes so strong that it frees itself eventually in a sudden jump. The necessity of a social revolution manifests itself, according to Dialectical Materialism, to everyone who attempts to get a real understanding of the origin of changes in the physical world.

If we analyze this conception of the physical universe as a symbol for rules of human behavior, we run into some difficulties which are evident to anybody who has done some "hard thinking" in the logic and epistemology of science. As we have pointed out, the picture of the physical world that is accepted at a certain period serves, in a symbolic way, as a source from which rules for human behavior can be derived. The shortest way of presenting these rules is to say that the physical universe can be interpreted as an ideal human society; every real human society attempts to become as similar as possible to this ideal, and this approach becomes the rule of its moral behavior.

If we describe this situation as a whole, we easily note that first, our picture of the physical universe is created by the human mind as an image of our actual human society; but that second, once this image is firmly established, it becomes an example by which human society is guided in its attempt to become an ideal society. This, however, is a clear example of circular thought; man creates the universe as an image of his own social organization, and then shapes his organization according to the image that he has himself created. It is logically clear that by this procedure no feasible rule for human behavior can be derived. Topitsch writes in the paper quoted above: "I tried to show that these procedures generally lead into purely analytical propositions which are either eternal truths because they are tautologies and disguised definitions, or eternal problems because they are self-contradictions." Historically, of course, the idea of the physical universe as a symbol for human society has had a great influence upon human behavior, because at every individual moment of history man has an individual picture of the universe; practically, the complete chain of reasoning is not conscious to man when he has to make a decision.

WINFRED E. GARRISON

Winfred E. Garrison was literary editor of the Christian Century *for 32 years (1923-55). A graduate of Eureka College and Yale and with higher degrees from the University of Chicago, he was a professor of church history at Chicago (1921-43) and also dean of the Disciples Divinity House (1921-27). Earlier he was president of Butler College and of New Mexico A. & M. College. He has been a professor of philosophy and religion at the University of Houston since 1951 and chairman of the department since 1955. He is a past president of the New Mexico Education Association and of the American Society of Church History and has been closely associated with the World Council of Churches and the conferences leading up to it. His books include:* Catholicism and the American Mind *(1928);* Intolerance *(1934);* The March of Faith *(1933);* A Protestant Manifesto *(1952); and* Christian Unity and Disciples of Christ *(1955).*

INTRODUCTION

I AM HOSPITABLE to the affirmative contributions of theism, science, and humanism to the clarification and confirmation of moral values, both personal and social, but am suspicious of the partisans of any one of these three the moment they begin to employ such terms as "only" and "nothing but." The margins of mystery about the theme are too great to permit the dogmatic assertion that any single formula is complete in itself and exclusive of all others. Personally I am a theist, by religious faith and also on what seem to me to be adequate rational grounds; but the positive elements contributed to an adequate value-structure by the application of rigorous scientific method to

73

natural and social phenomena and by the insights of the humanistic approach seem quite indispensable.[1]

The five questions to which the contributors to this symposium have been asked to address themselves are searching. They probe to the roots of religion and of philosophy, and also, in a somewhat different way, of science and of the social structure. Even though the inquiry begins with a question about the elements of permanent value (if any) in the Judaeo-Christian tradition and ends with one about the concept of God, it must not be assumed that it is only religion that is here being summoned to the bar of critical judgment and called upon to justify its existence. What are these varied, and sometimes competing, systems of thought with which we are here concerned?

The most general definition of religion, however it may be phrased, includes a recognition of man's dependence upon a power (or powers) higher than his individual self, some techniques of adjustment to this power by acts or attitudes designed to make its resources available to meet human needs, and some sense of a relationship between man's behavior and the nature or will of the higher power. In the higher religions, at least, these factors find expression in beliefs, forms of worship, and moral sanctions. Even more fundamental is an attitude of devotion to this higher power which underlies the specific beliefs, rituals of worship, and codes of behavior and lifts them to a level above that of mere devices for harnessing the higher power to the self-centered purposes of the individual or group.

Philosophy views critically the assumptions that underlie the beliefs, practices, and moral sanctions of religion. It explores the nature of ultimate reality, and thus questions the nature and existence of a "higher power" to which any adjustment might be possible other than conformity to the physical laws of the universe. It is critical of man's naive assumptions about the certainty and extent of his knowledge. It analyzes the sense of "oughtness" to see whether man's traditional ethical imperative is anything other than social pressure and a shrewd estimate of probable consequences for the individual immediately concerned.

[1] The author wishes to acknowledge, with thanks, many stimulating suggestions derived from *Religion and the Moral Life*, by A. Campbell Garnett (New York: The Ronald Press, 1954).

Science is concerned chiefly with the observation of phenomena and their arrangement in orderly patterns. It is descriptive rather than interpretative, and because it finds dependable sequences it can also be predictive. It tells how things happen, not why. It does not deal with values. When it seems to do so, it is actually showing that certain processes are useful in producing results which are assumed to be desirable but which it does not itself evaluate. It is not the function of science to decide what is ultimately desirable—that is, good not as a means but as an end. Science has developed such an intricate and extensive arrangement of phenomena in orderly sequence, reaching far back in time and spreading through the observable cosmos, that in spite of some difficult gaps (as between the inorganic and the organic) it seems to have woven the phenomena of nature together into one unbroken fabric manifesting the uniformity of natural law. By extrapolation at both ends of this vast series and by interpolation where chasms have not yet been bridged, such as the origin of life and the beginning of human personality, it may give the impression of having set up a perfect pattern of natural law reaching to the utmost bounds of time and space. But it has no answer to questions about the beginning of all things, or the design (if any) of the cosmos, or the nature of reality, or the ultimate values implicit in people, things, and events.

The existing structure of our society and what we call the democratic way of life command the allegiance of all right-thinking Americans, but these are instrumental rather than ultimate in their values. The democratic order is good because it is good for men. But why should it be assumed that what is good for men is *good*? The democratic philosophy has, of itself, no answer to that question. It must start with the presupposition that the welfare of men is of such value that it can properly be the objective of a social order. It must leave to other disciplines the establishment of a doctrine of the nature and value of man which justifies that assumption—if, indeed, any discipline can.

All these considerations are involved in a discussion of the questions that have been propounded. Before taking up the alternative theories or systems of thought that are before us (if they are alternatives), it should be noted that the whole argument about them must rest back upon some moral judgment that is common to the theistic, the humanistic, and the secularist interpretations of the cosmic order and the values in human life. There must be some generally accepted concept of a desirable social order and some agreement as to what one has a right to expect of any acceptable system of thought about it. It would doubtless be agreed that such a system of thought must: (1) take into account all the empirical data, including man's moral experience; (2) provide, or at least permit, moral ideas which will tend to the development of such a society as is held to be desirable by all parties to the inquiry; and (3) furnish adequate motivation for putting these moral ideas into action. I turn now to the five specific questions.

I

When we consider the values that are to be found in the Judaeo-Christian religions when they have been "stripped of their divergent ethnic, doctrinal, and structural factors," it must not be assumed either (a) that the features thus left outside our purview are in themselves unimportant, or (b) that they are alien accretions by which the original "pure" forms of these religions have become overlaid in the course of the centuries, or (c) that the three categories of excluded factors are coordinate. On each of these points there could be much argument which would be irrelevant to the present discussion. For our purpose it is sufficient to say that we are not considering the nature or value of what is being set aside, but are confining our attention to the elements common to these religions in all their forms. The notable fact is that there are such common elements and that they are of a fundamental nature.

It should be added at once that the elements which are common to Judaism and Christianity are also shared, to a great degree, by the other great ethnic religions. The limitations of the theme do not invite further discussion of this statement, but the truth behind it merits consideration in its proper place. Islam, Buddhism, and Hinduism may not be conspicuous factors in American culture, but it would be a grievous error to omit them in an audit of the spiritual resources that are available for meeting contemporary problems when these are viewed in a worldwide perspective.

The Hebrew and Christian religions, besides being much more, are ways of saying that man is important, has value, is not an accident or a by-product in the evolution of an impersonal cosmos, or a bubble of consciousness on the surface of the unconscious stream of physical reality. To those who held the Christian view of man's importance in the total scheme of things, it once seemed essential to think of the earth, since it is man's habitation, as the fixed center about which the rest of the cosmos revolves. That turned out to be a mistake. Under the circumstances it was a natural mistake since nearly everyone at that time, regardless of religious belief, thought that the earth was flat, fixed, and central. Religious thinkers presently discovered that the nature and value of man are not conditioned on the location or status of his habitat in relation to other astronomical bodies. A much less excusable mistake was later made by the nonreligious who, never having learned this liberating truth, concluded that the human race must be a fortuitous and negligible episode because its earth is a mere molecule in one among a myriad of galaxies.

The Judaeo-Christian tradition, then, starts with man's natural and naive sense of his own importance, but widens its dimensions by relating him to an eternal purpose of God, disciplines it by revealing to him his limitations, and socializes it by teaching him that other men are as important as he is and for the same reason, because they all stand in the same relation to God. The point of most importance for our present consideration is that the whole Judaeo-Christian system—with its God, its ritual procedures, and moral requirements, its concepts of sin, forgiveness, and redemption, and all its "doctrinal and structural factors"—is giving an impressive answer to the question, "What is man?" Whether its dogmas be divinely revealed truths or products of human speculation and imagination, whether its *Heilsgeschichte* be myth, legend, or a reliable history of God's acts for man's salvation, by all these things it is saying (though it is saying much more) that man, *as man,* has immeasurable worth, and that men are related to one another, as well as to God, in terms of mutual moral responsibility.

There have been times when the theological expression of this high estimate of man got so far out of hand that it defeated its social purpose by being so terribly concerned about the salvation of souls as to forget the worth of actual human life and the dignity and liberties of men here and now. Then the worth of man as he is and the splendid possibilities of life here on earth had to be rediscovered by the revival of interests and ideas not recognizably religious. The Renaissance was one such period.

Organized and institutional religion often resents and resists such invasion by "secular" influences and insists that, since it is of divine origin, it is both perfect and sufficient for all man's needs. Divine or not in its origin, religion works through men, and religious men are no more infallible than any others. The loftiest view of man as a child of God and a candidate for eternal bliss is no guarantee of good social arrangements on earth or of an intelligent and humane solution of the problems posed by an intricate industrialized society. Back of these technical problems relating to the formulation of a "good" way of life and the ordering of a "good" society there lies, however, the fundamental question as to what it means for a social order to be "good" and what are the ultimate values toward which it is directed. Merely believing in God does not answer that question, any more than does believing in the inviolability of natural law and the regularity of nature. The theist cannot fall back upon the easy definition of the good as conformity to the will of God, true as that proposition may be. Such a statement, if not further supported, drains all ethical significance from the proposition that "God is good," because it amounts to saying that whatever God wills is good because God wills it. It would be empty praise to say that "the king wills only what is lawful," if one had previously declared that "the law is whatever the king wills."

As a theist, therefore, I cannot say that man without the idea of God is a moral imbecile, or that religion is the source of the sense of "oughtness" and of that capacity to distinguish between right and wrong upon which the development of a moral order depends. Rather is it true that the idea of a good God could never arise if the "natural man"—man as the secularist and the humanist conceive him—did not have in him the root of the matter as a creature having what may be called a "moral experience" that is as natural to him as is the sensory experience out of which he constructs his knowledge of the physical world.

The existence of this kind of moral experience is a fact of which any philosophy must take account in its interpretation of the whole cosmic and human process. It points toward, if it does not demonstrate, the presence of a corresponding ethical quality in whatever it is that constitutes the basic and creative reality of the cosmos. It is not necessary to rehearse here the familiar "arguments for the existence of God." In their classic form—e.g., as set forth by St. Thomas Aquinas—they profess to prove only the existence of a Being infinite in power, wisdom, and goodness; but the "goodness" is a kind of metaphysical perfection having no ethical substance that man can recognize as akin to his own sense of moral obligation, and the infinitude hangs upon the tenuous argument that it really does require an infinite cause to account for an effect which, though immeasurably large, is still finite. On that line of argument, such moral qualities as love, kindness, disinterestedness, altruism are left wholly unsupported except by special revelation. In short, reason tells us that God is infinitely powerful; revelation tells us that he is infinitely good. I am not satisfied with that. I am more certain of God's goodness than I am of his infinite power, and that because the argument from man's moral nature and moral experience is more convincing than the argument for an infinite First Cause or an all-wise designer and director of the cosmos.

In the view which I am supporting then, the Hebrew-Christian tradition is not the source of the fundamental concept of a social order which is also a moral order. It does perform important functions in the development and support of such a concept and in its progressive realization.

First. It makes an important contribution to the statement of the principles that govern right relations among men and, in a less degree, to the formation of an acceptable code of moral behavior. It cannot be forgotten that "Thou shalt love thy neighbor as thyself" is both a Hebrew and a Christian injunction (Lev. 19:18; Matt. 22:39); and in both the affirmation of this basic principle of human relationship is explicitly connected with recognition of the reality of God and man's relation to him. For the implementation of this principle by specific decisions as to what love of neighbor requires under the varying conditions of the ever-changing human situation, men are of course chiefly dependent upon their own judgment in the light of their personal and social experience. However, the moral demands of Judaism and of Christianity are not left wholly in general terms. Even though much of the Hebrew law must be regarded as no longer applicable, there are elements of its moral code which stand with undiminished validity. "Thou shalt not kill," "Thou shalt not commit adultery," "Thou shalt not steal," "Thou shalt not bear false witness" are still sound rules of conduct. Christian ethics cannot be so readily reduced to rules, but it is not lacking in positive content and it may originally have been much more specific than is generally supposed (see *Gospel and Law,* by C. H. Dodd).[2] The question is not whether Jews and Christians have kept inviolate the moral teachings of their religions. Of course they have not. But always they have been confronted by these standards by which to measure their own delinquencies. The continued existence of this ethical tradition has been a factor of incalculable importance in the moral history of Western culture, and even today it confers its benefits not only on those who ascribe to it a divine origin but also to those who, denying this, yet live within a civilization that has been dominated by it.

Second. The Judaeo-Christian tradition, being theistic, provides a needed motivation for ethical action and an escape from the blind alley of purely utilitarian ethics. An ethical theism conceives of man's fundamental and natural "moral experience" as grounded in the existence of a God who is the source of that moral order in which man finds himself. To such a God man may—and the committed believer does—give himself in devotion. His motive for right action is therefore not the personal advantage he may gain by following such a course but the desire to live in harmony with that God to whom he has made this commitment. This is doubtless what Jesus meant when he said: "Thou shalt love the Lord thy God with all thy heart, and with all thy soul, and with all thy mind. This is the first and greatest commandment. And the second is like unto it, Thou shalt love thy neighbor as thyself." And it is what the writer of Leviticus meant when he wrote: "Thou shalt love thy neighbor as thyself; I am the Lord." The often repeated statement of the egoistic hedonist, that the martyr goes to the stake or the hero to certain death for his coun-

²   (New York: Columbia University Press, 1951).

try's cause because that is what they most enjoy, is a completely shallow remark with only the charm of paradox to commend it. The significance of the Judaeo-Christian tradition in relation to the moral and social order is that it lifts ethics above the level of the merely prudential into the realm of loyal commitment. It is not conditioned upon the recognition of "moral absolutes" in the sense of irreformable codes of behavior—a doctrine always imperiled by the discovery that, as a matter of history and present fact, codes of behavior are always largely the product of social experience and cultural evolution. Rising above the sterile dispute as to whether particular moral laws are "absolute" or "relative," it challenges man to be loyal to the best he knows about the morally right because only so can he be loyal to the God who is the source and ground of the moral order.

II

Modern science has given us a vastly increased knowledge of the physical world, of the incredibly intricate history of the development of living things, of the processes which manifest themselves in the stream of human consciousness, and of the correlations between biological structures and functions and mental states. Especially have the sciences of biology and psychology made indispensable contributions to man's understanding of himself and his world. The sciences are, in general, oriented toward (but not committed to) the concept of a monistic universe with a rigid and unvarying causality binding together all its parts and processes. This means the absolute dominance of "natural law" with the "uniformity of nature" as its result. A law of nature is, of course, thought of not as an edict or a superior force actually determining what shall happen, but as a purely descriptive statement of what does uniformly happen under given conditions. It is discovered inductively by observing the uniform behavior of things under identical circumstances. The laws are generalizations from the specific cases observed. A still wider induction from the discovery of many such laws may lead to the inference that phenomena of every kind are similarly linked, and consequently that the "reign of law" is universal.

When one considers how many superstitious notions and ignorant follies have been dispelled from the minds of all intelligent men by the application of the scientific method of observation, classification, and generalization, and how much more livable the world is when sequences of cause and effect can be safely relied upon than it would be if the forces of nature acted whimsically and all their operations were unpredictable, or were subject to random interruption, one cannot be too grateful to the generations of scientists who have discovered so much orderliness in nature. Without well-grounded confidence in that regularity every human effort would be futile, and life itself insupportable if not impossible. Before concluding, however, that science can speak the final word in regard to man as a moral being, some things must be considered.

First. If all existing things, including man, are rigidly controlled by causal forces which exclude choice and freedom, then man is not a moral being. Our questions about the grounds of the moral order would not be answered; they would be erased, for there would be no moral order.

Second. The inductive inference as to the universal sway of "natural law" necessarily falls considerably short of being a demonstration. When a principle that seems well established in one field (e.g., physics) is assumed to hold good in a very different field (e.g., the inner life of man), this is rather an argument from analogy than a valid induction, and arguments from analogy are notoriously precarious. This one is all the weaker because it requires the assumption that a vast body of primary data in the latter field (i.e., the whole of man's moral experience and his sense of "ought") is merely an illusion which science can ignore. This is not good scientific method.

Third. Science as such takes no account of *values.* It is keenly observant of the sequence of events, but it has no scale by which to measure the worth of any final end to which these events may lead. It is instrumental, not evaluative. This is true of both pure and applied science. The research scientist may be spurred by the conviction that it is "good" for men to know as much as possible about their world; but this is not a scientific conclusion. The question of value can be pushed along by showing that increase of knowledge is good because it leads to saving of labor, more leisure, more rapid transportation and communication. But are these ultimate values, or are they good because they are the means to other values? And what can science tell us about these? The medical scientist may discover means of combatting disease and prolonging life; but he must (and in practice he does) step outside of his role as scientist to decide that it is good to combat disease and prolong life. In short, science has no definition of the good except in terms of some other good which it is beyond its competence to define. I would hesitate to make this statement so absolutely if I had not checked it with an able and highly intelligent biologist who confirmed its accuracy. Science is therefore in no position to speak of "Nature's apparent indifference to the highest interests of man," because by the limitations of its own nature it knows nothing about the highest interests of man.

Nevertheless this "problem of evil," whoever propounds it, is a perpetual stumbling-block in the way of those who believe, or would like to believe, that the ultimate Reality of the universe is aware of man, is well disposed toward him, has a moral nature akin to his own, and also controls the day-by-day processes of nature which so often seem gratuitously disastrous to men. This was Job's problem. The glib answer of his friends—that suffering is always and only God's chastisement for sin—was indignantly repudiated not only by Job but also, according to the record, by God himself (Job 42:7). The Book of Job does not solve this perennial question as to why a good God permits sin and suffering in a world which he is said to have designed and to govern. It leaves the matter rather with a somewhat evasive statement to the effect that, if health and prosperity are what you consider the highest good, then you will never be able to understand why a friendly God does not give them to you.

I will not list the standard Christian answers to this question— none of them very satisfactory—but will merely mention three considerations which are part of the data in the total problem. First, the fact of good is as real as the fact of evil, and the problem of how the existence of evil can be reconciled with a good God is balanced by the problem of how the existence of so much good (especially man's sense of moral values and his strenuous moral endeavors) can be explained without one. Second, the hypothesis (to call it no more) of a transcendent Reality which is fundamentally a moral Being does not logically imply that this Being has either the disposition or the power to interrupt the orderly course of events in such a way as to guarantee to every person (or even to every "good" person) a safe and painless existence. Job's assumption that God caused his troubles can be questioned. Third, both the Jewish and the Christian religions teach that God is the eternal energy by which man lives and moves and has his being, even while he is responsible for his own choices since he has inherited a moral freedom akin to God's.

It seems futile to have recourse to either the methods or the findings of science when one is seeking the fundamental ground of the moral order, since science itself has no means of evaluating acts or events except as instrumental in relation to objectives which it may assume, but cannot prove, to be good, and since "good," "evil," "freedom," and "ought" are only borrowed words in its vocabulary.

One of the invaluable services that science has rendered, and for which it has been more often blamed than adequately thanked, has been to force a rethinking of the relation of God to the world. Theism has tended to carry over too much of the mythology of the prescientific age. In an early stage of human culture, polytheistic religions localized the divine power in superhuman persons with specialized functions in relation to physical nature and human activities—a separate god for each of the different types of natural phenomena (sea, wind, trees, fertility of the soil, lightning), or for particular areas or peoples, or for each kind of human interest (war, love, health, travel). Under this polytheistic system there was little thought of any possible connection between religion and morality, whether personal or social. The business of the gods was to exercise control, so far as they wished or could be persuaded, within the respective fields of their limited jurisdictions. Crude monotheism consolidated all these functions in the hands of one God and ascribed to him also the status and function of creator—a matter about which polytheism, in spite of its many creation myths, was generally vague and ambiguous. Ethical monotheism, the great contribution of the Hebrews, retained the attributes of divinity as the controller of all mundane events and natural phenomena and the determiner of human fortunes, but added such moral qualities as justice, mercy, love, and an abhorrence of everything that could be called 'sin." This was a great gain. It was a gain shared by all the great religions. With it, however, came the discovery of that baffling "problem of evil,"

the apparent inconsistency between God's goodness and his detailed
control of events in a world so marred by disaster and suffering.
Polytheists faced no such puzzle because their gods made no claim
to be either good or omnipotent. To Christians it has been a persistent problem.

In the midst of this bewilderment, science has sounded a clarifying
and, if rightly understood, a comforting note by exhibiting the
orderly sequence of natural phenomena and the proximate causes of
events. It has brought the good news that an earthquake killing
thousands, a death-dealing epidemic, or the birth of a child with a
deformity does not happen because God wills it that way. The
basically moral quality of the divine Reality is the central point in
an intelligent theism. The doctrine of creation is marginal, and
that of the divine omnipotence applied to the detailed direction
of natural and human events is a pious exaggeration. Science is to be
credited with forcing a reconsideration of the nature of God's relation
to man and the world, and the theologians have been reluctant to
face the question frankly in the light of modern scientific knowledge.
But science does not provide either a definition of the good or
adequate motivation for struggling toward it.

III

If religion is to be regarded as having any significance for man as
a moral being, and for society as a moral order, obviously "personal
character" is an intrinsic element in it. "Democracy" is a word with
many shades of meaning, but if we mean by it a social order in
which every individual is regarded as having a value that must be
respected and inalienable rights that cannot be invaded, then it
also is an intrinsic element in any religion worthy of man's acceptance.
The intelligent, or even semi-intelligent, adherents of any form of the
Judaeo-Christian tradition would doubtless be in substantial agreement on this. However, the question before us is whether the strictly
humanistic factor, including the democratic tradition as we know it
and the free man's normal sense of human rights and moral rightness,
is basic to a social order fit for men to live in, and whether this
by itself is an adequate basis. My answer is that this factor is
indispensable but insufficient. The main points in my own view

have already been indicated. With reference to this question they may, with some repetition, be summarized thus:

First. Man's native and natural sense of "oughtness" is fundamental to a moral order, and therefore to a good social order. In intricate ways that have been explored by social psychologists (notably by Mead), the human "self" is in large measure the product of society. The idea that fully self-conscious and completely egoistic and amoral individuals first exist separately, and then combine by a "social contract" to form a society in which each member has no other motive than to gain the greatest possible advantage for himself, is purely imaginary. It assumes that fully developed individuals first exist apart from society, that relationship among individuals begins when each discovers that all others are his enemies or his competitors, and that all social arrangements are merely devices by which each hopes to advance his own interests more easily and more effectively than he could by fighting for them. This is unhistorical, because no society ever came into existence through such a compact among previously independent and egoistic individuals. It is unpsychological for many reasons, one of which is that it leaves out of account certain universal elements of human consciousness which are the raw materials out of which morality is made or the seeds from which it grows. Darwin's "struggle for existence" is only one aspect of the natural history of man in his physical and social environment. Kropotkin's "mutual aid as a factor in evolution" is partly, but not wholly, a prudential adjustment by which cooperating individuals can be more successful in the struggle than they could be separately. Basic to the structure of any society is man's sense that there are things which he *ought* to do and things which he *ought not* to do. This is qualitatively different from the recognition that some acts are advantageous and some are not. Specific content and effective motivation are still to be supplied, but the elementary sense of "oughtness" with an altruistic reference is native to man as man.

Second. While this altruistic factor is as natural for man as is the egoistic drive for sustenance and security, the content of the codes of conduct in which it finds expression is determined by experience. "Experience" here is a very wide term. It includes the mores of the community and the whole tradition of the race insofar as this is accessible to those who are forming moral judgments. It is a characteristic of man—not shared, so far as we know, by the lower animals—not only to preserve his racial traditions and so to build up a funded body of experience, but also to criticize and alter his mores in the light of accumulating experience, changed conditions, and new knowledge of the experience of other (and sometimes of older) communities. It is no mere sentimentalism to say that mankind has been working its way, though with many backsets and wanderings, toward a clearer recognition of the principle, "Thou shalt love thy neighbor," as the full meaning of its elementary altruism and native sense of "oughtness." What specific acts and policies are the appropriate implementation of this principle in any given situation must be determined from time to time in the light of the relevant facts. What we call the "democratic way of life" is good because, and insofar as, it gives concrete expression to love of neighbor and takes the term "neighbor" in a comprehensive sense. No known democratic society—not even our own!—is a perfect embodiment of this principle. Every such society represents only a stage on the way. The merit of a democratic society, if it understands its own significance, is that it is headed the right way and that it is capable of self-criticism and self-improvement.

Third. A good social order, then, is based not upon self-interest but upon a sense of obligation to others; this altruistic concern is native to man considered empirically; and a social order so based implies the existence of a moral order—indeed, *is* a moral order so far as it goes. Devotion to such a social order is a religion, in the most general sense, since it calls upon man to give his highest loyalty to something larger than himself and to serve ends other than his own personal advantage. In my judgment it is neither an edequate religion nor does it provide adequate motivation for the acts and attitudes esssential to the best possible social order. The verdict of history is that man's moral and other-regarding impulses need the reinforcement of a loyalty directed toward something even greater than the whole of human society. "Religions of Humanity," however nobly conceived and eloquently expounded, never get off the drawing-boards of their architects. Consider Auguste Comte's beautiful design, and Lépeaux's Theophilanthropy. A religion that cannot get followers cannot have much effect on the social order. Many noble souls have truly loved and served humanity without conscious religious motivation, but such rare spirits are too few to form the basis for a generalization about the social order. The "religion of democracy" in practice too easily deteriorates into devotion to the interests of one's own class rather than of all the people. One has only to remember the familiar techniques of any political campaign. After unctuous words about the welfare of "the people," the farmers are assured that the policies of a given party or candidate will put more money in the pockets of farmers; laborers, that they will mean more take-home pay for labor; veterans, that the interests of veterans will be cared for. Class interests are only individual interests viewed collectively. The motive is egoistic—"more advantages for *my* class, and therefore more for *me*." Man's native altruistic impulse needs more effective reinforcement than it can get from a purely humanistic view of the world.

IV

The supreme values from whatever source *are* aspects of one basic Reality. God, science and humanitarian considerations all play their parts in the validation, definition, and pursuit of these values. The good life and the good social order are those in which love is the predominating principle. Man finds the germ of this principle in his own moral experience, the sense of "oughtness," which is as much a part of his human nature as is his capacity to have experience with the physical world. Therefore the natural man, as the humanist views him, knows himself as a moral being, recognizes the existence of moral imperatives and values, and by the accumulating experience of the race creates and corrects his codes of conduct.

This is what makes it possible for man to conceive of a moral order, and of God as a moral being. Science provides techniques for the attainment of those ends which man, by processes other than those of science, has found to be ultimate and unconditioned values. By increasing and organizing his store of knowledge it clarifies his thinking about the world and himself and relieves him of a burden of primitive fears, guesses, and superstitions about the nature of the forces with which he has to cope in his dealings with men and things.

God is the source and ground of the moral order, which man could not find in Him if he had not already found it in himself. Devotion to God provides the motivation which man constantly needs and which is not adequately supplied by abstract notions of "the good" or a generalized devotion to Humanity.

V

"God" *is* still a "useful concept." For this discussion it is not necessary to consider whether and in what sense God is the Creator of all things, or the uncaused "First Cause," or the unmoved "Prime Mover." Attention can rather be centered on the thought that God is the source and ground of that which makes man a moral being, and that He is thus the ground of the moral order and the guarantor of the ultimate values. An early Christian writer wrote: "Love is of God. . . . God is love." (I John 4:7–8). The second of these brief sentences defines the nature or character of God; the first asserts his existence as the source from which love originates. It is true that the existence of such a God as a separate entity somewhere in space or as a being transcending the category of space cannot be demonstrated by science or philosophy.

Belief in God as in any sense a "Being" requires a "leap of faith"— but not, as it seems to me, a blind or unreasonable leap. Love is a fact of history and experience. It is a value which requires no validation by showing that it is the means to something else of more ultimate value. However gradually its manifestations may have developed through the eons of evolution, its origin is not accounted for by any discoverable natural process. With man it assumes unique scope and importance and becomes the determining factor in his social structures, though still opposed by egoistic impulses and needing the support of the most powerful motivation it can get. The strongest motivation is wholehearted devotion to a God conceived as both the fountainhead and the exemplar of that love.

SIMON GREENBERG

*Born in Horoshen, Russia, Simon Greenberg, Vice-Chancellor of The
Jewish Theological Seminary of America and Vice-President of its
faculties, interprets the viewpoint of the Conservative Movement in
Judaism. He was educated at the College of the City of New York, Uni-
versity of Minnesota, The Jewish Theological Seminary, and Dropsie
College. Following graduate studies at Hebrew University in Jerusalem
and the American School for Oriental Research, he served many years as
Rabbi of Har Zion Temple, Philadelphia. For a time Executive Director
of the United Synagogue of America and a former president of the
Rabbinical Assembly of America, Dr. Greenberg is a Fellow of the Conference on Science, Philosophy and Religion. His publications include*
Living as a Jew Today *(1939),* Ideals and Values in the Jewish Prayer
Book *(1940),* The First Year in the Hebrew School: *A Teacher's Guide
(1945), and* The Conservative Movement in Judaism—An Introduction
(1954).

INTRODUCTION

THE catastrophes that have overtaken Western civilization in the
twentieth century could not but stimulate soul-searching
inquiries.

No institution of Western society—the state, the family, the
economic order, and religion—has escaped careful scrutiny. Each
one of these has by some one been adjudged as partly or primarily
responsible for the present debacle. Religion, however, has been
subjected to particularly sharp criticism and perhaps rightly so. It
above all was to have been the guardian of the moral climate of the

community, and in that it obviously failed. While at one time it may have appeared to some that the West would reject its religions, the attitude prevailing at present, particularly in the United States, is one more favorably disposed to religion than could have been foreseen a generation ago. The value of the institutions, dogmas, doctrines, and ceremonies of the various religions continues to be vigorously questioned. But no voice is today raised in America against what are generally spoken of as the goals and the ethical teachings of the Judaeo-Christian religions, that is, the religions that accept the Hebrew Bible as sacred scripture. This selective approach to religion is reflected in the frame of reference set for this inquiry. It is to be concerned with religious values "stripped of their divergent ethnic, doctrinal, and structural factors." We shall make every effort to keep this statement within the indicated boundaries. But we would not thereby want to give the impression that we in any way share what we consider to be two widespread and harmful misconceptions which such an approach may encourage.

The first is the notion that all things which have one or more significant characteristics in common are, "in essence" or "in reality," the same. In most instances in nature in which phenomena share a "common core," the attributes that distinguish the phenomena one from the other are as vital to each phenomenon separately as is its "common core." Bats, whales, and men are all mammals but what they share in common tells us mighty little about the real character of each of them.

The second is the notion that the common core of all Judaeo-Christian religions represents that which is most essential to any of them, or to religion generally. Hence, "ethnic, doctrinal, and structural factors" may, nay should be discarded as impedimenta.

One of the stumbling-blocks of our age is this search for the "essence" of things, a search motivated by the hope that the essence can in itself be an adequate substitute for the whole. We thus hope for the day when we will be emancipated from the need for bulk in our food. We would like to extract the vitamins, put them in pills, and live by them alone. But vital as vitamins are, man can not live even on vitamins alone.

We prefer to forget the second half of Hillel's answer to the gentile who wanted to be taught the whole Torah while standing on one foot. "That which is hateful to thee, do not unto thy neighbor. That," said Hillel, "is the Torah. All the rest is commentary. *Go and learn it.*" For various understandable reasons we may like to think that the commentary is not merely superfluous but a hindrance. Hence, while many are happy to accept Hillel's definition of the Torah they are reluctant to heed his admonition "to learn the commentary." But without the commentary, the Torah is a disembodied, ineffective idea. Without "ethnic, doctrinal, and structural factors" religious values are pious vacuities.

It does not, however, follow that an inquiry such as the one Mr. Cole has set for us is fruitless. On the contrary, it has much obvious merit. For the more conscious we are of the things we have in common the more likely are our common possessions to serve as bonds between us and as seminal seeds from which additional bonds of union may grow.

I

One can not discuss values without at once encountering the problem of whether these values are religious or secular. All our efforts to evade the question are of no avail. This aspect of the problem becomes all the more pressing because invariably the *argumentum ad hominem* is introduced. Mr. A. is a "religious" but unethical person, while Mr. B. is an ethical person but not "religious." One constantly hears this argument, though it should by now be obvious that the fact that one protests his atheism or agnosticism is no more reliable an index to the nature of the values by which he lives than is the fact that he protests his faith and piety. One of the most hopeful aspects of the human situation is the fact that for every one who "speaks better than he acts" there is another who "acts better than he speaks." Mr. Cole was apparently aware of this tendency to be diverted into the realm of defining religion. He, therefore, wisely directed each one to speak of "religious values" as "you use the term religion." We shall make every effort to follow that directive.

The religious values of the Judaeo-Christian religions which should be emphasized in contemporary thought are few in number, but indispensable to the future of civilization. First among them is the value of universal peace. Too many labor under the delusion that universal peace is an ideal either universally approved or generally believed feasible. The two attitudes are in a way different sides of the same coin. To believe that universal peace is inherently not feasible is to declare that the very nature of the universe or of man makes war inevitable. And that which the nature of the universe makes inevitable must in the final analysis be declared desirable, unless the universe itself is to be adjudged as inherently undesirable.

But not only has universal peace been rejected as an intrinsically impracticable ideal, it has also been adjudged as ethically undesirable. The moral arguments in behalf of war have been repeatedly stated by men in both high and low station. Hegel was neither an evil person nor one of narrow intellectual horizons. Yet it was he who declared that "the ethical health of nations is maintained" through war. He believed that "war prevents a corruption of nations which a perpetual, let alone an eternal, peace would produce." He rejected Kant's proposal to arbitrate the controversies between states as both undesirable in theory and as contrary to the nature of the universe.

The intensification of the horrors of war may make men hesitate longer before plunging into it, but it will not necessarily abolish it. The fear of death has never kept men from courting it in the hope of thus gaining honor, finding adventure, or enacting what they believed to be grandiose or noble roles. To one to whom human life per se, the life of the men, women, and children of his own generation is not intrinsically sacred, the destruction of half of mankind or more, holds no particular terror. Even a comparative handful of human beings can in time repopulate the world. To some it may even appear as a good thing drastically to reduce the globe's population, for there are many who believe that it has been increasing far too rapidly in the last two centuries.

We were ourselves witnesses to the grave evils suffered by the most "advanced" and "civilized" peoples of the earth because of the megalomaniacal visions of men determined either to usher in utopia in their day or to place all of mankind under the heels of the "super-race" of men. In both instances large numbers of all classes and walks of society zealously followed their leaders even unto death.

Hence to speak of universal peace as an ideal or value ardently believed in and sincerely accepted by men is to delude oneself. Peace as a supreme positive value, and not merely as the period of moral stagnation between wars, is an ideal we have not as yet really made our own. Nor should we close our eyes to the fact that, with the exception of Kant, none of the world's great philosophers, ancient or modern, have set universal peace as the ultimate and highest goal of the moral life of man. The prophets were the first to conceive it not merely as a desirable but as an ultimately inevitable goal, and the religious leaders who believed in the divine character of the prophetic vision were the ones who preached it most passionately down through the ages.

The second religious value indispensable to the future of civilization is that of the equality of all men. The generally accepted formulation of this religious value is that of the prophet Malachi. "Have we not one Father? Hath not one God created us? Why then do we deal treacherously one man against his neighbor?" The Fatherhood of God, we say, implies the brotherhood of man. But God is the creator not only of man but of all the animals. We do not deduce therefrom the equality of all the animals with man. The Rabbis, therefore, deduce the equality of man not from the concept of God as creator but rather from the narrative in Genesis which makes all men, regardless of race or color, descendants of the same original ancestors, Adam and Eve. "Therefore," they say, "did God create only one man and one woman, so that no one should be able to say my ancestors were greater than yours and therefore I am greater than you."

How far mankind still has to travel to accept this religious value even in theory, let alone in practice, is evidenced by the hold that the Nazi race theories had on the scientifically most advanced nation of the West, by what is happening in South Africa today, and by the daily experiences of the Negro population in the South and in other parts of our country. Religious institutions themselves leave much to be desired in this as in so many other aspects of their behavior. But though the constitution of the United States did not at once implement the bold pronouncement of the Declaration of Independence that all men are created equal, it could not remove from the conscience of America the vision of the mighty truth through which the Republic came into being. The vision of human equality rooted in the religious conception of the common human ancestry provided by the one just and merciful God, for all men, can also never be eradicated from the conscience of men. It will remain as a goal, giving neither rest nor peace to man until it is fulfilled in human society.

The third religious value that needs emphasis is that which sets the goal for the individual. Judaeo-Christian religions have from the beginning taught that the individual is to measure the success of his life not in terms of power, wealth, or worldly wisdom, but in terms of justice, mercy, and humility. "It hath been told thee, O man, what is good, and what the Lord doth require of thee: Only to do justly, and to love mercy, and to walk humbly with thy God." Anyone laboring under the illusion that this is a standard honestly accepted by large numbers even in theory, let alone in practice, is indeed deluding himself. There may be many who believe that "honesty is the best policy," that a proper admixture of "justice, mercy, and humility," is the most dependable means for the attainment of power and wealth. But that they are intrinsically superior to power and wealth and should therefore be more highly valued is an attitude unfortunately still too rare even among the followers of the Judaeo-Christian religions.

The ultimate salvation of mankind rests in the hearts and the hands of the individual men and women who constitute it. Neither universal peace nor human equality can ever be achieved unless a large enough number of individuals will them with all their hearts and souls. And only those who will first teach themselves to prefer mercy, justice, and humility to power, wealth, and mundane glory will have the spiritual resources to will universal peace and human equality effectively.

One can add other values whose religious significance is equal to these three. There are the values of love of God and man, of Holiness in personal life, of sacrifice and suffering in the service of God. The values of the Judaeo-Christian religions are organically so related that there exists no hierarchy among them. Any one of them when truly understood and followed would lead one to the morally good life. If we chose to speak of only the three values of universal peace, human equality, and personal ethical living, we did so because these essentially religious values are the ones already most widely known and at least formally widely accepted. If concretized in the structure of human society, they alone would be sufficient to set civilization on a path of unprecedented grandeur.

II

Of these three values the only one which is indispensable to an order of society which we would designate as democratic is the second—the equality of all men in their relationship to the society as a whole. It is the highest value envisaged by our Declaration of Independence. The Constitution of the United States unfortunately did not, in the beginning, even implement this one value. There is nothing in the democratic ideal as such, as thus far practised and propounded in history, which requires men to prefer the practice of mercy to the possession of wealth, or to be humble, or which implies that universal peace is a desirable or feasible goal. Hence religious values include "the human values expressed in the genius of the democratic movement," but the democratic values as thus far expounded and implemented are but one aspect of the far larger area of religious values. The democratic values, therefore, can not be the "sole ground" of a faith which belongs within the family of Judaeo-Christian religions." On the contrary, they are but one offshoot of such a faith.

III

The worldview that modern science is developing no more implies the reality of the religious values referred to above than did the worldview of the science of the nineteenth or eighteenth century.

Science can influence our attitude toward a value only when it is directly related to empirically established data. If data which was once believed to be factually true is demonstrated to be factually false, and the value can not be dissociated from that data, then obviously the value itself must either undergo modification or be rejected. If one's acceptance of the value of human equality is based on the assumption that the earth is the center of the universe, then science removed the ground from underneath that judgment. But the basic religious value that all men are to be treated as equals is not based on any empirical data. There is nothing in the identifiable nature of the world or of man that makes such treatment imperative or necessarily desirable.

Even more, neither modern nor ancient science has anything to say regarding a value which logically perhaps should precede the three we mentioned, namely, the value of life itself.

The will to live, the instinct of self-preservation, is undoubtedly the most powerful biological urge dominating the activities of any living organism. Man has, nevertheless, seriously questioned the value of life. He alone of all creatures commits suicide for an infinite number of known and unknown reasons. He shortens his life either by one dramatic act or by a series of outwardly imperceptible unheroic acts. Human sacrifice in early religious rites, death in dueling and in endless acts of violence climaxed by war, the refusal of many to bring children into the world, are in the last analysis expressions of man's rejection of or revolt against life. Ecclesiastes unequivocally declares non-life to be preferable to life. "Wherefore I praised the dead that are already dead more than the living that are yet alive; but better than they both is he that hath not yet been" (4:2-3). Death has been welcomed as a blessed relief not only by those "who weary-laden mourn." And yet the Bible is unique in its emphasis upon man's obligation to live. Man alone needs to be commanded to be fruitful and multiply and replenish the earth. All other creatures are merely blessed with the power to reproduce their kind. Man alone has to be commanded to choose life.

"See, I have set before thee this day life and good, and death and evil. . . . I have set before thee life and death, the blessing and the curse; and thou shalt choose life" (Deut. 30:15-19). All pagan philosophies view suicide as a legitimate moral act and man is given the moral right to decide when he may take leave of life upon this earth. The Judaeo-Christian religions alone declare unconditionally against it. Life is not ours to do with as we please. It is a sacred trust that must be kept by each one to the best of his ability. But science gives no assurance that life is anything more than a transient phenomenon to be extinguished eventually by the inexorable processes of lifeless cosmic forces. And where there is no assurance in regard to the essential goodness of life itself, there can be no assurance of the significance of any other religious values, for all religious values are related to this basic value.

Modern science has undoubtedly destroyed the preceding scientific worldview with its certainty that the world was a kind of clock or machine governed by immutable nonmoral forces, and that free will and moral values were only superimposed by fear-driven man. The modern scientific worldview grants greater plausibility to the theory of a universe within which there is room for ethical freedom. But it gives no scientific assurance of it. It has completely demolished all former materialistic conceptions of the universe and closed the previously unbridgeable chasm between matter and energy, time and space. But it has not been able to establish empirically that life per se is a blessing, or that values belong to the realm of being rather than merely to one realm of human imagination.

The greatest contribution that modern science has made to the advancement of religious values is through its marvelous technological advances which have made of the whole earth one community, and demonstrated in a manner more dramatic than ever before the interdependence of all men. And yet in the very generation in which these scientific triumphs have been won, racial persecution among "advanced" societies had reached new heights of intensity and depths of cruelty.

Religious values have need of science if they are to be kept from unfortunate involvement with ignorance, superstition, and falsehoods, and if their implementation in life is to be advanced. But in essence they are independent of science, and are in themselves adequate to chart a course for mankind leading towards its highest good. But scientific truths not only have need of religious values, they are indispensible to them, for without religious values scientific truths are ships without rudders, completely inadequate in themselves to give direction either to the individual or to human society.

There are no scientific grounds for our religious values. The most that can be said is that science does not invalidate them and tends rather to corroborate them. But there are sound logical grounds for these values. The logic implied lies in the simple proposition that the world we live in is either directly involved in moral and ethical values or it is not. If it is not, if justice, mercy, peace, brotherhood, and life itself are nothing more than the accidental concatenations of lifeless amoral electrons, then all our efforts to establish a better, happier order of society must ultimately end in futility and despair. To make sense out of a material inherently senseless is to engage in a Sisyphian task. It is to try to square the circle or build a perpetual motion machine.

Religious values, then, are postulates which science either of today or of yesterday cannot and could not validate or invalidate. Schweitzer's sense of the white man's debt to the Negro peoples is not rooted in scientific data or in a scientific worldview but in a religious faith transcending all the data accessible to the senses. Indeed, any act involving a sacrifice of any mundane satisfaction in behalf of another human being makes no sense and has no meaning except in a world whose essence is assumed to be moral or ethical in character. As our understanding of the structure of the universe becomes increasingly refined we may be able to identify our values with the very essence of the universe in a manner more susceptible to scientific validation than at the present. But that is only a hope. For the present we cannot speak of the basic religious values in terms of Knowledge but only of Faith. Human action over a period of time, if inspired by that faith, may some day supply the body of data needed to validate the values scientifically. But such a body of data will be brought into being only by those who are moved by the Faith.

IV-V

My faith in God in essence means to me faith that the values which alone give meaning to the whole of existence, the values of mercy, justice, equality, peace are not the creations of man, any more than the hosts of heaven are his creation. They are the creations of Him who created the physical world around us. He permits man to discover their reality even as He granted man the power to make contacts with the physical universe through his senses. He gives us no surety other than the surety which derives from the demands of reason for postulates that will make life meaningful. Even as the physical universe was opened to men by some among them endowed with greater courage, vision, and wisdom, even so have the religious values by which men are to live been revealed to the rest of mankind by those among them who were endowed with greater sensitivity to the presence of God and to His message for us. What the greatest amongst us have been granted to behold as the values by which human life should be advanced, they have recorded for us in the Sacred Scriptures. I know of no source containing more significant insight into the nature of man, the world, and the good life.

As to the nature of the relationship between these moral values and their source, I have neither knowledge nor conviction, but only opinion. Any form of pantheism or monism seems to me to be destructive of moral values. Man the creature, and God the creator may have that in common which may in some way be thought of as analogous to that which the poet and his poem, the architect and his building, have in common. But all analogies confuse as well as clarify. In this instance I incline to the opinion that the element of clarification is less than the element of confusion.

Men will triumph over the darkness that threatens to envelop them in our day not by an appeal to empirical data, which by its very nature is barren of all value, but by a great act of faith in the postulate which alone can provide a logical framework for a civilized society. These postulates are the religious values first propounded in the West by the Judaeo-Christian religions. Science has an indispensable role to play in our efforts to implement these postulates in the institutions and laws of our society. Without them science is bound to become the Frankenstein who will destroy his creator. With them, science may yet be the harbinger of the coming of God's Kingdom upon this earth.

THEODORE M. GREENE

Theodore M. Greene is one of America's well-known interpreters of philosophic thought in the field of religion. Born of American missionaries in Constantinople, Turkey, he graduated from Amherst College and the University of Edinborough, and has taught at Princeton, Stanford, Yale, and the Rice Institute. A former traveling Fellow of the American Council of Learned Societies and a member of various learned societies, Dr. Greene's publications include: Meaning of the Humanities (1938); Liberal Education Re-Examined (1943); Liberal Education Reconsidered (1953); The Arts and the Art of Criticism (1947). He has also contributed articles on religion to various volumes, including: The Christian Answer (Van Dusen) (1948); Religious Perspectives in College Teaching (Fairchild) (1952); Christianity and Reason (Myers), 1951; Modern Philosophies and Education (Henry), 1955; Goals of Economic Life (Ward), 1953. In 1955 he joined the Faculty of Scripps College, California, as Hartley Burr Alexander Professor in the Humanities.

I

I AM SORRY that my first answer to this question must be critical and negative. The wording seems to imply that when the "divergent ethnic, doctrinal, and structural factors" of a religion are "stripped" away, its "religious values" are left. I must reject any such interpretation of religion. A religion's "doctrines" and its "structural factors" (presumably, its ritualistic forms and practices) are among its *essential* components; without them it is not only structureless but meaningless. Religious "doctrines" are basic religious beliefs. Strip away these beliefs and all you have left are mere attitudes and feelings without religious content, mere ritual without religious meaning. Ritual, in turn, is a necessary vehicle for public (and often for private) worship. Worship, as an expressive *act* of reverence, becomes impossible without some sort of ritual. When doctrine and ritual are excluded, therefore, religion ceases to be the actual *process* of *communion* with God which it purports to be. It loses all its religious values and becomes a secular or humanistic echo of its former self.

Consider, for example, Judaism and Christianity. What chiefly differentiates them? The belief (or doctrine) that Jesus was the Christ, the Son of the living God. Their distinctive forms of worship clearly reflect the Jewish rejection and the Christian acceptance of this doctrine. How, in turn, do they most closely resemble one another? In their common belief in, and worship of, a God of righteous love. If we strip away this belief and this worship, both are "reduced" (I use the word advisedly) to a strictly humanistic respect for man and a concern for his welfare. Many people today accept humanism as their ultimate faith, their religion. They insist (as *their* basic doctrine) that such a humanism is the *essence* of both historic Faiths. They may be right. But what they have discarded is so crucially important to both Faiths, and what they have kept differs so profoundly from the corresponding factor in each, that the net result merits, in all honesty, a new name, e.g., "humanism."

I think, however, that I understand what Mr. Cole was after in formulating this question as he did. He had in mind, I believe, the following undeniable facts—that religions tend to multiply their doctrines and to elaborate their rituals, that these doctrines and rituals come to be accepted dogmatically and legalistically, and that, in the process, the living spirit of religious dedication is very apt to be warped and stifled. Mr. Cole is also aware of the many doctrinal and other divergencies within Judaism and within Christianity. He is therefore, I believe, asking us to go beneath these rigidities and divergencies and to describe what seems to us to be of abiding and crucial importance in these great Faiths. What, in short, is the living spirit of Judaism and of Christianity which their representative doctrines attempt to formulate theologically and which each seeks to celebrate ritualistically?

The only way in which I can answer this important question is to restate some of the central doctrines of Judaism and Christianity—doctrines which constitute the very *structure* of these Faiths.

(a) Our physical world of nature is not the whole reality, as naturalism insists, nor are we human beings nature's highest product, as humanism maintains. Nature and man are both the creation of God.

(b) God differs *in kind* from all His finite "creatures," both natural and human, not only in His infinitude but also in His absolute holiness. He thus "transcends" His finite creation. He is the "Ground and the Abyss" of all finite reality, partly knowable (as Ground) and partly unknowable and mysterious (as Abyss). He alone is holy; He alone is worthy of our reverence and our absolute devotion.

(c) God does not merely create and sustain the "world." He enters human history, revealing Himself to men in countless ways as Righteous Love, inviting man's responsive love, and making available to all men His redemptive Grace.

(d) Christianity differs from Judaism in its central belief that God has also revealed Himself to man uniquely in Jesus Christ. He has thus enabled men to know Him and to respond to His love (by loving Him and one another) as they would be unable to do without this unique Revelation.

(e) In this perspective we can see ourselves as "free" moral agents, able to accept or reject God's love, to worship Him or not, as we choose. We can thus understand our need for forgiveness and for redemption from our multiple idolatries.

(f) Men have always searched for God and worshipped Him as they conceived of Him. Witness the universality of "religion" in all cultures. Not only has man's understanding of God differed profoundly from age to age and culture to culture; *no* finite understanding of Him *can*, in the nature of the case, be wholly adequate. Hence the "pious idolatry" of absolutizing *any* conception of God, even the loftiest, *any* ritual, even the most revered, any "Church" or "Scripture," even the most inspired. The *only* God worthy of our complete loyalty and worship is the "God behind all gods" (Paul Tillich), the God whom all men hunger for and partially apprehend and largely misapprehend. Hence the crucial importance of man's continuing search and the compelling need for humility regarding *all* human apprehension of, and response to, the Divine.

(g) Man's age-old religious quest is thus his "ultimate concern for the Ultimate" (Tillich). This is no idle quest, for God *does* reveal Himself to us in countless ways, however imperfect our human apprehension and response. The God we thus encounter is *not* just a man-made ideal but the *power* of righteous redeeming Love. This power can enter our lives and transform us as we are unable to transform ourselves by our own efforts. God is our supreme Source of spiritual light and strength, our sole refuge from sin, and our only hope of salvation.

These are some of the familiar doctrines about God and His revelation to the world and to mankind which are so essential to the Jewish and Christian Faiths. They constitute the credal essence of these Faiths, the credal basis of their vital spiritual power. It is *because* we believe these things that we are impelled to worship God as holy righteous Love and that we feel obligated to love one another as He loves us. Whatever in our creeds, our rituals, and our behavior to one another fails to express these basic spiritual affirmations should be discarded or revised and revitalized. That Judaism and Christianity both stand in perennial need of such purification and spiritual revitalization is clear. But the "religious values" we cherish will be lost, not purified, if they are abstracted from the rich historical traditions in which they have arisen and developed.

It seems to us, therefore, idle to say, "Disbelieve in God if you like but obey His commandments!" How can a man obey His commandments if he does not know Him and believe in Him? How can he battle against his own sinfulness without His help? The sincere humanist does not believe in God and does believe that man is "on his own." If the humanist is right, the Jew and the Christian are wrong; their basic beliefs are illusory, their reliance on God's help is pathetically futile, their worship of Him is a waste of precious time and energy. Each of us is here confronted with a crucial and ultimate either/or. We must decide as best we can and take the consequences, whatever they may be. I can see no way of avoiding the issue; consciously or unconsciously, thoughtfully or thoughtlessly, we *must* "take sides" and live our lives accordingly.

This does not mean, however, that the sincere "secularist" who continues to search for "God" in reverent humility, and the sincere

Jew or Christian who keeps on trying to comprehend more fully and to worship more truly the God he believes he has found, are poles apart. They are far nearer each other, spiritually, than they are to the smug, self-righteous and dogmatic secularist *or* believer. For what is *most* crucial of all in the life of the spirit is a faith which sustains man's continuing spiritual quest, a profound sense of finitude and sin which instills humility, and a capacity for self-sacrificial, outgoing love. These are, par excellence, the stigmata of the spirit, as arrogance and self-righteousness, in whatever guise, are the damning hell-marks of the anti-spiritual. True humility, whether credal or sceptical, always involves the refusal to "play God"; it reflects man's awareness of his own finitude and his realization that there is, or that there may be, in the universe that which somehow transcends all human power, knowledge, and virtue—a "something" which is "holy" and therefore worthy of our reverence.

II

Here again my first answer must be negative. I believe that what we get out of the mill of reflection is determined by the kind of experience we feed into the mill. If the experiences we seek to interpret are devoid of religious values or overtones, the principles we invoke to explain these experiences will themselves lack religious content and significance. The experiences upon which the scientist relies are primarily sensory observations; his approach is essentially quantitative; his conceptual apparatus is, so far as possible, mathematical. The questions he puts to nature are questions of fact, not of value; his initial approach to nature is respectful but not reverent. No wonder, then, that the cosmos which unfolds itself to the scientist's view is essentially a cosmos indifferent to human hopes and fears, neutral with respect to the values which men most prize. I therefore find in modern science, *as such*, no grounds for any affirmative *religious* convictions about cosmic reality. If science were our only source of knowledge about reality we would, I believe, have *no* reliable basis for belief in a God of religious worship or in cosmic Justice or Love.

This does not mean that science contradicts our deepest spiritual insights. It is merely neutral to them; it neither supports nor disproves them. Science has, of course, repeatedly contradicted *factual* propositions (e.g., regarding the age of our globe and the emergence of animal and human life) which organized religions have mistakenly felt impelled to assert. The religious doctrines which I have summarized above are not of this type; they are doctrines regarding man's *spiritual* nature and the Spirit we call Divine. They, too, claim factual validity, but what they factually assert are propositions concerning the nature and significance of spirit, human and Divine, not concerning our spatiotemporal world in all its "physical" detail and scope. Science and religion, both properly conceived, do not contradict one another because their approaches to reality are so radically, and properly, different.

Many people today would question this statement. I refer here not to the Fundamentalists who insist on the literal inerrancy of every sentence in the Bible read as factual prose. I refer to those who find in the wonders of our cosmos evidence of a God of religious worship. Is not nature's incredible size, they say, and the unbelievable minuteness of its smallest parts, and its universal complexity and orderliness, evidence of an infinite Divine intelligence and power? We are indeed impelled to envisage an almost infinite "intelligence" and power as the ultimate source of nature, but why, on strictly scientific grounds, distinguish these from nature itself? And why, even if they are somehow distinct from nature, conceive of them as Divine? And even if we postulate a Divine First Cause, what possible scientific reason have we for ascribing righteous love to such a Being? Nature in all her power and immensity can indeed awaken in us a kind of awe, but only what is intrinsically good can evoke our reverence.

Modern scientists are speculating today as to the age of our cosmos; they are invoking the concepts of "creation out of nothing" and of cosmic entropy which, of itself, would bring the cosmos, as we know it, i.e., as impregnated with energy, to an end. Such theories as these, if they could really be established scientifically, might be taken to substantiate certain theological statements regarding the beginning and end of our universe. But even here the scientist can merely tell us something about *when* our universe got started and *whether* and *when* it may "run down" and *how* these events can be *physically* understood. Science, *as such,* can tell us *nothing* about the spiritual significance, if any, of these or any other physical events and processes. A truly religious doctrine of creation differs *in kind* from a purely physical or scientific doctrine of creation, for it asserts that God, as *righteous love*, created the world and declared it to be *good* and continues to sustain it and direct it. Science can neither support nor contradict such a theological assertion.

We are also invited to argue from natural beauty, or from the marvels of functional adaptation, to the existence of a good God. We may even be reminded that the Psalmist believed that the heavens declare the "glory of God" and that the firmament "sheweth His handiwork." What is here forgotten is that the Psalmist already believed in God when he viewed the heavens and the firmament; he never dreamt of basing his faith or God on this natural evidence. A long succession of honest philosophers have cogently criticized the so-called teleological argument to God from natural order by pointing out that this order is both kindly and cruel, cooperative and predatory, beautiful and ugly, creative and destructive. Nature, honestly interpreted, points not to one good omnipotent Deity but to a Power neutral to all our values, or else to a finite good God in eternal conflict with neutral or evil powers which He has not created.

What, then, of the problem of evil? Nature does indeed seem to be indifferent to man's highest interests; it often injures him and it eventually destroys him as a psychophysical being. It is no adequate answer to say that much of the evil which befalls him is of his own making, because so much of it is not; or that he can, if he will, bring good out of evil, because this still leaves evil evil—compensation for evil cannot make evil good. No less undeniable is widespread animal suffering which our sense of decency and compassion must also judge to be evil.

Here, I believe, we must be honest and admit that we, who believe in a good God, have no explanation. Those who disbelieve in God are right in saying that this is not a problem for them but only for us. They can acknowledge the fact of evil and avoid the necessity of "exploring" it; they can say that this is just the way our universe functions. They know no more than we do *why* it is the way it is, but they are not bothered by the presence of evil in a world created by a good God. This *is*, however, a problem for us, and one for which we have no adequate solution. Our only recourse is faith that the God in whom we believe does, in His own way (which we cannot fathom), make His righteousness "somehow" prevail. Here religious believers have little cause for self-righteous complacency in their own wisdom.

III

The genius of democracy is indeed integral to my religious faith. It is, however, not the basis of this faith but rather one of its crucial secular corollaries.

Democracy, as I interpret it, presupposes (a) the ability of a people, at a certain cultural level, to govern themselves, and (b) their moral obligation, as a community of free and responsible moral agents, to do so. Both propositions follow logically from the Hebraic-Christian conception of man as a being with talents which invite development and as a being who can and should relate himself to his fellow men in justice and love. If God did in fact endow us with freedom, it is right that we should be in a position to exercise this freedom politically and socially; it would not be right for us to be prepetually enslaved to human masters, however benevolent, or for some of us to enslave some of our fellow men, even "for their own good." Democracy is more in line with the Christian conception of man than any other form of government known to us.

This does *not* mean that all people, at all cultural levels, are automatically ready for democracy. Democracy is the most difficult and challenging of all forms of government; it calls for more self-discipline and enlightenment than many societies actually possess. A people conditioned from time immemorial to paternalistic control and passive obedience is not ready for democracy. Democracy can succeed only in a society which has learned to value freedom and to use it, on the whole, wisely and with restraint; in the hands of the totally unprepared, freedom is bound to degenerate into license. Even our western forms of democracy, which are only partially successful, are beyond the immediate reach of many peoples on our globe today. But there is no reason to believe that any people is intrinsically incapable of growing up to democracy, and there is every reason for believing that this is their proper human destiny.

Judaism and Christianity, in view of their conception of human nature, should do everything they can to prepare people for responsi-

ble self-government and to help people in a democracy to rule themselves as wisely and justly as possible. We must be careful, however,
not to absolutize democracy and make religion merely a means for
the achievement of democratic ends. Democracy is not, from the
Hebraic-Christian point of view, an end in itself; it is a precious means
whereby man can progressively develop his moral character and realize his proper destiny on earth.

In its respect for man's intrinsic dignity and for his freedom, democracy is more able than any other form of government to assure
man's freedom of worship and the sanctity of his conscience. An
authoritarian state may support freedom of worship, but there is no
a priori reason to expect it to do so. It is more likely to support one
religion by giving it official status. All authoritarian religions would,
of course, like to be in this privileged position. A true democracy, in
contrast, will by its very nature defend each man's right to worship
God or not to worship Him, as his own conscience dictates. It will try
to implement the religious wishes of the majority while honoring the
religious rights of the minority. It is thus the ideal political champion
of man's free spiritual search.

How autonomous are the values upon which democracy rests?
Authentic democracies have arisen and endured only in Christendom;
their historical indebtedness to our Hebaric-Christian tradition cannot
be disputed. Can the requisite respect for man and for truth and
justice continue without the vitalizing support of these Faiths? It is
my own conviction that this respect is bound to weaken if its spiritual
roots are cut. A people without faith in a God of righteous love will
find it increasingly difficult to cherish social justice and to feel genuine
concern for their fellowmen. Some significant spiritual orientation to
the ultimate is in the long run, I believe, the prerequisite for the basic
moral values without which a democracy must eventually collapse.

IV

The more I study the course of human history and survey man's
progressive insights in every area of human wisdom, the more am I
compelled to believe in *one* ultimate spiritual reality which reveals
itself to man in different but complementary ways. The more we learn
about truth, the more evident is it that authentic truths do not con-

flict but harmonize. The more we consider the nature of goodness, the more is authentic goodness found to be rooted in reality itself. If beauty be defined as harmony of form and function, we find beauty in nature and we create beauty whenever we aesthetically express an authentic vision of the good. The more adequately we apprehend and realize truth, beauty, and goodness in our lives, the richer and more meaningful life becomes. How can we explain this demonstrable fact without appealing to a common spiritual source of these values?

A survey of man's generic types of experience points to the same conclusion. Scientific inquiry presupposes intellectual and moral integrity, a respect for nature, and a concern for human welfare. Reversely, science has contributed immeasurably to our understanding of ourselves and of nature and to our physical and mental welfare. Art at its best is both realistically oriented and truthful; its expressed insights complement the insights of science. Our social and political experiments are significant and successful in proportion as they are based upon a valid understanding of human nature and man's need for, and capacity for, justice and love. These in turn are precisely what the higher religions exhort us to strive for and exemplify in our daily conduct. We would be in a bad way if religion, art, science, and democracy, each at its enlightened best, pulled us in different directions. In fact, in their respective ways they all emphasize our inescapable dependence on truth and harmony, justice, and love. Could this be so if our universe were itself wholly indifferent to, or hostile to, these abiding values?

How are these values ultimately related to one another and to the world of physical fact? This is the ultimate problem of metaphysics, the problem which speculative thinkers must deal with anew in every generation. To cope with it successfully we must do justice to the infinite diversity of fact, the multiplicity of apprehended values, the actual discrepancy of fact and value, and their ideal potential harmony. We must believe that the ideal, though rooted in reality, requires actualization in space and time; we must take cognizance of continuing creation at every level, the actuality of evil, and the perpetual possibility of replacing evil with good. We must also acknowledge the limits of human insight and the necessity for humility. A metaphysic *must*, therefore, be tentative and provisional.

The three great human ventures here under review, that is, science, democracy, and the Christian and Jewish religions, are natural allies in man's all-embracing spiritual quest *so long as* each is honest, enlightened, and aware of its own limitations. They become hostile enemies whenever they become arrogant and self-righteous, that is, untrue to themselves. Each, *at its best*, is essentially liberal and humble. The more each exemplifies this spirit, the more will it contribute to man's total enlightenment and welfare.

V

It should be clear from what I have said, especially in my answer to Question I, that my own philosophy is essentially theocentric, with God as the ultimate Source and Ground of all reality. I can see no way of avoiding the concept of God in a philosophy which conceives of ultimate reality as spiritual. The use of this concept is indeed fraught with danger, for God has been conceived in many ways and because no conception of Him can be adequate. All human knowledge is finite and fallible; all human apprehension of God is, of necessity, anthropomorphic; we cannot help seeing reality through human eyes. But this need not discourage us. We can continue man's age old struggle to apprehend ultimate reality even *more* realistically. "Nature" is, in its way, as ambiguous a term as "God"; science, too, is essentially anthropomorphic and necessarily inadequate to nature's mysteries. But this does not impel us to give up the term "nature" or to cease to perfect our scientific understanding of nature's structure and processes. Let us, in the same spirit, continue our search for God and our effort to worship Him more adequately and to serve Him more perfectly.

Science and democracy are both, at their best, self-corrective. So is religion at its humble spiritual best. Its task is not only to affirm man's positive spiritual insights but also to reiterate the limits of these insights. God is simultaneously our assurance and our hope; He is the Being we encounter and "know" but also the Being who eludes us and whom we can never comprehend in all His length and breadth and depth. What higher quest could men have than the quest for God, in assured faith and honest humility?

A. EUSTACE HAYDON

-»»)«<-

A. Eustace Haydon was Head of the Department of Comparative Religion and teacher of the history of religions at the University of Chicago for twenty-six years (1919-45). Born in Canada and a graduate of McMaster University and the University of Chicago, he became a Fellow of the American Association for the Advancement of Science and a member of other learned societies. From 1918 to 1924 Dr. Haydon was minister of the First Unitarian Church, Madison, Wisconsin, and since 1945 he has been the leader of the Chicago Ethical Society. His books include: The Quest of the Ages *(1929);* Man's Search for the Good Life *(1937);* and Biography of the Gods *(1941), as well as contributions to various dictionaries and encyclopaedias of the social sciences and religion.*

I

To LIVE is to desire. All living things reach out tirelessly for fulfillment, man most eagerly of all. The religions of all ages in all lands embody a great hope, the hope that some time, somehow, somewhere, human life will be crowned with complete happiness. Any religion may be described as man's shared quest for the good life; the cultural form of the human thrust of planetary life seeking fulfillment on the social level. Religions are the modes, endlessly varied and changing, in which the desires of men have been socially oriented by approved means toward ideal values in relation to a cosmic background.

Every religion has come down the centuries in a threefold embodiment of ideal, techniques, and worldview or theology. The values of the ideal are those things which satisfy the manifold desires of men.

112

The techniques are the practical and ceremonial means of acquiring the values. The worldview relates the religious adventure to the environing universe. Both worldview and technique changed through the centuries as man learned more about himself and his world and achieved greater control over the natural and social environment. The values of the ideal were always relatively stable since they were determined by human desires. These desires were of three kinds— physical, personal, and social. The values satisfying physical desires were food, sex fulfillment, shelter, safety from danger, security. The values which satisfied personal desires were recognition, friendly response, prestige, status, honor, a sense of worthfulness in the group. Unlike the physical and personal desires, social desires are not innate. They must be learned. The social values related to them are loyalty, filial piety, love, peace, justice, generosity, brotherhood. These abstract words translated into patterns of behavior mean social harmony, satisfactory human relations, a cultural environment in which all the potentialities of individuals may be led to full flowering and happy creative expression.

Since the values are common to man's adventure in all cultures there is no need to tie them up to the Judaeo-Christian tradition. It is unfortunate that all religions have passed through an era of frustration when the hope of building a good world in which a good life might be lived faded. Then the ideal was projected to a future age, to a heaven realm, or to an eternal spiritual reality beyond both earth and heaven. The scars of that experience still cling to the old religions. But today the religious quest has come back to earth. We take up the task begun a million years ago, interrupted for a little while by the failure of nerve. We seek to integrate the values distilled by the experience of the ages—justice, love, peace, brotherhood, kindness, loyalty, cooperation—into social institutions. When we learn how to give these words effective meaning in practical patterns of behavior we shall have given embodiment to man's age-old dream.

II

There seems to be no adequate evidence that the universe is interested in man's well-being. Faith in gods was the man's daring hope that the universe in its deepest meaning was on the side of human ideals. But that was faith, not knowledge. Certainly the universe is not consciously hostile, indifferent, or friendly to man.

It is important to remember, however, that man is at home on the planet. He is a phase of nature, a terminal thrust of planetary development moving through time as a social process. He is the material of the universe come alive, consciously able to survey the past and direct the future. He is earth material coming to a focus in intelligence, with capacity to feel, to enjoy, to think, to choose between good and evil. The planet came to consciousness of itself in him. He carries within him the learning of millions of years on the biological level, hundreds of thousands of years on the social level. He bears the heritage of the ages creatively through the present into the future. He belongs so completely to his world that he may be justified in thinking that the planetary process is willing to give him a chance for further development. Innumerable forms of life failed in the adventure of life. Tens of thousands could not endure the ice ages—man came through. He swings with the rhythm of the universe. There is a mystic glow in the presence of sunlit meadows after rain, the magic of moonlit nights, the springtime foliage, birds' songs, and the swinging surge of the ocean. Man is part of it all and echoes of the ages of his climb through time haunt him still. All this was the result of adjustment.

But at some auspicious moment in the morning of history man ceased to be content to adjust his desires to nature and ventured the attempt to adjust nature to his desires. He was determined to have a hand in the shaping of his own destiny. In that moment he took his first faltering step in the march to mastery of the planet. The long ages have revealed the meaning of this human adventure in all its breath-taking splendor. Man, the thinking animal, has dared to try to lay the reins of an intelligent, human purpose on a cosmic process, to shape the material resources of nature into a home of beauty and physical fulfillment, to mold the undying social process into ever lovelier forms as sun and soil for the perfecting of the art of living. Man has learned that he can make ever nearer to the heart's desire both the natural and social environments. He finds no steel ribs, no eternal decrees, no rigidity of karma to halt his plans. Long ago F. C. S. Schiller said, "You never can tell what reality will stand for until you try." It was always easier to believe that "good will be the final goal of ill" than to fight to make the good prevail. It was easier to believe that "truth crushed to earth will rise again" than to exalt truth and defend it. It was easier to believe that "all things work together for good" than to order things the righteous way. It was easier to believe that a divine purpose through all creation runs than to use intelligence to put purpose in to the flow of human events. If man can organize social institutions to achieve a guiding intelligence for the world, thoughtful providence, and a world conscience, the cosmic social process may be harnessed to human well-being.

Beyond our little planet, our fourth-rate sun, and our solar system is the vast universe. Before its swinging galaxies, its immensities of space and time, the imagination reels. In this universe man's individual life is brief as the flickering of summer lightning, his whole racial history only a moment. It would be supreme egotism to think that this universe is interested in man. But even if it were hostile to man's puny planning, the children of earth, like Prometheus, would defy its might and still try to build out a little, sunlit valley of happiness in their sequestered nook of space until time tolled the closing of man's day.

III

For two centuries vital religion has been flowing away from the traditional religious institutions into a thousand social forms and moving into the future under the banner of democracy. Religion comes back to earth from its otherworldly wanderings to become the dynamic, synthesizing, direction-giving force in the secular world.

Christianity followed a unique pattern which was set when its leaders abandoned the religion of Jesus, set aside the Jewish law, and made it a religion of salvation to immortal life through faith in a dying and risen savior. The emphasis was on correct belief, in contrast to all other religions which stressed a way of living rather than a way of believing.

There was a time, however, when Christianity seemed to be flowing into the pattern of other world religions. After the fall of Rome, the great dominion held together by the Roman peace and the far-flung network of Roman rule disintegrated. Later the Moslems threw their crescent around the Mediterranean, cutting the trade routes and isolating Europe from the old centers of culture and learning. The only institution that had unity in the Empire was the Christian Church. Between the sixth and the twelfth centuries the Church became the teacher and guide of Europe. One after another all phases of culture came under her control until the sciences, philosophy, politics, trade and business, morality, education, and art all felt the hand of the great Church controlling and unifying them.

But this Medieval synthesis began to break up after the twelfth century. The system of Thomas Aquinas was made to adjust Christian belief to the science and philosophy of the newly discovered Aristotle. This adjustment was the last effort at creative change in the Roman Church. After that the Christian system crystallized as belief and refused to move to come to terms with the disturbing ferments which transformed the Medieval world—the Renaissance, the new physical sciences, the new philosophy, expanding trade, the discovery of a new world and the ancient Oriental cultures, the new emphasis upon the values of life in this world. No branch of the Christian Church responded to the need. Roman, Eastern Orthodox, and Protestant alike entrenched themselves behind their barricades of eternal truth and allowed the secular realm to escape the control of a unifying philosophy of life.

Science, with much anguish and bittter struggle, broke free and went its own way without any sense of social responsibility. Philosophy followed science, always feeling the tug of the apron-strings of its mother, theology, but proudly conscious of its separateness from religion. Education, to be based on verified knowledge, was forced to remove the dead hand of Church control. The revival of the trade routes gave rise to new opportunities for business expansion. Business men would no longer tolerate the restrictions of the Church. So business became business, with not so much as a side glance of deference to the ideals of religion. The national states asserted their independence. The hand of the Church was removed from the helm of state, and politics lost its bond to religion and its sense of responsibility to the human ideal. Art also refused any longer to accept specifications from priestly authority.

All of this meant that for centuries in the western world every area of culture controlling the destiny of the individual in society has been moving under its own directive with no sense of duty to a common objective, no unifying philosophy of life, no loyalty to social values, no feeling of being weighted with responsibility to the commonweal. Herein lies the great tragedy of our western culture, the creation of our amazing civilization with its contrasts of splendor, and poverty, beauty and squalor, luxury and drabness, hope and the menace of doom.

During the last two centuries religion has been trying to find a new embodiment in the world of everyday living. We are moving toward a new synthesis of culture following the democratic ideal. Democracy is spreading to include not only political democracy but economic, educational, ethnic democracy, and democracy of the sexes. The ideal includes all the the values revered through the ages— justice, love, peace, brotherhood, loyalty, with the addition of freedom, equality of opportunity, and the supreme worth of each individual. We call these "religious" values but when religious values are analyzed they always turn out to be economic values, political values, moral values, truth values, aesthetic values—the values of the secular life of man in society. The religious ideal of the new age will be a synthesis of all the values which make for human fulfillment.

The program will challenge every phase of our culture to loyalty in a new unity of human social living. Science, philosophy, business, education, art will all serve the common cause. These elements of civilization are no more than instruments of culture—servants of the good life—and must find their justification at the bar of religion and morality in terms of their contribution to the common weal. They are not a law unto themselves. They must bow to the reason for their existence, as creations of man for the service of man. The goal is the achievement of human happiness. The task, in Professor Perry's words, is "to satisfy man's needs abundantly and justly, the needs of all men everywhere, by the combined efforts and resources of all men everywhere." That means the physical needs of food, sex, clothing, health, shelter, and security. It means satisfaction of the needs of comradeship. It means release of all the potentialities of man's nature. It means the cultural need for fulfillment of the total personality as a bearer of the human heritage. It means meeting the needs on a world scale of all men as citizens and creators, sharers in the welfare of all mankind. This is secular religion. It is also democracy.

IV

I would like to drop the word "spiritual" from our religious vocabulary until it can be purged of its dualistic taint. It would be difficult to exaggerate the far-reaching effect upon the history of religions of the epochal blunder of primitive man when his imagination gave him the idea of a ghost and a separable soul. It split the universe in two, creating all the later dualisms—soul-body, spirit-matter, supernatural-natural, heaven-earth. It made possible the continued life of the gods as spiritual beings after the nature powers from which they sprang had been drawn into the known world of familiar fact. It created the spiritual realm as the secure harbor of supreme values. It gave rise to the many theories of existence after death—eternal existence on the wheel of rebirth, resurrection, and immortality. It crowded the unseen with innumerable heavens and hells as residences for human souls. It peopled the environment of man with every imaginable form of spirit and demon capable of bringing him weal and woe. In times of cultural defeat, it invited prophet and seer to project the ideal into the spiritual world, forever safe from the tribulations and ravages of time. It provided some of the most important building blocks with which theologians and metaphysicians have delighted to erect their marvelous architectonic systems. The word "spiritual" still wears the dualistic aura of thousands of years of history.

If "spiritual" can be made to mean the intellectual, emotional, aesthetic, and social phases of the higher life of man, I would say that "reality" is not now one but that it may be unified as man learns to harness the natural and social environment in the service of the religious ideal. Evil still dogs man's footsteps, a sign of maladjustments not yet overcome, but today 95 per cent of all evils he suffers are the result of faulty human relations. The progressively perfected social order of the good society may be able to provide all needful and desirable values to each individual in ways that are socially safe. The social structure will furnish and guarantee by practical means what men have so long waited with wistful eyes to receive from the "spiritual" realm.

V

I have no need of the concept "god" in my "rationale of religion." It is better to understand the gods than to believe in them. The gods are the aristocrats of history, but like man they are earth-born. It seems strange that we should expect knowledge and guidance from them at this point in world history. "Thus saith the Lord" is now a figure of speech, not a theophany.

There is a deep pathos in the story of man's outreach for help and guidance from the unseen. A son sleeping on the grave of the father who had given him guidance in life hoping for wise counsel was a natural and widespread form. Dream revelations in the temple of a god, at the grave of a saint, or at the shrine of an oracle, divination in its manifold modes, were common ways of finding assurance. Anxiety regarding the future, helplessness in the presence of unknown powers, pathetic eagerness for good fortune, lack of knowledge, urged man to grasp at any promise of wise leading. Mystical experience and sacred scriptures which are esteemed as the "word of god" are more sophisticated ways of getting guidance from the unseen world.

The mystic in every age escaped the limitations of formal religion. He did not need to bow to the authority of priest or scripture or institution for assurance in his religious life. But the truth the mystic found in his ecstatic experiences was exactly what he had accepted from his social environment. The mystic brings no news from another realm of being. Mystical states are purely subjective. Their value lies in giving a warm glow of certainty to whatever worldview the individual may hold.

Infallible scriptures claiming to reveal the divine will always need interpreters. Their authoritative status was illusory. The effective authority was in the social group of official interpreters. And their interpretations, claiming divine guidance, were actually dictated by the knowledge and problems of the social situation. Interpretations often clashed and contradicted each other. It is clear that revelation was only a means of reinforcing the best wisdom of man.

There is always a moral danger that an individual, a church, or a nation may identify personal or group interests with the will of god. Gods do not talk directly to man. Long centuries ago Confucius said, "Heaven does not say any thing." Only the interpreters speak. When a church talks with the authority of god, it may block a path of progress, freeze the status quo, and command acquiescence and a resigned attitude in the presence of crying abuses. Radical reform may seem to be rebellion against god, or the quest of new truth a repudiation of intellectual pride.

What is needed is an intelligent and trustworthy method of guiding the human adventure by practical programs to the attainment of selected goals. For that task we now have a new instrument—the method of science. Moreover, it is the only authority that may hope to command the loyalty and cooperation of thinking men. It can give both knowledge and guidance.

Science is illumination. Its searchlight reaches into the deepest space and its microscopic eye penetrates into the infinitely little. It sweeps the ages to tell the story of the earth, the history of man and his civilizations. The whole drama of human history appears to modern eyes in a new light. Gods and dogmas and institutions and moral codes fall into proper perspective as phases of the social life of man. Gone are the ultimates, absolutes, and finalities of the earlier ages. The steely rigidities of eternal truth are replaced by a view of reality as plastic, and therefore capable of being molded by good will and intelligence to the purposes of man.

But science is also method—the sure, objective way of thinking through problems, the democratic way of thinking, open to all and capable of being tested and accepted by all literate minds. It meets with confidence the tangled mysteries of nature, of human nature, and of social structure. Its record of achievement in the physical realm gives hope of still more thrilling victories over the age-old evils that have saddened the pilgrimage of man through all his adventures as a builder of culture.

Realizing that the only security that man has ever had has been in the warm enfoldment of the natural and social environment, we may visualize the time when the progressive perfecting of this enfoldment may provide him with an actual guide, guardian, providence, and guarantor of fulfillment.

If religion were simply a commerce with the supernatural, which could only be transacted through specially qualified persons and institutions or by means of mystical technique, it would be meaningless to talk of scientific method. But faith reaching to the heavens is of no avail. More important than faith in the gods is devotion to the human values of which they have been the symbol. Too long man has loaded down his gods with his burdens. Too long he has healed the sickness of hope deferred by more passionate faith. What the gods were expected to do, and failed to do, man must find the courage and intelligence to do for himself. More necessary than faith in the gods is faith that man can give justice, brotherhood, peace, and all his beloved moral values embodiment in human relations. Lack of that faith is the only real atheism. Without it belief in all the millions of gods of history is mere futility. With it, and the action that flows from it, man need not mourn the lack of guidance from the gods.

HUDSON HOAGLAND*

Executive Director and co-founder of the Worcester Foundation for Experimental Biology since 1944, Hudson Hoagland is a distinguished leader in the field of biological research. A graduate of Columbia, Massachusetts Institute of Technology, and Harvard, he was a Fellow of the National Research Council at Harvard (1927-28) and a Parker Fellow at Cambridge, England (1930-31). Dr. Hoagland has taught physiology and biology at Harvard, Clark University, Tufts Medical School, and Boston University. Since 1954 he has been chairman of the Josiah Macy Jr. Conference on Neuropharmacology. A Fellow of the American Association for the Advancement of Science, the Conference on Science, Philosophy and Religion, and Vice-President of the American Academy of Arts and Sciences, he has served as co-editor of Experimental Biology Monographs *and on the editorial board of* Physiological Reviews.

IT IS OFTEN said that a major reason for the decline of leadership in the western world is our loss of religious faith, and that since our ethical and moral standards have been built upon divine sanctions, revealed through the Judaic-Christian tradition, this loss in the faith of our fathers leaves us floundering like a rudderless ship in a storm. Arnold Toynbee, in the last volume of his *Study of History,* expresses the view that only a renaissance of religion can save our civilization from further decline, and this view is held by many thoughtful people. The advancement of science is often blamed for our loss of religious faith and this in large measure may be justified. It is my belief, how-

* The reader will note that Mr. Hoagland has decided not to subdivide his essay following the proposed plan of the inquiry.

ever, that the loss of traditional religious faith does not in itself imply the analogy of a rudderless ship or a collapse of ethics, and that the values by which men live are not contingent upon supernatural sanctions.

A recent study by Anne Roe, called *The Making of a Scientist*,[1] consisted of interviews and psychological tests applied to sixty-four eminent American men of science. The group was selected by a sound sampling procedure in terms of criteria of eminence in the physical, biological, and social sciences. Nothing was known of the religious backgrounds of the men when they were chosen for the study. In the group of sixty-four, five were from Jewish homes, the parents of one were strong "free-thinkers," and fifty-eight came from Protestant families. None had Catholic backgrounds. Of the scientists themselves, only three of the sixty-four were at all active in church affairs and a few others attended church occasionally but were not concerned with institutionalized religion. These findings are in general agreement with the personal experiences of many of us. Scientists for the most part are agnostics and reasons for this are not hard to find.

I have heard the physicist P. W. Bridgman define science as intelligence in action with no holds barred. Over the past three centuries accompanying the development of science, there has been repeatedly tested and satisfactorily confirmed an hypothesis that the most fruitful way to knowledge is limited by one's capacity to ask meaningful questions, to observe objectively, and to reach conclusions based on shareable observations relevant to the questions asked. Experimental procedures with adequate controls, logic, and mathematics are tools to assist this process and to enable one to draw tentative conclusions and proceed to more questions and testable hypotheses. But logic of the best can give no better answers than are inherent in the observations to which it is applied and no amount of skillful reasoning can reach sound conclusions if the questions are meaningless, the assumptions invalid, the operational procedures faulty, or the observations inadequate. Most scientists have had the experience of working on highly limited problems in their fields of special competence and arriving at convincing conclusions only to find later that the answers were wrong because of errors in assumptions or technique.

[1] (New York: Dodd, Mead & Company, 1953).

The progress of science itself and its relativity in terms of the intellectual atmosphere of the times illustrate the tentative nature of scientific advance. The views about phlogiston of eighteenth-century chemists, Lamarkianism and its modern abortive counterpart, present day Lysenkoism, are examples of this sort of thing on a grand scale. Most experienced scientists can give examples of erroneous conclusions of their own on a lesser scale. As a result of experiences with the elusiveness of truth in limited fields in which much is known and where technics are highly developed, the scientist is skeptical of conclusions arrived at by methods devoid of control and independent of his criteria of evidence. Thus logical proofs of the existence of a beneficient personal God are to most scientists meaningless because they cannot accept the assumptions upon which the logic operates. The historical bases of revelation are devoid of the evidential qualities essential for conclusions. Psychological interpretations of religious experience offer to many a more probable foundation for these phenomena than do the interpretations of the theologian.

In 1942, in that year's volume of the Second Conference on Science, Philosophy and Religion, I wrote:

All that we know is a product of the functioning of our nervous system. Our neurosensory apparatus is itself a direct product of biological evolution. We, together with other contemporary living organisms, are here today as the resultant of an extremely inefficient process of elimination. For every surviving species, many thousands of species have perished. For every living organism, many billions of potential organisms in the form of their parents' germ cells have perished. Animals eliminated in the course of evolution are, in large measure, ones that as a result of genetic accidents have failed to develop suitable physiological mechanisms to cope with the vicissitudes of their environments. All knowledge of our universe, including a knowledge of God, comes to us strained, if you will, through a series of highly involved physiochemical events, constituting sensory reception and responses mediated by the central nervous system (the brain). We experience not the properties of objects but the properties of our own nervous systems. We can thus have no direct knowledge of reality beyond the symbols that we learn to agree upon with others who have similar nervous systems. Since all normal men have in general similar nervous systems, it is impossible for some of us to accept indefinable and unsharable ways to a superior knowledge of God. In addition, naturalistic interpretations of religious phenomena in anthropological and psychological terms preclude for many of us the type of faith enjoyed by others.

Mystical experience appears to be no less a product of the nervous system than is the reflex reaction to a pinprick or the appreciation of a Beethoven symphony. Experiences of transcendent mysticism may be produced by the action of drugs on the brain. Thus the ingestion of half a gram of mescaline can produce remarkable aesthetic and mystical experiences, as Aldous Huxley has so well described in relation to his own experience, in his little book *The Doors of Perception*.[2] This substance, a product of the cactus plant, has long been used by the Indians of the Southwest for the purpose of inducing mystical experience in conjunction with religious rites. One of a number of other interesting substances producing psychological changes is lysergic acid diethylamide. A thirty-millionth of a gram of this substance, diluted in the body to one part in two billion, can produce in normal men by its action on brain chemistry weird and psychotic-like experiences lasting for eight to ten hours. Thus subjective mystical experiences can be brought about experimentally by subtle modifications of brain chemistry, and interpretations of religious experience based upon functional properties of brain mechanisms seem to some of us more probable than their interpretation as insights revealed by a supernatural external agent.

One property that nervous systems have is an ability to coordinate response of the organism as a whole in terms of the total environment. This ability to react to total environmental configurations on the part of animals, including man, has had great biological survival value. In the 1942 Conference volume referred to above, I suggested that man's drive to explain and make sense of his world and his relation to it may be a consequence of this fundamental property of his functioning brain, a property necessary for his survival as an individual and as a species. Thus the drive for a monistic viewpoint and a monotheistic god may be an attempt on our part to close a Gestalt and to unify our universe. There are primitive counterparts of this tendency to unify the environment in the behavior of animals. Similar motivation, in the main subconscious, may play a role in much of science and art.

[2] (New York: Harper & Brothers, 1954).

While we know all too little about the nervous system, intensive work of the last century and a half has never necessitated an hypothesis concerning its action that transcends physicochemical concepts of its workings. Modern views of mechanism are quite different from the materialistic clockwork concepts of the nineteenth century, and seem adequate to account for elements of purposive behavior, memory, and even learning, since these functions have been incorporated in electronic devices containing appropriate feedback circuits. This matter has been interestingly discussed by, among others, F. C. S. Northrop.[3]

The scientist cannot accept revelation as a way to knowledge. Revelation based on either secular or theological authority is alien to his way of life and thought. It is clearly alien to Bridgman's definition of science mentioned earlier since it insists that some "holds be barred" and such authoritarian restriction destroys objective inquiry.

Man appears to be one form of a large number of organisms that inhabit a minor planet which is a satellite of one of many billions of stars in one of many billions of galaxies. Because of its mass, distance from the sun, and rotation, the earth happens to present a set of remarkably restricted physical conditions that make life upon it possible. Ever since 1828 when Wöhler synthesized in the laboratory the first carbon compound (urea) it became clear that organic compounds do not require any vital principle for their formation, as had been thought, but follow the laws of chemistry. Organic compounds (i.e., the carbon compounds), of which hundreds of thousands are known, can be made in the laboratory as well as in living cells. In 1936 A. L. Oparin discussed from a fresh point of view the possibility of the spontaneous generation of carbon compounds as the beginners of life in the remote geologic past. Such compounds might serve as the building blocks of living organisms. Based upon considered geological evidence, he suggested that in very remote times the earth's atmosphere lacked free oxygen but was rich in methane (CH_4), ammonia (NH_3), and water vapor (H_2O). He postulated that electrical discharges in the form of lightning might produce a synthesis

[3] "The Neurological and Behavioristic Basis of the Ordering of Society by Means of Ideas," *Science* 107, 1948, p. 411.

of amino acids, the building blocks of proteins. Recently Harold Urey and S. L. Miller have tested Oparin's hypothesis. They circulated a mixture of these gases continuously for a week in an enclosed glass apparatus past an electric spark. At the end of the week it was found that amino acids had indeed been formed with a surprisingly high yield. Glycine and alanine, most prevalent building blocks of proteins, were found, with lesser amounts of aspartic acid and two other amino acids. In an excellent article on the origin of life, George Wald[4] has discussed these findings together with other important aspects of the problem, including probability considerations and energetics. While the nature of the origin of life has certainly not been proved, the probability of its chance spontaneous generation without the intervention of a directing agency is certainly strongly indicated.

It is believed that primitive life could begin from soups of protein molecules in primordial pools, each molecule made of chance arrangements of amino acids, and with the operation of natural selection and vast eons of time a wide variety of organisms, including ourselves, could have developed. Man seems nowhere to display a break in his continuity with nature. Thus viruses, which display many properties of living organisms, have been shown by Wendell Stanley and others to be large protein molecules composed of amino acids linked together. Viruses can be crystallized and, when put in a bottle, the virus looks like so much salt. Inside the congenial environment of a suitable host organism, these molecules reproduce themselves and produce diseases after the manner of bacteria.

In a sense, living organisms including man appear to be by-products of natural selection based primarily upon the chemical properties of carbon, nitrogen, oxygen, and hydrogen chancing to exist on the highly limited surface of our planet. Man has become most differentiated in the course of evolution from other animals by the elaboration of his brain, rich in complex electrical feedback and control mechanisms. Both conscious and unconscious drives are properties of his brain's action and he is aware of himself and of aspects of his relation to his environment. He, along with other contemporary animals and plants, seems to be the end product of entirely chance variations in the arrangements of the special protein

[4] "Origin of Life," *Scientific American* 191, 1954, p. 44.

molecules constituting the genes. Natural selection has eliminated innumerable less well-adapted genetic mutations. As a result of this, man appears to have been selected by design, as do all other forms of life that have survived the inefficient process of elimination resulting from chance variations in genetic mutation. Accounting for the order man sees about him in terms of Divine purpose fulfills a basic biological urge to unify himself with his threatening environment and to put himself in an especially favored position. While these views may seem bleak, they cannot be removed by wishful thinking. They may, of course, also be wrong, but the general picture is consistent with the results of scientific inquiry.

This brief consideration of the nature of man is presented not to convince anyone that it is correct but merely to indicate some lines of thought that may help account for why many scientists are agnostics. Science deals with probabilities. Absolute and final truth is not within its province. But science can ultimately yield so high a degree of probability as to become certainty for all practical purposes. Thus, for example, it is certain that the earth is round, not flat. Biological evolution by natural selection of mutants is no longer a theory but is so highly probable that debating its general validity has become futile. Newtonian mechanics as a first approximation for phenomena of intermediate dimensions is true despite relativity and quantum mechanics with their different views of the physics of the very large and the very small. The social sciences are as yet too young and their phenomena too poorly controlled to have given answers of a degree of assurance characteristic of the physical and biological sciences, but much may ultimately be expected from them. Some events are more probable than others, and to many the phenomena of religious experience and beliefs are more probably explicable along naturalistic lines than in terms of the traditional views of theologians. To many the existence of God can neither be proved nor disproved and honest agnosticism becomes the only answer in spite of the will to believe. It seems probable that, for better or for worse, agnosticism may increase in the future rather than diminish. If this is so, a frank facing of the situation is in order. If we assume as a working hypothesis that good and evil are purely products of man and his relation to his environment, particularly to his social environment, what can he do in support of the good life?

In terms of the above views on the nature of man, what becomes of human dignity and ethics? In the Judaic-Christian tradition and in that of other of the great religions such as Mohammedanism and Buddhism, man has dignity because he is made by God in His own image. His ethics have been a result of his religious sanctions as interpreted for him by theologians. God has revealed a way of life, for example in His commandments given to Moses, and this is the justification of ethical conduct. If we reject this idea of revealed truth, what have we left in the way of values?

I suggest that in practice the agnostic scientist is an ethical person. His conduct is not different from that of those who profess conventional religious beliefs. The scientist has developed a high regard for truth and spends much time in trying to ascertain it, but this alone hardly accounts for his basic set of values. He has learned to say "I do not know" to questions where others are sure they do know the answers on the basis of meager evidence or no evidence acceptable to him. He knows that some of the most unethical conduct of history has been the result of religious belief. He recalls the cruelty of the Crusades and of the Protestant and Catholic wars of the Middle Ages. Surely witchcraft, superstition, and the tyranny of organized religion, as featured by the Inquisition, have contributed little to human dignity.

Communism in operation may be thought of as a modern secular religion with its doctrines according to Marx and its icon worship of pictures of political leaders and symbols. A monolithic state replaces God and its worship degrades the individual. Science and the arts become slaves of the state. Authoritarian communism represents an unusually vicious form of dishonest tyranny. The intolerances of great faiths have generally resulted in concentration of power in the hands of a few to the suppression of the many. As Lord Acton said, "Power corrupts and absolute power corrupts absolutely." More blood may well have been shed in the name of religion than over any other issue. In view of all this, it is reasonable to ask if there is any enduring, positive relationship between restrictive authoritarian faith and the good life.

In many ways the findings of modern science validate the conception of the brotherhood of man and of democracy. It furnishes no comfort for race and caste prejudice. While marked differences exist between achievements of, let us say, Englishmen and those of

South Sea islanders, these differences appear to be due to environmental, cultural, and historic factors rather than to intrinsic biological genetic differences. Within any given group of people, intelligence as measured by tests that are reasonably culture-free indicate no significant racial differences. A similar bell-shaped distribution curve seems to apply to members of all racial groups in terms of measures of abilties. Man is one species displaying marked individual differences in abilities and endowments, but these differences are intracultural. When racial groups are compared, evidence indicates there are as many brilliant people and morons in one racial group as in another.

Just as a locomotive will continue to run for a time along the track after the fire under its boiler has been extinguished, it might be maintained that most agnostics are well behaved because of the momentum given to their ethical values by the Judaic-Christian tradition and that this momentum will be lost in time by a society that loses its belief in a personal, beneficent deity. There are many who sincerely believe that only a revival of belief in a supreme personal God on the part of secular leaders and people in general can save western civilization. Many scientists, schooled in rigorous views of validity of evidence, find it is not possible to have faith in the existence of something for which there is to them inadequate evidence. Such persons are humbly aware of the mysteries of the unknown at every hand and of the inadequacies of knowledge and of science to give certainty. But to accept a faith in a personal Deity who has specific concern for personal problems of good and evil on the basis of ignorance and mystification is simply not possible for many persons. Mystification humbles us but for many of us it cannot in itself interpret and yield a basis for positive faith.

Since the existence of God can neither be proved nor disproved by methods acceptable to most scientists it might be held that empirically the assumption of a beneficent personal God makes for a better and more workable society, and on pragmatic grounds therefore confirms the hypothesis of the existence of God. We have considered reasons for questioning the validity of the generalization that religious dogmas make for better societies and to many the concept of revelation is intrinsically unacceptable. It might also be maintained that belief in divine revelation was historically important in leading men to higher standards of values. These values of ethical conduct have then withstood the operational test of use so that the scaffolding of supernaturalism used in building them is no longer necessary. The completed ethical structure can stand by itself in terms of the important role it plays in daily living. Thus, for example, it matters little how the use of traffic control lights came about. Their continued use as a form of ethical regulation is assured because of their merit in an automotive age.

Altruistic behavior is not limited to man. The sacrifice of life of mother animals in protecting their young, the protection of members of the herd by the organized behavior of animals, even at the cost of their own lives, are forms of conduct which in us would be called ethical. Such behavior has survival value, preserving the group and the species in a hostile world. Symbiosis among plants and animals is of great significance in survival and advancement, both of the individual and of the species. The remarkable ecological aids afforded to each other by plants and animals, even between widely different species, can teach us much about the essential value of mutual co-operation in human societies. Evolutionary progress may in a sense be measured by the development of complex multicellular plants and animals from primitive single cell forms. The service of individual cells in special organs and tissues to the functioning of the total organism characterizes the metazoan and emphasizes the dependence of each cell upon the activities of the others. In all of these considerations the concepts of teleology and entelechy have added nothing to our understanding of biological phenomena. Such hypotheses have only confused the issues.

In the course of evolution within a system various writers have pointed out that new properties of the system emerge. These properties are intrinsic to the system but as emergents they may be entirely novel. Thus, modification in the course of evolution of the anatomy of the forelimbs of certain terrestrial animals has resulted in the novel property of flight. In man elaboration of the brain has brought about properties of behavior found only in rudimentary form or not at all in other animals. Man's use of the spoken and written symbol is a case in point. The use of language, an emergent property of his highly developed brain, has been essential for social evolution and the developments of civilizations. It has been suggested that the vast elaboration of the human cerebral cortex may result in the ultimate elimination of man as a species, that phylogenetically the great brain may be a sort of cancer operating to produce nuclear weapons, bacterial warfare, and other forms of destruction that could eliminate him as a species. An oversize brain may be as great a phylogenetic liability as may have been the great bulk of the dinosaurs. Just as animals and plants have used their special physiological and anatomical advantages to survive and prosper, so must man use his especially advanced brain to control himself in relation to his fellows if he is to survive and prosper. His great forebrain makes possible the binding of time—past, present, and future—for his advantage. It also serves to inhibit and modulate appropriately the basic drives of brain stem and midbrain mechanisms. Thus, control for long time objectives of aggressions, appetites, and fears is possible as in no other species. In other terminology, man has developed in the course of emergent evolution a conscience. If one wishes to use Freudian terminology, his id and ego are controllable by his superego.

Of all the concepts of ethics, that of the dignity of the individual seems to me to be most essential for advancement of man's welfare. The value of this concept appears to run through all historical human progress. This value seems to be an emergent property in man as a social organism. Nothing quite analogous to it seems to exist in ant and bee colonies or in the wasteful propagation of species in which only two of billions of germ cells form an embryo and become an adult organism, whether man or fish. The value of the individual per se does not seem to be inherent in the principles of natural selection responsible for survival of the species.

In many animal societies and in human societies individuals stand in certain relations of dominance and submission to each other—the pecking order in birds is a case in point. But the concept of the dignity and value of the individual man as it operates in ethics is more than this, and tempers the human pecking order in favor of a better life for all. It seems to me that this is the result of the operation of values based upon intelligent appraisal of their consequences and that this, after centuries of testing, sanctions the values. Slavery has been abolished because of man's belief in individual human worth.

Nazism has been destroyed because of man's belief in the dignity of
the individual. Tyranny has repeatedly surrendered to this belief, and
we hope in the case of the Communist tyranny that it will cease to
exist without a devastating nuclear war. There are many crucial tests
of the workability of value concepts that are part of the historical
record of the past 3000 years. Intelligent appraisal and insistence on
these values and their modifications when they fail to work seem to
be the best hope for man. Civilization depends upon social life controlled by accepted values. In the past, through ignorance and its
accompanying prejudices, hatreds, and fears, men often lost for
generations their earlier advances. The rapid decline in ancient Greek
civilization is one example in point. Science can be of inestimable
value if applied objectively to the testing and evaluation of values
as they operate in society. There certainly can be a science of values.
The social sciences deserve every encouragement lest our advanced
knowledge in the physical fields prove our undoing through devastating world wars with modern weapons.

I believe that basic values from our cultural heritage contain the
ingredients needed to solve the problems that plague our world. From
the ancient Greeks primarily came our belief in the importance of
intellectual honesty and free inquiry. From Judaism and Christianity
has come our faith in the brotherhood of man—this means man as
such, not just members of the tribe or nation or race. Primarily from
England we have derived our humane legal code which holds that
a man is innocent until proved guilty, and is not guilty when charged.
From Magna Charta on through eighteenth- and nineteenth-century
liberalism and our Bill of Rights has come our conception of the
rights of man. The state is for man and man must not be a pawn
of the state. All of these things add up to our belief in the dignity
of the individual with his freedom to choose and, if he wishes, to be
unorthodox in the honest choice of his opinions.

What Chief Justice Holmes has referred to as the right of dissent
—the right to disagree with authority—is essential for the survival
and advancement both of science and of the democratic society. Without the exercise of this right knowledge ceases to grow and democracy
is turned to tyranny. The norms of ethics, the purposes and values
by which we live, are not static but dynamic and subject to education
and evolution, and we have a moral obligation to be intelligent, as

well as honest, in appraising the consequences of action and so directing our values in terms of these consequences. Much that ails the
world today appears to be a result of the fact that many people
everywhere have surrendered their freedom of choice in favor of the
easy, ready-made ideologies and slogans of dictators with their false
solutions and authoritarian panaceas. These surrenders are in part
a consequence of the failure of traditional religious beliefs. They are
probably more the result of anti-intellectualism, ignorance, and dis-
respect for the tested values that have given men dignity and integrity
over the ages.

Since I have spent a quarter of a century doing research in the
biological and medical sciences, it is inevitable that my beliefs should
be colored by this background. Science and democracy have advanced
hand-in-hand over the last three hundred years. Without the cultural
climate of democracy, science, with its wide impact on human affairs,
could not have developed. German science deteriorated under the
Nazis and the science of genetics has been destroyed behind the iron
curtain. While I believe that science is a technique of the greatest
importance for the acquisition of knowledge and that truth is intrinsically good, I am fully cognizant of the limitations of science.

In our daily activities we must usually act upon the basis of evidence
that would not withstand the tests of scientific validity. The frontiers
of the unknown hem us in on all sides and we are aware that according to the rigorous criteria of the laboratory we know little about
many things. These limitations are especially conspicuous in the
realm of values and human relationships. Aside from the austere,
rigorous approach of science there are other approaches to reality.
Thus, literature, history, the arts, and the experiences that come from
living with one's fellows offer different aspects of great importance
of the world about us. An objective, scientific approach to human
relations has much promise for mankind. It has never really been tried
on a large scale or for a significant period of time.

Reason and the basic sciences have emancipated us from the
superstitions of the dark ages. I believe that reason and loyalty to our
historically tested values, derived by the struggles of free men over
the centuries, can do more than anything else to resolve the tragic
problems of our generation. This is not an easy road but I know of
no short cut.

ERNEST HOCKING

*William Ernest Hocking is "dean" of contemporary American philoso-
phers and has traveled widely in Europe and the Orient in the interest of
positive and religious thought. A graduate of Harvard and a graduate
student at Göttingen, Berlin, and Heidelberg, he has taught philosophy at
Harvard (1914-43), and has been the Gifford, Hibbert, Flint, and William
James' lecturers at Glasgow, Oxford and Cambridge, the University of
California at Los Angeles, and Harvard, respectively. A member of the
American Philosophical Society, the History of Science Society, the
British Institute of Philosophy and the Society of Dutch Letters, Dr.
Hocking has written, among others, the following volumes:* The Meaning
of God in Human Experience *(1912);* Human Nature and its Remaking
(1918); Types of Philosophy *(1929);* Living Religions and a World Faith
(1940); What Man Can Make of Man *(1942); and* Science and the Idea of
God *(1944).*

I

B Y RELIGION I mean a passion for right living, and for the spread
of right living, conceived as a cosmic demand.

The passion for right living is an ethical impulse; every man at
some time or other finds it in himself. It may be transitory; it is likely
to be a lonely and disturbing realization of the human situation—that
there is a right way of taking hold of life, easily missed since there
are numerous wrong ways; and that having but one life to live, there
are few issues more important than to take hold of this one by the
right handle. So far, ethics.

If this ethical impulse is joined with a sense that something in the
world I spring from *expects me to make a good job of it* (as "Eng-

land expects every man to do his duty."), ethics shades over into
religion. Religion brings the universe into my private business as a
party; it introduces a new responsibility into the situation, and a new
horizon. It is the passion-filled carrying on of the effort to find and
follow right ways, in the spirit of a responsible companionship with
the sources of my life—call them "the cosmos."

The new responsibility adds a certain weight to the natural impulse
to share with others what one perceives of "right living." What the
cosmos expects of me, it expects of all men. And one of the tests
that I have discerned a right way is that I can get your corroboration.
In fact, it is part of the right way of living that it is a sharing of the
right way! Religion thus tends, out of loneliness, to establish a
mutuality; and if the joy in discovery is great, one might find a group
starting, persisting. And the members, not ceasing to explore the hard
paths of "right living," might keep reminding each other of their
beginnings, "the old times we had together," and incipient "tradition."

This tendency to sharing, or group-making, does not cancel the
necessity that each person has to keep open his private path to his
own insights. And among those insights there may be some individual
demand upon him, *a "task" which is his alone*. Indeed, whatever
insight one gains as to the right way of living involves at that moment
a purely private and individual responsibility—the task of sharing it.
As Confucius put it: "Heaven has appointed me to teach this doctrine;
and until I have done so, what can the inhabitants of X [the mob]
do to me?"

Religion is thus an extraordinary union of the most intimate and
private with the most universal. We might put it into the form of
propositions which will help to answer the question before us:

1. There can be no religion unless it is original in each one for
himself: it is each man's private sense of the cosmic-expectation that
attends his impulse of duty. No man can use or borrow, or adopt
any other man's insight here; still less can he accept any other's
authority. Religion begins in the absolute intimacy and solitude of
individuality, reinforcing the uniqueness of the self, its aloneness in
presence of the mystery of Being.

2. There can be no religion that continues as a purely private
possession. For its sense of the Real that is over against it is its sense

of everyman's Real. Its nature is to communicate itself, with a "passion for the spread of right living." To settle down in one's solitary enjoyment of the "right way" is to deny the right way, whose essence is sharing of the most important. The most intimate has in it the need to become the most universal.

3. Hence every man, as right living takes on its cosmic bearing, faces an alternative. He must either form a group, sharing his insight, or recognize his own findings in an existing group, and join it. The third alternative, to which (especially as an American citizen) he may be inclined, namely, to be religious in his own way, enjoying his private sense of rightness and letting other folks alone, is excluded as contradicting the nature of religion. For that course is another way of saying that differences in religion are not important; implying that one's own findings are not important; and this, in turn, implies that religion has become for him an amiable sentiment which, after all, makes little difference. Its "passion" is gone; and for this reason, all talk about "the destiny of the soul" has become an exaggerated worry, intruding on the normal business of being a decent citizen. This is the real antithesis to religion—the cooling off of passion, the loss of "potential energy," the entropy of the soul, the second law of thermodynamics for the inner life of man—all temperatures tend to an equilibrium with the environment, in which no *work* is possible.

At the opposite extreme, in which religion is the integrating force of life, the alternative may be felt with extreme sharpness: either to find oneself at home in an existing religion or to start a new one!

In view of the obstacles which all well-established religious societies offer to this feeling-at-home on the part of strongly original souls, it is not surprising that so many "new" religious movements spring up, but rather that so few are heard of. The number of young men who begin movements of this sort, which live for awhile and vanish, would be astonishing if records could be kept. There was one in my own student days at Harvard: it called itself "The Brotherhood"; its motto was "Fraternity, Enlightenment, Progress"; I was in it. I will not further reveal its secrets except to say that its aim was to substitute for or reform existing religious societies, including Christianity, encrusted with ancient observances and outgrown cosmologies, with the example of a free society, animated by true social passion and consistent with the advancements of science.

I believe in movements of this sort; they represent the true spirit of religion, always original, always tending to regenerate the life of man—for religion, contrary to its repute, is the innovating force in society. Such movements never vanish without trace; they leave their mark on their membership, and through them on the life around them. But as divergent organizations they tend to disappear; and for one reason, among others, that the society needed by each one's religious impulse must create a fellowship, *enduring through time and reaching back to the birthdays of truth,* which one can recognize as one's own truth. It is the nature of religion to give truth effect, not simply to hold it as a creed; to make truth a working factor in history. Insofar as this has already been done, it belongs to truth to acknowledge it. It belongs to religion, I say, to be absolutely original; but originality and truth do not comport with failure to appreciate that same originality and truth in one's predecessors and in actual operation. It belongs to a true originality to realize the authority, i.e., the guidance and leadership, of an earlier and deeper exploration, where it exists. To trumpet a truth as one's own when it has already been proclaimed and embodied in action is not truth but falsehood.

So I now answer the first question in this inquiry.

If you look around for a perfect organization, you will not find it. The trail of the serpent is over all human organization. If you look around for a perfect membership, you cannot find it. You can enjoy the freedom of aloofness, keeping one's garments clean. It is the freedom which the perfectionist, the scholar, the scientist, the philosopher, the philanthropist in all ages tends to hold, as against traditional religious societies. It is a fine, and often noble, but inferior kind of freedom. It asks the wrong question. The question to ask is not whether a given organization is perfect, or what I would like it to be, but whether it was *born from truth,* from discovered and essential truth; whether it has given and gives that truth a working hold on the growing community; and especially whether it is self-renovating, so that reform can hopefully work from within—self-renewing, instead of encasing itself in a shell that can only be enlarged or rectified by being broken.

Apply these tests to the present situation:

¶If one finds that the unique simplification of the way of right living in the rule "Love God and your neighbor as a spark of God" is a valid induction; and if one further finds that the early Christian proposal of working toward a Kingdom of God on earth, in which love and good will are the animating forces, marks a birthday of indispensable truth in religion still held to and working as a leaven, it is honester to work with that tradition than to work apart from it.

¶ If one further finds that religion, as an organized force in history, needs an assurance that its difficult right-way is possible for men— an assurance arising from the fact that its way of life *has been lived* at least once; and if one finds that the crucial paradox of Christian morals, "He that loseth his life shall find it," was actually exemplified in the visible failure and ultimate success of the original teacher; it is better to accept the gift of this historic embodiment of the truth than not to accept it.

¶ If, again, as one examines the history of his own civilization one finds, here and there, discoverers, innovators, reformers who have had the same complaints of the then-existing pieties and organizations as one now has; and who have left on the institutions of their time and ours effects which must be credited to a rebirth of the original insights, and to faith in the infinite futurities of human nature, he would be untrue to his own original sense of religion if he did not reach out for fellowship in the historic succession of those originating and devoted spirits.

In sum, the contemporary religious value that I find in the existing western tradition is the value of having, not merely religiousness, but "a" religion as a going concern—working, historical, and embodied in an actual life, serving as an adequate symbol.

As I consider these things, the alternative of founding a new religion seems a contradiction in terms, since a new religion by definition would fail to include these beginnings.

But the relation of any thinker to an existing religious tradition has one absolute condition; he cannot subscribe to any dogma which he considers doubtful or false. If, desiring and needing to identify himself with an historic community of faith, he is confronted with this dilemma, he must adopt the course of dissent as a condition of his

own integrity; and believing, if he can believe, that the existing institution will find the way to its own truth, including his truth, he
may count himself a member of the church of the future.

II

The second of these questions simply expands the first, if, as I believe, the "religious conviction about cosmic reality" is that it "cares."
Unless the cosmos somehow "cares" about human life and motives,
any religion which consists in taking "right living" as a cosmic demand
is a fallacy. My answer to the second question is Yes; and the
grounds are—in a word—experience.

The first point to be clear about is that science has nothing to say
on the subject, pro or con. Strictly speaking, science has no worldview: it has a nature-view. And in its nature-view there is and can be
no "caring," because caring is excluded in advance by scientific
method. Science is occupied solely with measurable relations between measurable events; and "caring" offers no hold for mathematical description. Modern science, as far more definite about its methods
than earlier science, is also far more definite about its limitations. The
true scientist today, knowing as any other man knows that human
beings "care," has no theory about how they came to care, nor even
how they came to be conscious at all. He knows, furthermore, that to
say that "Nature is all there is" in the universe, is a wholly unscientific
assertion.

A second point is this: that science does not provide its own facts—
it finds them; it does not ask how there happen to be any facts at all,
rather than nothing at all. This implies that all "facts," including the
most important facts, are known not first by science but by experience. Each man knows his own existence, important to him not by
science but by experience—self-awareness. The most important facts
of the universe are consciousness and caring; for without them nothing
is "important," nor of any value whatever.

And just these two facts are very bothersome to science. Physics
and chemistry can get along quite well without them. Biology could be
much more comfortable if organisms would be organisms and do their
reacting as they do without the intrusion of an invisible, unmeasurable,
unverifiable entity called consciousness. And even psychology, pre-

sumably occupied with the "soul," lists heavily to starboard, that is to the "behavior" which can be traced in the laboratory, in preference to the subjective experiences which elude the experimenter and can only be gauged through the unreliable medium of the subject's self-reporting. It would be far simpler if the "soul" could be eliminated! And perhaps in the ideal future laboratory it will be.

While science walks among these facts-of-first-importance with uneasy tread, the common man has a certain right to do his own thinking. He is likely to consider that, since consciousness and caring are here, they could hardly have occurred by pure chance or have slipped in incidentally as minor "variations." The general notion of which science makes much use, that nothing comes from nothing, tends to persuade him that the fact of "caring" could not have come from a non-caring cosmos. To say that they have arrived by "emergent evolution" or, still worse, by "creative evolution," seems to him a pedantic way of extracting something from nothing, and on the whole very poor science; for science cannot extract the more from the less, nor the new quality from the old, nor awareness of fact from simple fact. Science knows nothing of "creation."

Nor does it know anything about freedom, a scientific nuisance which physics gladly hands over to psychology, and psychology, playing with Heisenberg's indeterminacy, would like to hand back again. Spinoza, who mistakenly made Nature equivalent to the whole world, *Natura sive Deus,* shut freedom out, and made the highest virtue consist of accepting necessity with gratitude and love as *amor intellectualis Dei.* Spinoza has the great merit of having made the conscious-and-caring side of reality an integral part of his worldview; but since for him physical Nature and mental Nature had to march along together he excluded freedom. And therewith he excluded empirical fact; for freedom is there, and it is the very making of humanity's character. Without free choice there is no duty, and none of that constantly perilous, often tragic, interest that makes human history the scene of the world's meaning. We must include freedom, even though the problem of how, in a world with science-charted Nature, freedom is possible is obligatory business for the scrupulous thinker.

And with freedom there is another important fact, an almost invisible fact, one on which science builds and yet which eludes scientific accounting—each person's *awareness of other persons*. No one doubts the fact; but how we are aware, science has no answer. Our senses report other human bodies in action; but the consciousness animating that action is imperceptible by any sense. Today, we talk much of "intersubjectivity," the consciousness of "we": nothing is more spontaneous than "Here we are!" As my colleague Whitehead put it, in one of our joint seminars, "Hang it all; *here we are*; we don't go behind that, we begin with it!" Right: but where do we get that self-evident "we"? Descartes didn't find it, in his search for an undoubtable fact; yet he used it! What he found was that "I exist"; literally, "I, Descartes, exist." Yet he *published* his finding for others to corroborate! And in publishing he showed that he, too, was sure of the "we." We must include the "we" in our factual data, without the prior support of science and, so far, very little from philosophy, though philosophers are waking up to it!

This "we" is, for us, the most significant of all these pre-scientific facts. For the "we" awareness does not arrive; it is there from the beginning of conscious life. Were there no "Thou-consciousness," there would be no "I-consciousness." With the first awakening of conscious life in mere uninterpreted sensations as of "something there," there is also a dim realization that there is something to do about the sensations; that the life of the dawning self calls for more than sensing, namely, for *thinking*: sensation must become a sign of "things in a world." And that world is, from the first, not "my" world; it is "our world"—a common region of experience. In other words, there is a "Thou" in the situation, working as a summons to become fully human, not simply a sensing, moment-to-moment consciousness. But in that relation of invitation-to-become, there is on one side *duty*, on the other side *caring*.

This is the account of the "we"-mystery which I find to be the true account: the "we" is a part of our most primitive consciousness. To be alive is to exist in an environment which is a common world for self and others; its "space" is your space as well as mine; its events are events for us and for all others. And the original and permanent Other-self is the "Thou" of the world. And in that inescapable companionship, entirely unintrusive, to live is to care and to be cared for, inseparably and immediately.

If this account is valid, the "caring" of the cosmos is, as I said at first, a simple *deliverance of experience,* and like all pervasive things easily overlooked and lost in the run of the day's events.

And while science has no specific part in this perception, its own path is evidently made clearer by it; for science depends on each observer's ability to report his own perceptions as verifiable by any others who share the identical space-time world of nature. Science can therefore have no objection to the acceptance of what we find as primitive datum.

As for "Nature's apparent indifference and destructive treatment" —this question in the inquiry is central and should be treated at greater length than I can give. Let me say simply (1) that Nature, as environment for human living, while silent as it has to be, is not indifferent in its constitution. As affording possibilities for the "highest interests" and also for the highest calamities, ergo for the gravest choices men are called on to make—as the present crisis exemplifies— Nature is not unsuited to a developing human order. In this sense the "fitness of the environment," as L. J. Henderson put it, is part of the picture. (2) That the critical factor for human happiness is not the negative fact of the presence of risk and the possibility of suffering, but the affirmative fact of cosmic concern. This fact *holds the balance* of the positive and negative values of living; for it has the capacity of making suffering significant, where insignificant suffering would be intolerable.

III

I presume this question is answered by implication in what has gone before. If religion has the nature of recognizing a summons from the cosmos to everyman to a life of duty, the task of working out right living in a community of fellow seekers is implied. This community, which is at first the community of the church in a broad sense, has its direct bearing on the political community. Historically the bases of western democracy are first moral (as in Solon's legislation) and then religious, as in Locke's derivation of human rights.

The broad aspect of evolution and the place of man in the series, together with the disposition of all human societies to remake the typical man in the image of their developing ideal of character (as I have pointed out in *What Man Can Make of Man*)[1] strongly suggest that the working out of personal moral character is the goal of the cosmic process.

The humanitarian impulse based on a passionate regard for the ideal possibilities of human nature is capable of rising to religious intensity, as Father Bienvenu saw when he asked the blessing of the dying Conventionist. When one encounters this spirit in human beings, apart from religious commitments, it is apt to elicit a peculiar reverence, as if the lover of mankind were taking on himself the work our imagination ascribes to deity. I often felt that way toward "Daddy" George of the George Junior Republic, in whom I recognized an unalloyed passion for "saving souls," lifting the youngsters-in-trouble, as if by main strength of his own devotion, to the level of the possibilities he saw in them. I also felt that this love and faith had its own background in his vision of the cosmos, with which he—almost subconsciously—felt himself cooperating. Here the struggle for better things needed no apology, no philosophy, no theology: this "lifting" was its own reason for existence; whatever the reality of the cosmos might be, here it was actively at work in dealing with a curable misery, here was intense happiness shining out in the midst of intense trouble. The world was good, and nothing else mattered.

These things are not "the sole grounds of religious faith"; they are manifestations of religion, and it is through religion in its cosmic reach that one understands why one feels in them, through the particular personal or social preoccupation, the presence of the holiness at the center of Being.

IV

Since it is the function of religion to *integrate* the impulses and purposes of a human will under a dominant affection or loyalty, whatever phases of religion one finds—in Nature's travail to beget and nurture human life, in history's travail to beget a society of, for, and by free men, and in the traditional religion of love to men—must of necessity belong together.

The causes are many: the spirit of religion is one. But that spirit has to contend with the plurality of the causes, and may be splintered

[1] (New York: Harper & Brothers, 1942).

by their partiality. The economic contest with nature's reluctance, combined with the fight against poverty, greed, injustice; the struggle for a society not alone of freedom but of dignity and beauty; the long-drawn-out effort for relations of peace and good-will among nations—all these and others give rise to enthusiasms taking on religious coloring, calling out sacrifice, heroism, and prophetic vision. At the same time each tends to fill the horizon to the exclusion of others, and so to provincialize the religious spirit with which it seeks identification. Each needs the constant reminder of an over-all unity of aim, beyond the warping inherent in every concrete human enterprise.

Each one also encounters, partly through its own error, check, frustration, the temptation to despair. Here it needs the sustaining guidance of a life-giving source beyond the sphere of its particular effort. It has a need for morale such as the human resources of faith and hope may not supply. This is a further function for that non-local conception of a developing Kingdom of God on earth, defined in terms of a spirit rather than of an ideology, and supplying an absolute prohibition against giving up the fight.

V

Question V is essentially answered in the concept of religion itself as involving a cosmic concern in individual right living. This implies an individual center of caring; for only an individual can apprehend an individual. We have further identified this individual as a "Thou," an Other-self to all finite selves at all times. With this, the pictorial conception of the cosmic Carer as a person limited to one position in space and time is discarded; and all the pictorial images are relegated to the realm of symbol, myth, or poetry, without disparaging their value as symbols. The center of the "meaning of God in human experience" is, and must remain, precisely in the realm of intimate personal awareness of a sustaining Other-selfhood, coextensive with the experience of Nature presented to each finite self, whose presence transforms the impact of sense-data from brute fact to the building material of thought, at once an opportunity and an obligation. An aboriginal "ought" is carried with the sense-stuff, a summons to live on the level of thought, not of sensation alone, and thus to participate in a world which is also a world for others. This is the birth of science, which is thus literally an offspring of the religious consciousness.

Since it is this primitive community of the moral sense, which is the basis of all further community, this conception is indispensable, even while we accept the judgment of all mystics that it is also ineffable and all that we say about it suffers the distortion of finitizing the infinite: as Spinoza put it, all determination is negation. The conception is indispensable, certainly *not the name!* And when Gandhi says that "law and the lawgiver are one," the ultimate "moral law of truth and love," he gives a touch, at once specifying and liberating, to our concept of the living fountain of life perennially summoning man to universality of mind and universality of sympathy.

HORACE M. KALLEN

Horace M. Kallen is Research Professor in Social Philosophy and Professor Emeritus of Philosophy and Psychology in the Graduate Faculty of Political and Social Science at The New School for Social Research in New York. A favorite pupil of William James, he has been identified with the pragmatic movement in American philosophy almost since its inception. He has extended the pragmatic outlook in his own special way to the economy of culture, of the arts, of education, and of religion. His central emphasis has been on the role of individuality and freedom in these fields. Among his books are: William James and Henri Bergson *(1916);* The Book of Job as a Greek Tragedy *(1917);* Culture and Democracy in the United States *(1926);* Why Religion *(1927);* Art and Freedom *(1942);* The Liberal Spirit *(1948);* The Education of Free Men *(1949);* Secularism is the Will of God *(1953).*

INTRODUCTION

IN REFLECTING upon the questions to which this paper is a proffer of answers, I undergo a feeling of irony that spans their entire theme. The very subject—"the foundations of human purpose and values"—starts it. "Foundations" suggests permanent grounds for stable superstructures. It implies that the grounds are somehow inalterably the same, however the superstructures differ from one another. The particle "the" accents the suggestion. It implies for the reader that, whatever be their nature, there are, there can be, no other foundations. They are *the* foundations, infallibly such-and-such, always and everywhere the same one eternal and universal order behind and beneath the world's multitudes of peoples; its manifold configurations of beliefs, preferences, and performances supporting, holding up their "purposes" and "values" as Atlas supports the world. By implication, foundations are the unchanging ground of change, the safe and certain matrix of the changes and chances of the human struggle for existence which the words "purpose," "value," signalize. By implication, their changeless substance is more valuable and meaningful than the processes of ongoing change, of hazards and challenges which are the stuff of history and biography. Unitary origin counts for more than diversifying consequences in the diverse struggles of the diversities of *homo sap.* for their diverse survivals.

"Purposes" and "values" signify these diversities; they name formations of the matters, the media, the satisfactions and frustrations which men's struggles come to and go from. In any individual life, they signify the shape of its ongoing propulsions; they are terms of passage with significances that only the future can validate, and the future enters everybody's experience as a diversification of familiar sameness into surprising difference; an individual's future is the news in his life. To live on, and by living on, presently to suffuse and alter the ongoing past with events and experiences which neither repeat it nor inevitably follow from it, is to create this news, which differs from individual to individual, and compounds into the indefeasible uniqueness wherein each distinguishes himself from every other. The self-creation is also what we usually call "struggle for self-preservation," "struggle for survival"; it is what the diversifications of being born, growing up, and growing old diversely count up to, at the stoppage whose other name is death.

These consummations, at once unique and manifold, are, however, what the religious and philosophical systems of our "great tradition" refuse to accept. They call them mere appearances, deny that they truly evince the human condition, and argue variously and inconsistently with one another to prove that the experience of life and death is an experience of unreality, and the reality is an external and universal foundation that repeats itself in man as inalterable soul which cannot die. Their aspiration continues to be one of replacing the human condition with a set of foregone conclusions: that though it is to live on, yet it is not to change; to purpose, yet to have its purpose already realized; to desire, yet already to be possessed of what is desired; to value, yet not to need to struggle for the existence of values. They argue that we cannot want what we do not already have, nor become what we already are not, and that the contrary witness of experience is *maya,* illusion.

A common symbol of this reality behind and beneath the apparent human condition is "Heaven." With it go a whole congeries of terms, bespoken by such expressions as "supernatural," "immortal soul," "spirit," "angel," "God," "Devil," all receiving meanings as concrete and singular as the cultures they figure in, and all in themselves constituting, for the meaners of those meanings, "the substance of things hoped-for, and the evidence of things not seen." In the discourse of their users, they serve as value-words: that is, words whose meanings are inward to the words themselves. Searchers for something else than the words, for forces and forms that the words signify, regularly come back to individual or collective attitudes, actions, hopes, fears, facilitations, frustrations, or their configuration into churches and other institutions. They never attain to any open sharable experience of "objective" substances and evidences, such as commonsense and the sciences rely upon. The words and other symbols are terms of faith, not knowledge; themselves all the objects, the substances, and the evidences that faiths are faiths in. They bespeak the ever-insecure and troubled human person, struggling to be safe and untroubled yet alive at last. But they do not purport the endlessly varying circumambience of nonhuman things and events amid and with which the sons of Adam wrestle, as Jacob, with the Lord.

That nonhuman is usually called "nature", and its stuffs and sequences can be discerned, explored, defined, and known. The entities postulated by the value-words are usually called "supernatural", and can only be believed-in. "Nature" is equated to "existence," the "supernatural" is equated to "value." Thus "value" would be one of the differentiae, perhaps the most critical differentia, which signalizes the humanity of the human being—the difference wherewith human existence distinguishes itself from other existences, the natural singularity of *genus humanum.*

It would follow that a humanism which, whether as a philosophy or as a religion, concerns itself with that in men which establishes them as human, would first and last value the entire diversity of valuations.

To deny or condemn any one of them for what it is, and not for its consequential relations with different valuations, would be to cultivate a defective and less-than-human humanism. If, as Protagoras is said to have held, man is the measure of all things, of things that are, that they are, of things that are not, that they are not, then he "values" wherewith the sorts and conditions of mankind measure themselves, their fellow-men, and their nonhuman circumambience are the constituting energies of their being as men, each different from the others and none more privileged to be itself than any other.

The maxim of Protagoras would be falsified if any by original nature had a better title to struggle for its existence than any other, or freely to endeavor to excel in the consequential arts of measurement than any other. Those are the arts whose tests in experience are the diversifications of unfree and narrowly conscious human existence into ever freer, ever more dynamically comprehensive awareness of self and the world. The Biblical term for this propulsive self-orchestration of diversifying consciousness is "the life more abundant." Albert Schweitzer, proclaiming "reverence for life," embodies this intention of "man the measure" alike in his personal history and in his reasoned faith.

I now turn to the five questions. What answers I can produce will be congruent, at least to the extent that my intention and desire can make them so, with the beliefs I have just set down.

I

If "religion" signifies what I perceive it to signify, then to strip "the Judaeo-Christian religions" or any other, of "their divergent ethnic, doctrinal, and structural factors" would be to denature them. It would be to treat them as a chemist treats a compound when he deprives it of its qualities *as* compound, and reduces it to simpler residues. His analysis destroys; it neither discloses nor discovers the compound's *identifying* characteristics, for that compound is a whole whose parts are so related to one another that each has come to be qualified by all. Its concrete identity is a consequence of those relations. When they are severed, it perishes. What ensues is something quite other, in quality and action as different from the compound as hydrogen and oxygen are different from the water into which they are usually combined. The religions of mankind are complex historical growths. They do not put on and take off their divergent ethnic, doctrinal, and structural factors as a man his clothes. Rather, the factors figure for the religions of the world as a living man's lungs and liver and other organs figure for the man. Together with the residual creeds and codes, rites and rotes, they compose the diverse "organic" configurations that are the distinguishing *whats* of the global multitude of religions, of which the Judaeo-Christian ones are a few.

History records sequences of such configurations, all altering as they struggle to live and grow, some carrying the tradition which their alterations compose through millennia, others failing and falling apart in the course of a few centuries, a few generations, a few years.

That which makes the difference between long life or short, survival or extinction, is not *what* the configurations are, but *how* their faithful believe in them. Any person, any image, any idea, any pattern of behavior, any social institution, and any configuration of them becomes an object of religious faith when a believer so believes in its bearing on his existence and destiny that he bets his life on it; and it is reliably *his* religion only so long as he bets his life. Then, be it a theism, an atheism, or any other *ism,* he trusts it as the insurance of his victory in his struggle to live, even when he dies. Thereby he endows it with supreme value, and he will talk and work and fight for it against the other faiths of different believers. To him the latter are then infidels, heretics, rebels, traitors, and foes of eternal life who must be extirpated if possible, and silenced, or contained and restricted, if not.

Now a certain phase of contemporary thought and practice recognizes that in such a war of all religions against all, each believer intends for himself what he would deprive the others of. Each insists that the end on which all agree can be attained by his means and only by his means. All want life more abundant, each according to his kind, and each insists that the way to this life is his way and no other. Since the Protestant Reformation men have come to recognize that any and all religions, however set up, are diverse communities of collective means for the consummation of the life more abundant as a distributive end. They have come to recognize that religions are made for men, not men for religions. So they have come, in their thought and practice, to pass from mutual aggression and warfare to the grudging balance of power which is the first form of toleration, from that to the more generous rule of *live and let live* which is toleration's second form. And they are now at points in passage to the third form, whose rule is *live and help live*.

In this passage, the emphasis properly falls:

First: On perceiving each religion as a cultural whole of faith and works.

Second: On endeavoring to understand sympathetically the individuality of this whole: to accept and respect its existence; not to aim to conform it to one's own religion on pretensions to exclusive God-given superiority and truth.

Third: On cultivating such free and friendly communication between different religions as would consummate in a union of each with all that would guarantee to each alike its freedom to live and to grow in safety and equality. As I have shown in *Secularism Is the Will of God,*[1] such a union of all faiths—*in pluribus unum*—would compose a global communion that could grant no favors to any nor commit itself to one more than to any other; it would be a whole, with qualities and functions different from those of its member parts, and *Secularism* is the word which signifies these qualities and functions.

II

I do not consider that modern science is unfolding one and only one worldview, or that it is committed to any. Science, insofar as it *is* science, is an ongoing method of inquiry, changing and improving as it goes on. The reliability of *what* a science discloses accrues to it not from *what* is disclosed but from *how* it is disclosed; from the trust in the method, not the character of the object. Just now some men of science are monists and determinists who work in the faith that all differences can be liquidated in an identity such as "energy" and all changes conformed to unchanging laws of change. Other men of science are atomistic pluralists and indeterminists who work in the faith that "reality" is a manifold of fluidities and processes that compound as they continue, and that cosmic evolution and human history

[1] (New York: Twayse Publishers Inc., 1955).

are better accounted for when new beginnings are added to ongoing
sequences, and chance and probability complement invariant laws.
And there are other scientific worldviews less postulated on the disclosures of scientific method. All may, as such, become "religious
convictions," and do; or they may be used, as by Compton, Jeans,
Eddington, Whittaker, and others, to supplement or to confirm the
more conventional "religious convictions" which assert that some
immanent or transcendent total consciousness similar to human reason
or will or feeling is an all-ruling providence which benevolently shapes
all ends, whoever rough-hews them and however.

But there are also those who believe in a Devil as well as a God,
a hell as well as a heaven, to say nothing of a purgatory, and to these,
Malevolence can be as real and as rational as Benevolence. For some,
like the Manicheans, all existence is a practically equal struggle between the two, in which the final victory of Benevolence is inscrutably
remote. On the other hand, for persons whose faith is firm that God
is omnipotent Benevolence, their faith creates the well-known "problem of evil." So far as any man's personal history is concerned—he
is born, he grows up, he grows old, he dies. From birth to death his
existence consists of a struggle to go on existing. The struggle enacts
itself as a gathering, making, storing, using, consuming whatever supports it; as dispersing, destroying, shutting out, and cutting off whatever is felt to be seeking to quell it. During some of its phases life is
heightened and advanced; during others, life is contracted and re-
treats. Often, the forward phases occur at the cost of the freedom and
existence of other men, always at the cost of soil and sea, of animals,
plants, microorganisms. During phases of recession, these others reverse the roles; earthquakes, storms, eruptions, floods, plagues, and
poisons destroy the works and flesh, and check and subdue the spirit
of man. If "indifference"[2] means that "Nature" evinces no hierarchy

[2] See, for example, Chapter XII, on "Altruism" in Sir Charles Sherrington's
Man on His Nature, (Cambridge: Cambridge University Press, 1951), where
he recounts from "almost countless many" the life-cycles of Redia, the
parasite of sheep-rot and of plasmodium, the parasite of malaria, with their
ravening, torturing blind pilgrimages from host to host, animal or human.
"Life's prize," Sherrington comments, "is given to the aggressive and inferior
life, destructive of other lives at the expense of suffering in them, and sad as it
may seem to us, suffering in proportion as they are lives high in life's scale."

of values, plays no favorites, has no chosen breed, human or non-human, then nature is "indifferent." That whatever is born dies, whatever begins ends, and that nothing on earth is seen as unbegun and as going to no end, is an observation tempered also by another observation: that the sequences between beginning and end often do compose themselves into orders of excellence, better and worse, and that because this happens, philosophers and theologians and historians do choose one such order to use as the measure of praise and blame for all: one need only mention St. Augustine, or Oswald Spengler, or Houston Stewart Chamberlain, or Henry Adams, or Arnold Toynbee. In the context of their worldviews, "indifference" would mean deterioration or rejection. But in other contexts it also could mean the formation and growth of excellences without any care for their duration: they could come to perfection and perish. There are people who bet their lives that God is both good and omnipotent whatever happens; their faith is, "Though he slay me yet will I trust in him." If they die trusting, have their values been invalidated? Can existence for them be said to have been indifferent or malevolent?

III

I presume that "genius of the democratic movement and of personal moral character," refer to the ideals of human nature and human relations set down in such public credos as the American Declaration of Independence and the global Universal Declaration of Human Rights, and to ongoing struggles to incarnate the ideals in the works and ways of the world's peoples. I think I can say that they underlie the creed and code I bet my life on. I believe with a firm faith:

(1) that people are irreducibly different from one another and that this difference is an inalienable right, to be exercised by all alike, without fear or favor, safely and freely,

(2) that the right extends to every form of the human enterprise—religious, cultural, educational, political, economic, scientific, and so on,

(3) that people best secure these rights to themselves and to one another by joining together in corresponding societies, little and great, which serve them as collective means to their distributive ends.

Yet, if I were a Brahmin, I might concede and reverence the right to be different without penalty to cattle and vermin, but would penalize certain categories of other human beings for their difference. If I were a Buddhist, I might concede the right to all living things and contract my own existence as man to the mystic's minimum, ultimately to the nullification of my humanity. If I were a fellow of some one of the "Judaeo-Christian" communions, I might concede the parity of those groups whose rights I was not strong enough to disregard to overrule. Then I might "tolerate" their differences, but condemn or deprecate and scheme to translate them into agreement with mine, whether in their hearts they agreed or no. If I were a certain species of Humanist, I might take either attitude toward non-Humanists.

As a Secularist, however, I recognize the equal right of all the world's different faiths to be what they are as they are, so long as they do not cancel this right for themselves by refusing it to others. Although it cannot be said that the world was more made for man than for any other living thing, the world's peoples, when they unite their different strengths and skills and wisdoms, can and do remake it for themselves. As their local cooperative unions associate into a global one, the remaking becomes global, *in pluribus unum*.

IV

There are assumptions in Question IV as put whose disclosure and analysis my present task has no room for. Just now I can only say: Mankind being what it is, the "moral man" of one society may be, and is, the "immoral" or "unmoral" man of another, and that the "supreme values" of one may be, and are, condemned as the reverse, by another—that, in some, different groupings manifest different ways of life, different standards of living, different personal embodiments of both.[3] The values are many and the moralities are many, each varying from the others, each having the others for near or distant neighbors. The neighborly relationship may be tantamount to a warfare of moral ideals. It may consist of hot war of all with all. It may pass from that to cold war, thence to "coexistence," and at last to the free trade in things, thoughts, and beliefs wherein neigh-

[3] See the article "Morals," *Encyclopedia of the Social Sciences* (New York: The Macmillan Company, 1948), Vol. 10, p. 643.

bors become "good neighbors." The relationship between "good neighbors" may be described as a pooling of means in a shared endeavor to help each other attain their individual unsharable ends. It is the collective or public table which satisfies the singular and private hungers. Insofar as any oneness comes here into play, it is a consequence, not an initiation. The initiation is in the indefeasible plural hungers; the oneness in the consequently pooled means of their satisfaction; it follows from and resides in the union of the many, and its reality has for its sufficient reason the reality of the many.

Whether I should regard such a reality as "spiritual" would depend on what is meant by this many-valued word. Assume that it is being used as priests and other churchly people use it. Then it signifies an Otherworld of one or more substances, each an individuality invisible, imponderable, impenetrable, indestructible, always and everywhere the same. The conventional names of such substances are God, Devil, angels, demons, souls, and the like. Collectively they compose "the Supernatural." By definition utterly different from the natural Thisworld of matter where we struggle for our existence, this supernatural Otherworld of spirits providentially infiltrates, permeates, and surrounds Thisworld, influencing our motives and conduct, shaping our fortunes for both worlds. But the action is not one-way, down from the heights of spirit to the abysms of matter. Enfleshed man can affect discarnate spirit, prevent it from hurting, persuade it to helping. Such working on the supernatural becomes the specialized vocation known as priestcraft, that expertise in doctrines and disciplines which is required for the profession of middleman between Supernatural persons and natural human beings. The means and tools of the profession are nature's lands and buildings and other properties, vessels, vestments, meats, breads, wines, and other sacrifices, chants, songs, preachments, all ordered into the rites and rotes, the modes of worship and prayer, which diversely signalize the diverse cults of the supernatural. By their means, the specialist in the manifestation of the supernatural practices his art on behalf of the "material" and "spiritual" needs and wants of his cure of souls.

"Spiritual" here has a meaning organically related to the economy of a religious corporation, competing, like other corporations, for more abundant material support, prestige, property, and power. Different meanings go with different configurations of experience and organization. All might be regarded as changes whose matrix is a man's primal awareness of his own breathing. His *in*-spiration and *ex*-piration are movements and pressures felt, heard, but not seen. The Old Testament word for spirit is *ruah*; Greek *pneuma*, and it variously signifies invisible wind, the hot blow and the cold. Within man, *ruah* is the angry, the sad, the fearful blow of his breath, or the zealous, the hopeful, the triumphant one. Outside man, *ruah* signifies the invisible élan which pours itself out upon, rushes or falls upon, passes over upon men—who thereupon prophesy—and which is here, there, everywhere, nowhere, beyond beholding or imaging. The *what* of *ruah* is a passage too mobile for perception to catch; only the *how* of its passing is felt and the consequence of its passage known.

In the New Testament—essentially the Pauline documents— *pneuma* figures as that indiscernible inbreathing (ultimately the Holy Ghost) which sets Christian apart from non-Christian—God's grace, the free gift he gives, or pours out into, the true believer, who thereby becomes one "reborn into the Kingdom." Finally spirit as invisible mobility ends up in Spirit as invisible immobility. It is consolidated into that unitary, impenetrable, imperishable entity for which the commonest name is Soul.

Now, although a soul's mortal span is crowned by an immortal destiny, its theological identity is unaltered and unalterable in both. Although it thinks and wills and feels, it does not change; only its place and status change. Yet its mortal breath of life consists of a sequence of Thisworldly transactions, conscious and unconscious, with Thisworld's material circumambience, whereby it both learns and forgets. The transactions diversify and combine as refinements of perception, as discriminations ever more delicate and precise among thoughts and things and events, as their orchestration into a confluent pattern where in each is appreciated via its relations with all. On occasion, this ongoing process enters a phase when it is suffused and lit up by a glow of positive feeling which signalizes a kind of closure; the individual has wholly committed himself to the vision he beholds, and his seeing has become his conspectus of understanding and guidance for his life, his light upon existence and destiny. This event is the individual's *auto da fé*. That which he now affirms has become the object of his faith on which he bets his life—the substance of things hoped for, the evidence of things not seen, and so the substance of spirituality. It is this not in virtue of *what* it intends, but in virtue of the *how* of its intending, and of its uses. So, we speak of the spirit of a people, a culture, or a cultus, the scientific spirit, the spirit of the laws. These are not primal stuffs but ongoing attitudes and behaviors, leaving residues in the works and institutions of men. Students of the past may infer them from the residues; but as the life of living men they are addressed to the breeding of the unborn future. The sacerdotal Otherworld of souls and spirits appears, in the light of such spirituality, a materialism addressed to accumulating property, prestige, power, and people. Organic relations between that supernaturalism and this spirituality are as rare and accidental as such relations with any of the separate and distinct Thisworlds, which together compose the nature that science studies and the arts remake in order to meet the exigencies of human nature.

V

From what I have already set down, it would follow that the symbol "God" has multiple roles in my "rationale of religion," and that these roles are attributes of the multitudinous concretions—some seventeen hundred different major divinities alone have been counted— of image, attitude, idea, force, function, and mystic experience all given the name "God." Conceptually, "God" is used to designate one chosen from the multitude to the exclusion of all the others— indeed, in enmity and warfare with all the others—and thereby in recognition that they are, and are rivals of the preferred divinity. That one is the "true God" of his faithful devotee because the latter is betting his life on his God's grace to save him from the compulsions of fate, and on his God's providence to save him from the accidents of fortune. The believer's religion is his theory and practice of bringing grace and providence to his aid.

The symbol "God" may also be used to denote all the gods of all the faiths taken together, not pantheistically, but as a free, federal union acknowledging, respecting, and conserving their individualities but orchestrating their functions in such wise that the faithful of any may feel assurance of help in need from the faithful of every other. Or, like certain mystics, a believer may feel that the Divine Many, with all their diversities of conception, image, creed, code, rote, and rite, are but protean disclosures of an ineffable One utterly opaque to conception and imagining, and endlessly reshaping itself into concepts and images, all symbols, none disclosures. The experience on which this view draws is beyond verification. Being unique and ineffable with each mystic, it is incommunicable and beyond proof and disproof. But unless disproved, its authenticity may not be doubted. The faiths of which it is the matrix are another matter: their deliverances and practices can be set beside each other, analyzed, and compared, and their singularities, overlappings, and inconsistencies displayed.

On the other hand, to their incommunicable and hence indiscernible mystic matrices, Leibnitz's rule of "the identity of indiscernibles" may be applied. This would compenetrate the ineffable Many into an ineffable One, the source of the Many. So the devout Hindu mystic, Ramakrishna, committed himself wholly to the divinities of his own land, to Allah of the Moslems, to the Christian pantheon, and "realized God" in all alike. He went from the Many to the One.

But the many creeds and codes and cults which are assumed to issue by interpretation of the One cannot be rendered thus identical. Their diversifications continue indefeasible. Oneness for them all must be, as for Ramakrishna, eventual free achievement, not necessary antecedent condition. The Godhead of their discourse is the diversity of Gods whose faithful tend to war against each other for the greater glory of their chosen One, whose reign on earth hence is not, but is ever to come. Bringing the state of war among religions to a covenant of peace between them requires at once the obsolescence of the conception "God" as a primal unity of which the world's multiple pantheons are shadows and reflections, and its replacement by the idea of Godhead as a free union whose diverse members are acknowledged for the realities they are in the cultural economies of their faithful. In that union is their peace. Religious pluralism is the *sine qua non* of interreligious peace, even as cultural and national pluralism underlies intercultural and international peace. For peace can be had only in a union of the different wherein all covenant equal freedom and security to each.

I do not, however, find in the record any unquestionable ground for connecting this belief, or any other with either "the highest type of human being" or the "lowest." Different families and ages of mankind are still far from a consensus regarding "highest" and "lowest" and are always likely to be. For these appraisals are differentials of the singularity of the struggle to live and to grow of each individual, of each society of individuals, and of each society of societies. The course of the struggle may exalt now one type, now another, as the Christian Gospels suggest.

For myself, I would rather dispense with such invidious terms of appraisal, which denote alterable relationships to altering interests, not unalienable qualities and rights. I prefer to place my faith in the parity of the different, the equality of the unlike, and their collective guarantee of this equality to one another: this is the thing not seen that I hope for, and its substance and evidence I gather from the record of the peoples of the world. I am well aware of how selective and *ad hoc* is my gathering.

ADOLPH KELLER

━━➤➤)《《←━━

*For half a century Adolph Keller has been studying international trends
in social thought and interpreting European and American Protestantism
to each other. A native of Zurich, Switzerland, a student at the Universities of Basle, Geneva, and Berlin, and a graduate of Basle, he has been a
minister of Protestant Churches in Cairo, Geneva, and Zurich. One of the
two former general secretaries of the Ecumenical Council on "Life and
Work" and one of the secretaries of the first Ecumenical Church Conference at Stockholm, Dr. Keller has been a consultant to the World Council
of Churches and a special lecturer on religion in colleges and universities
throughout Europe and America. His publications include* A Philosophy
of Life *(1914);* The Churches and Peace *(1927);* Church and State On the
European Continent *(1936);* Five Minutes to Twelve: *A Spiritual Interpretation of the World Conferences at Oxford and Edinburgh (1938);*
Christian Europe Today *(1942);* Amerikanisches Christentum Heute
(1943) and Zeit-Wende *(1946).*

I

OUR WAY out of the present political, economic, and cultural chaos
in the world toward a hopeful future for mankind is uncertain
and dangerous. We are today at a turning point of history. A re-
orientation of human thinking and planning is unavoidable. It is
clear, however, that the present challenge is not merely an intellectual
task. It must concern the attitudes of man toward his own inner world
discovered by the "depth" psychology, as well as toward the universe
whose silence and extension "frighteneth us" (Pascal).

Where can we find the principles to guide us in the new orientation
of human life in a universe which we can no longer understand in
terms of our traditional beliefs? On examination of these principles

we will doubtless discover not only the profundities of the human personality and the cosmic Unknown, but also the chaotic character of the current social world through which we have to grope our way. Furthermore, opposing tendencies in human society seem to be pushing us toward a crisis in social affairs. We do not yet know in what measure they can be constructive or destructive, divine or demonic, helpful or hostile.

Not only our former categories of space and time are changing; our notion of reality itself is being modified. It may be replaced by a new term, Being, whose meaning is still doubtful and whose application in human thinking has still to be made, in spite of efforts already attempts by a Christian or a pagan "existentialism." Furthermore, what we considered hitherto as a continuity inherent in human history may today be regarded as a discontinuity, which raises basic questions about our political and cultural traditions.

It has become questionable to what extent these former traditions are *idola fori,* to use a phrase of Bacon, or whether they contain values which we must conserve for the interpretation of a new world-in-the-making. Many of these values seem to have lost their significance. We are therefore confronted with a dilemma; whether to give up these values and try to create or adopt new ones, or to reinterpret them in order to make them understandable to a new generation speaking a new language and using more efficient means of meeting the new tasks with which man is confronted.

These opportunities of a renewal or a rethinking of our commanding values have already been attempted in various ways. In either instance they reflect one of the major problems of our time. That is, they must come to terms with a condition of profound conflict in society. It goes without saying that conflict provides the pattern in which any relationship between the old and the new in our cultural development must be worked out. It appears, for instance, in the dialectical formula of Arnold Toynbee as a "challenge and response." The death or the need for profound change in our basic values is in every way a challenge not simply to our thinking but to our individual and collective attitudes toward life. Historically, the replacing of old values by new ones has often been arrived at by a revolution in the social and cultural standards of the masses.

We mention here, by way of example, a few of these revolutions. You will observe that they occur at the end of an era and, therefore, with the demise of certain values which have lost their guiding influence for the masses.

The first of these revolutions was the challenge which the Christian Gospel threw into the face of the antiquated faiths of ancient Rome. The invasion of a new oriental religion within the Roman Empire proved the end of the indigenous religion. Julianus Apostata made a last minute attempt to save it, but it was already being replaced by early Christianity: *Tandem vicisti Galilee!* The acute cultural change was already manifest in the type of defense and mediation practised by the Christian apologists. They faced a dilemma: were they dealing with a continuity or a discontinuity of history? A problem of which Clemens Alexandrinus and Origenes were fully conscious, as were later Kierkegaard, Dostoievsky, Unamuno, Barth, and Brunner.

A second revolution, concerning Western man's basic values, occurred when the Renaissance and the new spirit of science began to declare that there were only such values as are discovered in the human mind. They challenged the Protestant Reformation which claimed that human values centered in the transcendent world. When Nietzsche declared God as dead he did it as a spokesman of this new era which sought all values resolutely within man himself.

A third wave of revolution in human values is being observed after many forerunners in the challenge with which the world is confronted by the threat of nuclear energy. This challenge is questioning the value of life itself. Christianity, as well as secular humanism, is opposed to such a declaration. The higher Asiatic religions, except Buddhism, would concur in a common defense of life itself, as Albert Schweitzer so signally affirms.

The most progressive minds in the Christian and the higher Asiatic religions would agree that this third situation should be met effectively. How can the historic values of the various religions be reinterpreted to serve the present need of mankind?

Although I shall develop this theme later, I would like to say at this juncture that one evidence of this rethinking is the new emphasis upon transcendence in the thinking of the religious world. It takes account of the mystery of God and his universe, stressing not so much apocalyptic eschatology as the notion of the otherness of God. God stands over against man and his world. He is also the *Deus absconditus,* safeguarding His secret nature as well as His liberty. When Rudolf Bultmann speaks of a "demythologisation" of the Gospel, he proposes such a reinterpretation. He tries, for example, to preserve the essential elements among old values and yet to recognize the significance of certain historic accessions to the Christian faith. Another reinterpretation of human values is under way in the Ecumenical Movement. It is attempting to safeguard the modern liberty of conscience, so far as the churches are concerned, against the intrusion of dogmatic intolerance or of a stereotyped expression of the highest values in Christianity.

II

Modern science in the last three centuries has not been free from dogmatic tendencies. However, in the recent development of nuclear physics, scientists permit a place for personal religious convictions in three directions. This is true for those who consider modern science either as a wealth of scientific data or as the interpretation of a cosmic system subject to mathematical laws. The first leeway lies in the fact that scientific thought has not explained the ultimate mystery of the universe, either its infinite extension of space and time or its infinite concentration of secrecy in cells and atoms. The ultimate mystery of the beginning and the end of reality remains unsolved, as for instance the problems of the origin of movement, life, and consciousness. Even if some of the questions raised by Dubois—Reymond were answered, we are faced with an eternal "ignoramus." The initial and essential mystery which we may call *otherness,* the transcendent, the third of the three dialectics submitted by the French philosopher Gourd remains, and the potential ground for a belief in a higher Being has not been diminished but rather intensified. The mystery seems to recede deeper into a beyond of the things measurable by space and time.

The differentiation between the fields of natural science and *Geisteswissenschaft,* mental science, suggests a second opening for religious faith. The teachings of "depth" psychology reveal in an increasing measure that, beside the scientific approach to man based on mathematical formula, there are other parallel paths uncovering a more comprehensive understanding of the inner universe of body-mind-spirit. This is true even though this psychology is entirely based on empirical evidence. Since the contributions of Vico, the Neo-vitalist School and Hans Driesch, and the philosophies of Henri Bergson and Whitehead, the exclusive rationalistic claims of natural science, based on experience and reason, have been paralleled by other equally significant affirmations. Intuition, instinct, and symbolism dominate the viewpoints of Freud and Jung and the teachings of depth psychology. These claims contain a cognitive element which has won a place even in natural science, as observe the writings of Arthur Compton, Millikan, Schroedinger, von Weizsaecker, Pauli, Rhine, Portman, Jordan, Pascal, and others.

The condensation of our knowledge of the universe in fewer and fewer mathematical formulae leads to the replacing of a *weltbild,* an image of the world, by a world formula which eliminates aesthetic, moral, and religious considerations. However, these elements do form a part of our conception of a multiform or pluralistic universe, of which William James wrote. History has always kept a door open, not simply for a mathematical oversimplification of man's relationship to the universe, but for other aspects of human interest which we call epistemology, analogy, coexistence, synchronism, and symbolism. These remain valuable referents in our theoretical and practical interpretation of the world, and pave the way for a third ground of support for religious faith. Immanuel Kant defended this point of view when he insisted that man is not simply interested in the question, What can we know? but also in What ought we to do? and What can we hope for?

Theology is therefore in good company when it does not give up the stand for "religious convictions about cosmic reality." It cannot be denied that the anonymous character of natural science seems to prove nature's "apparent indifference" towards the highest aspirations of man. But in the face of such "apparent indifference" of nature, history points out astounding moments when the mystery of the world seems to reveal itself to man. It does so not in the form of general laws, which are those of nature, but in the inner life of individuals, in specific historical phenomena, or in a particular personal confrontation, rather than in a logical cogency of *universalia* of which it was said *dolus est in generalibus.*

Here a differentiation between Greek thought and Hebrew thinking becomes manifest, to which Martin Buber as well as Emil Brunner have drawn our attention. Greek thinking seeks to determine the absolute idea by which God can be expressed. It is the idea of a supreme reality to whose perfection being as such must be ascribed. For Plato, for instance, this supreme Being is the highest essence, the οὐσία, and its ideological expression is the τὸ ὄντος ὄν, that which exists in reality. On the other hand, Hebrew thought does not search for such an ontological determination of Divinity; but man is confronted with God not in an idea but in an existential encounter.

William James in his *Varieties of Religious Experience* points out this difference, which may be seen in a comparison between the roles of the philosopher and the prophet. The experience of the latter is not simply an historic fact, often described in the prophetic books of the Old Testament and in the gospel record of Jesus of Nazareth; the prophet believes that he is brought face to face with a living God. Such a belief is in the mind of Pascal, who in his *Memorial* describes in detail a fundamental religious experience he encountered as in the night of November 23, 1624.[1]

Pascal's point of departure in his religious thinking was Augustine's question which even today is the problem of thinking men: Is man qualified to understand or to express God? *Homo capax Dei?* Pascal referred to the *"incapacité de l'homme,"* which seems to be the position of modern positivism and secular skepticism. He corrected this word and substituted "disproportion," as Theophil Spoerri has pointed out. We have in this alteration a suggested key to modern symbolistic thought. That is, subjective religious experiences and even intellectual and dogmatic convictions have a symbolic character and serve a purpose in human thinking. These symbols do not express the supreme reality, the Absolute, but they represent a human effort to approximate it. Religious truth is therefore not so much the logical truth of an idea, but the moral truth of a real confrontation or encounter with reality.

[1] See Theophil Spoerri, *Der verborgene Pascal* (Hamburg: Furche-Verlag, 1955), pp. 167-68.

While official church doctrine maintains, following an Aristotelian, and therefore Greek tradition, the dogmatic character of revealed absolutes (which leads toward intolerance), modern religious groups stress religion as an encounter with a transcendent Power. Their spokesmen, instead of reopening the dogmatic conflicts of the third and fourth centuries, give a prominent place in their thinking to the Holy Spirit by whom this encounter receives its dynamic, decisive, and volitional significance.

Psychology's approach to the unconscious deals with this same phenomenon. Freud stresses the incapacity of man for grasping a transcendent reality, calling it "an illusion." On the contrary, C. G. Jung, in agreement with the historian Arnold Toynbee, speaks of the religious encounter as the challenge of a superior power transcending the conscious mind and the human response to such an appeal. A similar symbolism is recognized in the theological school of Bowne and Bridgeman. These parallel approaches to reality permit the scientific mind to discover in religion much of human challenge, encouragement, and inspiration. Thus the finest emphasis in the Judaeo-Christian tradition seems to be justified and is harmonious with the principles of modern thought.

III

The question whether our highest moral convictions have an affinity with a special form of human society, with democracy, also requires rethinking. In recent years so-called democratic forms of society have developed which seem to deny some of man's highest moral principles. The term democracy is like liberty, justice, or love. We need to examine whether these ideas have the same content as when they were an inspiration to earlier generations. The term democracy today represents in part a kind of new secular religion, with a dogma, certain rites, prophets, and ethical implications. The critics of this democracy, especially in the West, call it an illusion or even a failure when compared with the original ideals and promises already mentioned in Greek thought. The latter has taken political form since 1291 in the Swiss Republic, as well as in the Western revolutionary movements in the seventeenth, eighteenth, and nineteenth centuries. On the other hand, in what is called the "people's democracy" in modern Eastern Marxist systems, the democratic pattern developed contrary to the position established through the English and French revolutions. A historian like Jacob Burckhardt considers the practical application of the original democratic ideals incompatible with the size and development of the great Western democratic powers. Is pure democracy possible only in smaller states or with those of a special structure, but inconsistent with world powers or even with what is attempted in a universal society in one indivisible world of which Wendell Willkie dreamed?

The unsuccessful effort of a special committee of the United Nations Organizations to present in the "rights of man" an acceptable philosophy or a moral basis for human society, the resistance with respect to moral purposes which the United Nations meets in the Eastern world, and the deplorable facts of corruption and commercialization of high democratic ideals within the contemporary "free" state systems, make it appear doubtful whether modern democracies possess the ethical ideals that are inherent in real democracy. The situation suggests, especially when one turns to juvenile delinquency, that our educational methods need thorough rethinking and that our age-long optimistic belief in the efficacy of education requires revision. The optimism which goes back to Pestalozzi, Rousseau, the idealism of Emerson, and the pragmatism of John Dewey does not appear to be corroborated by the results of "democratic" education.

It is a question whether secular education based on immanentist human values is adequate for a democratic society. In principle it excludes the higher moral and religious ideals. This does not mean that the present religious education as provided by Jewish and Christian organizations is qualified to meet the present educational situation. The problem remains one of the first magnitude in our chaotic times where even the finest ethical values seem to have lost their power of challenge and educational influence upon whole segments of the population.

If democracy has become a kind of self-sufficient religion or a supposedly valid ethical code for mankind, it is manifest today in such phenomena as the anxiety of the people, the disintegration of traditional values, crime waves, and wars; in brief, in the "quiet desperation" of man, of which Thoreau wrote. Such a religion of human self-sufficiency, of an imminent evolutionist moralism, and of limitless optimism, can no longer offer to contemporary society the protection it needs or the inspiration and guidance it requires.

We do not enter here into a discussion of confessional religious influence in our schools. The rethinking of the relationship between our moral ideals and the democratic structure of our state systems has certainly not weakened the challenge of such ideas as liberty, justice, or fraternity. Rather, it compels us to seek a new type of man and a new form of society corresponding more closely to what has been meant historically by democracy.

In this effort we may expect some help from "depth" psychology, which excludes today Victorian self-sufficiency and a perfectionist ideal of the "good society." The viewpoint of C. G. Jung, for instance, is much better prepared for understanding the deep polarity within the soul of man than are the stoic or humanistic interpreters of our educational task. Considering, for instance, the psychology of compensation and integration, it offers a religious comprehension of the manifest opposing drives in human nature, the open conflicts in the soul of man, and the manner of their solution not in an anticipated absolute and perfect society but in patient and hopeful progress toward a meliorist position. Such individual and collective progress cannot be achieved merely by resort to humanistic self-redemption; it requires that spiritual help and cooperation provided by the personalistic influence of Jesus Christ and the inspiration and belief in the never-ending challenge of the Holy Spirit.

IV

The answer which I give to this question is not in terms of a philosophical theory but as a personal expression of Christian faith. I have abandoned any attempt to enter into such a discussion as the question suggests. How can we speak of a general concept of the phenomenon of religion and apply such a resulting abstraction to our empirical situation? I am no longer so confident that moral man can so simply dispose of supreme values, or that they are so easily available to him.

Traditionally, our religious and moral situation insured certitude for the believer. The Victorian or Puritan tradition, as well as the infallibility of judgment attributed to the head of a church, gave to men a sure faith, an indubitable credo, a specific moral way of life, and a clear eschatological promise. They were conceived in terms of certainty, supported by an ensemble of indisputable facts.

The situation today invites another viewpoint: religion as uncertainty involving personal decision, morality as a risk or a heroic adventure, and hope not as an apocalyptic and dated event but as a turning to that total otherness of the transcendent God whom man may meet through personal encounter. To refer to this Being as "spiritual reality," implying some manner of metaphysical "system" or totalitarian unity of the values of Christianity, Judaism, science, and philosophy, seems to me premature in the present confusion and disintegration of human values. There was a time for such a monistic philosophy when we had an infallible dogma, a positive science, and believed firmly in the "one world" idea. But today we are living in a situation compelling us to recognize our dialectical position, our suspense between opposing alternative ways of life, whose polarity can no longer be reduced in a simple abstract monism. The cataclysm, which today has shaken the political and social world, with the bomb threatening an end of civilization, reaches deeper into our personal faith than the official life of State or Church. It also shakes our former categories of time and space, and causality and being, as well as of religion and denominations, and creeds and myths.

Before we start to rebuild with the remnants of our traditional values, let us realize that our situation has a dialectical character as long as we live in time. We should learn to accept a certain "coexistence" in our religious and moral life. This is a new position reflecting a new humility of the human mind. It acknowledges that we face a new frontier along which new problems and new tasks are arising. In such a state of coexistence, a minimum of intellectual success in reconciling differences does not mean that we are uninterested in that "spiritual reality" which operates behind the phenomenal world. We believe in it, even if we are unable to express it in an abstraction or in a totalitarian system. The changing situation requires us to try new reinterpretations of old values and hopes.

V

It has become problematic whether our task with respect to a search for God is a conceptual one. We need to bear in mind the kind of encounter of which the prophets, Jesus, Pascal, Kierkegaard, Buber, Barth, and Brunner have spoken. Of course, there certainly is a place for an intellectual approach to religion within the limits of pure reason, as Immanuel Kant, Troeltsch, and Paul Tillich attempt it. But our first task, so far as human effort is concerned, is not ontological but "existential," in the sense of Christian existentialism as Bultmann uses this term. That is, man faces a new responsibility which is born out of his real encounter with that spiritual reality which we call God. I would not give up this personalistic concept for an abstract idea although it must remain clear that this term contains a symbolic element and that the Finite is sometimes *capax infiniti* and sometimes *non capax*.

God conserves his character as the Mystery, on the one hand behind the cosmic manifestation, and on the other behind the phenomenal world of the conscious and subconscious human soul. Man's mind is not *capax*, capable of eliminating or explaining the Mystery, the *Deus absconditus*. However, the Mystery does manifest himself as *capax infiniti* to man whenever an awe-inspiring "encounter" takes place.

WILLIAM H. KILPATRICK

Possibly more than any other educator in our generation, William H. Kilpatrick has affected the course of professional leadership in the public schools of America. For some thirty years he taught at Teachers College, Columbia University, specializing in the philosophy of education. During these years, and since, he has served as visiting professor and leader of educational conferences throughout the United States. He also served as president of the board of trustees of Bennington College, as chairman of the New York Urban League, and as chairman of the Bureau for Intercultural Education. His publications include, among others, The Montessori System Examined *(1914);* Source Book in the Philosophy of Education *(1923 and 1934);* Foundations of Method *(1925);* Education for a Changing Civilization *(1926);* Education and the Social Crisis *(1932);* Selfhood and Civilization *(1941); and* Philosophy of Education *(1951).*

INTRODUCTION

MY RELIGION consists of the deepest and most fundamental aims, meanings, and values that I have been able to find for life and the universe. If such an aggregate were only intellectually held, I might call it my philosophy of life, but it is much more than that. Because I not only believe it intellectually, but have given to it my deepest commitment for determining all that I feel and do, it therefore constitutes my religion. In the degree that I live up to my commitment, I will value all else in terms of this committed outlook and on it as a basis make all of life's decisions. This then is what I mean by religion: that to which I give supreme value and in terms of which I decide my life.

172

In keeping with the foregoing, the term faith is not taken as a sub-stitute for important knowledge which man otherwise lacks. Rather is faith the correlative of serious effort to face properly and effectively a troubled and uncertain world. Suppose a given situation in such a world seems to require action, but what to do is uncertain. A fair canvass of this situation may show grounds for hope, hope that action along a suggested line may take care of the situation. Faith then, acting on the belief that effort counts, is the active will to risk the effort and pursue the hope. Such a faith not only hopes, it actively resolves that the hope shall be made a fact. So, in a precarious and uncertain situation a man makes up his mind in faith to put forth appropriate effort. Faith is thus both an act of courage and the will to take a thoughtful risk. In such a faith one wills to make the de-sirable possibility come true.

But the term faith is also used, and properly so, in a wider sense as a correlative and a characteristic of one's religion. The term faith in this broader sense repeats the personal acceptance of the risk and hope involved in religion, the acceptance with a simultaneous will on my part to make my religion, in spite of the risk involved, the inclusive hope and pattern of my life. In this sense faith is an es-sential part of the commitment which raises my philosophy into my religion.

The foregoing discussion, it should be stated, was influenced by the ideas of the late Dr. George A. Coe, long-time professor of religious education at Union Theological Seminary and at Teachers College, Columbia University.

Dr. Cole, in proposing the series of which this paper is one, asked certain questions to guide the discussion.

I

As to what aspects of the Judaeo-Christian religion my personal outlook would emphasize, the answer seems clear. It would stress what is called "the social gospel" as against the eschatological empha-sis given by many in the late conference in Evanston. Specifically, it would reject Sir Thomas Browne's 1643 statement: "I give no alms to satisfy the hunger of my brother, but to fulfill . . . the command of my God." The grounds for such rejection seem clear; in accepting the religion sketched above, I must, if I am true to its leading, consider not merely or even principally what it will do for me as an individual person—though that result will inherently follow—but rather what it enables me to do with myself for the welfare of mankind. And this is true, "for none of us liveth to himself," but we are "every one members one of another." The rule to follow is explicit, "thou shalt love thy neighbor as thyself," "cease to do evil, learn to do well, seek judgment, relieve the oppressed, judge the fatherless, plead for the widow."

And in this religion the stress must be on the spirit and not the letter, "the letter killeth, but the spirit giveth life." "As a man thinketh in his heart, so is he"; out of the heart "are the issues of life." "As we have opportunity then, let us do good unto all men." "And as ye would that men shall do to you, do ye also to them likewise." And "the work of righteousness shall be peace and the effect of righteousness peace and confidence forever."

> They shall beat their swords into plowshares
> And their spears into pruning hooks;
> Nation shall not lift up sword against nation.
> Neither shall they learn war any more.
> They shall sit every man under his vine and under his fig tree,
> And none shall make them afraid.

II

Dr. Cole asks about science and its relation to religion. I would answer that in the content of my religion, my committed outlook on life, science plays a definite part. This science serves, however, not as an aggregate of conclusion but as a method of inquiry, a method which furnishes a way of learning by experiment and observation what to expect in connection with our hopes and our acts. This method of inquiry by experiment and observation is available in all our endeavors. Nature, it appears, biological as truly as physical, supplies the conditions under which all events happen in the world and accordingly the conditions under which man lives and has his being. If at times Nature seems destructive of man's interests, it then becomes the duty of man to study more thoroughly the ways of Nature so as to avoid its dangers and utilize its possibilities. It is the uniformities of Nature which on the one hand constitute the object of our study, and on the other hand furnish us, through our successful study, with the means to use in conducting life. Such a view of Nature becomes then the central nucleus of man's inclusive view of life and of the universe as discussed at the beginning of this paper.

III

A more spiritual aspect of my religion holds that the central feature of man's social relations is, and must be, morality, the obligation upon each one so to live and act that all who are affected thereby shall in their turn live more finely and grow best. Certain freedoms are essential to good social relations: freedom of thought, freedom of assembly, freedom of speech, freedom of action consistent with morality.

These things mean, in William James's suggestive phrase, "the sovereignty of the living individual." They further mean that personality should be respected as the most sacred thing known among men. And the same things also mean that "the supreme test of all political institutions and industrial arrangements shall be the contribution they make to the all-round growth of every member of society" (John Dewey), and "equal rights for all, special privileges for none" (Thomas Jefferson), and "I will accept nothing which all cannot have the counterpart of on the same terms" (Walt Whitman).

In effect, all these things mean the rule among men of the spirit of democracy and of personal morality. They are at the same time intrinsic elements in my religious faith, made so because from all the study I have given, and can give, to the matter, both current and historic, I can see nothing more essential to proper human behavior.

IV

The question is asked as to "one spiritual reality," whether all the varying aspects of my accepted outlook on life join together to form one such reality. The answer I give is yes. So far as I can see, all the essential parts of my faith join consistently together to support and reinforce each other. This does not mean that I have no problems, that there do not remain unsolved difficulties. There are many such. But I have found an outlook on life to which I can give supreme commitment. This outlook I hope to improve as I study further. One essential part of my overruling commitment is to keep an open mind for new evidence, new insights, and consequent enrichment and improvement of my inclusive outlook. Provision for such correction and growth is a very essential part of my outlook.

As to the source of knowledge and insight for what I am to believe, this comes as was said above from experience and observation. These with consequent suggestions made by me and by others from experience and observation and the most careful study and criticism of such in order to make the most constructive and defensible use of the suggestions—these constitute the source of whatever I accept to believe.

Such then is the religion which I hold and trust to guide me as I face the problems of life.

M. F. ASHLEY MONTAGU

→»)(«←

M. F. Ashley Montagu was born in London, England, and studied at the Universities of London and Florence. He came to the United States in 1927, took his Ph.D. in anthropology at Columbia, and has taught at New York University, Hahnemann Medical College and Hospital, Philadelphia, Rutgers University, The New School for Social Research, and Harvard. A Fellow of the American Association for the Advancement of Science, Hon. Corresponding Member of the Anthropological Societies of Paris and Florence, Member of the American Association of Physical Anthropologists, American Association of Anatomists, The Society for the Study of Child Growth and Development and The History of Science Society. Dr. Montagu's publications include Coming Into Being Among the Australian Aborigines *(1937);* Man's Most Dangerous Myth: *The Fallacy of Race (1943);* Introduction to Physical Anthropology *(1945);* Darwin, Competition and Cooperation *(1952);* On Being Human *(1953);* The Natural Superiority of Women *(1953);* The Direction of Human Development *(1955).*

I

THE ESSENCE of the Hebraic-Christian religious teachings is Love. Divested of all the theological, doctrinal, ethnic, and secular accretions under which this essential truth has well-nigh been overwhelmed, Love will always remain the supreme religious value, and in contemporary thought and practice it is this essential principle which requires most attention and emphasis.

We are in a rather better position than ever before to begin utilizing this principle in our daily lives, the reason for this being that science, the secular religion of our own time has, or at least some practitioners of that religion have, something at once enlightening and convincing to say about the nature of that principle.

Anthropologists have offered as a minimal definition of religion the proposition that it constitutes the belief in spirits. That definition is, as its framer, Edward Tylor, would have acknowledged, too narrow. I like to think of religion as man's attempt to penetrate the mystery of life and man's own relatedness to all things, to the world stuff which unites all things in the community and commonality of being. The religious attitude is that in which the person, with reverence, respect, and humility, accepting the fundamental unity of all things, asks questions of the world in which he lives which are calculated to show how they came to exhibit their infinitely interesting present differences.

But this is not all. The genesis of this attitude may have come about in different ways, but the essence of the religious attitude is the feeling of the mystery which binds all living things together, and which man can only approach in the spirit of humility and which he can hope to penetrate only partially. The whole mystery he may never penetrate—the secrets of the universe man will never completely know—it is the recognition of his own ignorance, and the combination of what used to be called "being in tune with the infinite," which should give a man that feeling toward the universe which I would call religious.

Such a feeling is, of course, possible in innumerable persons who would not call themselves religious in the ordinary sense. The secular scientist, for example, often denies that he is religious, and in doing so he may be sound. There are, however, many secular scientists who are deeply religious in the sense in which I use the term. Their interest in life is devoted to penetrating a mystery. They begin with wonder, and through a rigorous and ascetic devotion to the scientific method they proceed toward the penetration of the mystery which elicited their original wonder.

For scientists the method has become the message, the means is part and parcel of the end. For such scientists scientific method has become the equivalent of religion, they do not sickly o'er their methods with the pale cast of thought. Sufficient for the day is the method thereof. In this way many scientists have grown indifferent to the consequences of their methods. Science, they say, is ethically neutral.

I do not believe this for one moment, and I say this as a scientist whom the scientific method has led to the conclusion that the scientific method is not enough, that reason is not enough, but that it is only through the scientific method and the rigorous use of reason that we can come to know this to be true. Scientific method and reason are not the only ways to the attainment of truth, but for Western Man, in the position in which he now finds himself and because of the route by which he has achieved it, these remain the ways to the discovery of truth—the truth about himself and his relation to his fellow beings.

It is because this truth leads us to the discovery that Love is the main principle by which men must direct their lives and develop their values, that I see the value in the Hebraic-Christian concept of love. Not only this, I see here the platform upon which the traditional religious and the scientific viewpoints may be dramatically reconciled. This is a matter to which I shall return later in this paper.

II

The elementary particles which constitute the structure of the atom are, in their different forms, common to all things whatsoever, living and nonliving. This constitutes the ultimate reality, the ultimate cosmic reality. This is the cosmic bond which unites every human being not only to every other human being and living thing within the cosmos, but to all things whatsoever. Hence I regard the truly religious man as one who recognizes his relationship and relatedness to all things whatsoever, and acts accordingly. Based upon his understanding of the unity of all things the attitude of the religious man is one of reverence toward all things whatsoever. By reverence I mean esteem and respect—I do not mean obeisance. By esteem I mean the act of cherishing, of favorable regard. By respect I mean the act of having deference, of prizing, and of consideration for the other.

Man alone is capable of reverence in this sense. Certainly in his capacity for reverence man has reached the summit of the evolutionary process. It is in the further development of this capacity for reverence that man's future as a religious being lies.

The grounds for my belief in the reality and the unity of the cosmos are scientific and they are simple. As a scientist who has been especially interested in the origin and development of human nature I have been concerned with the study of living things from the simplest to the most complex. The conclusion to which I have been led as a consequence is that the cosmos which in microcosm one sees in the living organism is a harmonic one, and all the evidence, so far as I am able to read such of it as is available, indicates that the macrocosmos is a harmonic one too. This belief is not an act of faith but a reasoned conclusion from the evidence. I see that even the particles that constitute the nucleus of the atom function in harmonic relation to each other. I see that single-celled organisms are mutually attracted to each other. I see that the cells which comprise the multicellular organism are in continuous cooperation with each other. And I see that all living things are preserved by cooperation and destroyed by disoperation. Throughout the whole realm of animated nature life exhibits increasingly more complex and higher levels of integration at the cooperative level, culminating in man—unquestionably, in some of his present cultural forms, the most destructive creature on the face of the earth, the creature that possesses the highest capacities for cooperation! Original sin, the innate depravity of humanity and brattishness of human nature, and all similar doctrines are nothing but unhappy guesses calculated to explain the disordered or evil conduct of some human beings.

I now understand as a scientist, and can explain to others, the cause of human disoperative behavior—and it has nothing to do with "original sin" or innate depravity. On the other hand, it has everything to do with the fact that human beings are *not* innately disoperative but that they are caused—some of them—to behave disoperatively by other human beings. To this, too, I shall return for further discussion. Meanwhile, I make the point that man does not stand alone against the cosmos, but rather that the cosmos is an environmental necessity of man without which he could not for a moment exist, and that he is, in fact, a product of the cosmos.

To the extent that man obeys and utilizes the natural processes of the cosmos both outside and inside himself, man remains in harmony with the cosmos, *healthy*. When he attempts to oppose the cosmic process he becomes disharmonic, unhealthy, and destructive. It was Francis Bacon who wrote, some three hundred and fifty years ago, that Nature to be commanded must be obeyed. I do not think it is correct to say that Nature is ethically neutral or that the cosmos is so, for both Nature and the cosmos clearly favor the cooperative. On the short run the competitors may sometimes appear to be favored, but there can be little doubt that it is the cooperators who are favored in the long run.

There are several forms of competition, and some of them are harmonic and desirable; these may be briefly resuméd under the rubric cooperative competition. In cooperative competition the competitors strive *with* each other, rather than in competitive competition *against* each other, to achieve desirable ends or goals. Such competition is in harmony with the cosmic process. It is competitive competition that is opposed to it. On the short run competitive competition may appear successful, but in the long run and by the measure of cosmis time it is in opposition to the cosmic process.

It is not that the cosmic process is concerned with the welfare of human beings. It is absurd, even metaphorically, to personify the cosmic process and to speak of it as caring for the wellbeing of man. It is equally absurd to speak of Nature's apparent indifference to the highest interests of man and its occasional destructive treatment of him. Man is neither an object of Nature nor of the cosmos, *he is a part of them*. When men behave as if they were the whole and the rest of the cosmos were the part, it is because they are unhealthy. The healthy person thinks of himself as a part of a larger whole. And this is what each human being is, a unique and unreduplicable part of the cosmos. If for no other reason than this, every human being would merit the interest and respect of every other human being.

The cosmos is neither concerned with nor indifferent to the welfare of man, but it is involved in that welfare as providing all the opportunities by means of which man may realize his richest potentialities. As Stephen Crane put it:

> A man said to the universe:
> "Sir, I exist!"
> "However," replied the universe,
> "The fact has not created in me
> "A sense of obligation."

Personified or not, the cosmos is in no sense obligated to anyone or anything. It is the cosmos that has made all living things possible—*not* the living things that have made the cosmos possible. The possibilities have been realized in a universe which is completely free, and the cosmos, as it were, grants humanity the freedom to develop howsoever it will—and humanity is the only form of life which has developed this capacity for self-determination. The obligation, then, is toward himself. Man owes it to himself—*not* to the cosmos—to realize his own potentialities for being human, and for being human "in tune with the infinite."

III

I regard democracy as the best form of government for human beings because it affords human beings the maximum amount of freedom for personal and group development. The democratic process is a mirror of the cosmic process to the extent that it exhibits a well-organized series of systems for the maximization of order and freedom. There are no fundamental values without choice, and democracy is the form of government which affords the maximum of freedom of choice for the person.

I have never been able to dissociate politics from life, as so many politicians seem to be able to do, and as an even greater number of ordinary citizens have been able to do. For me politics is a major part of the living scheme of things and, as we have only too tragically seen in the recent past, politics may mean the difference between life and death for tens of millions of human beings. Nor can I dissociate politics as an intrinsic element of my religious faith, anymore than I can dissociate my religious life from my secular life. I can understand and deplore these dissociations in others—I could not tolerate them in myself. Hence, I consider the democratic way of life part and parcel of the process of daily living, and this of course involves my view of personal moral character and of religion—and I consider them all but aspects of the functioning of a unitary whole, the person. It is only for purely arbitrary purposes that I would make any distinction between any of these aspects of the human personality. A person's political, moral, and religious beliefs should hang together. Alas, too often they present the picture of a group of pseudological rationalizations based on unanalyzed systems of value. It is for this, among other reasons, that I regard the ability to use one's mind critically and soundly in the evaluation of evidence as an obligation of every human being toward himself and toward his fellow human beings. Not only this, I regard such an obligation as a moral one—the obligation of right conduct. In this age of expanding freedoms and tightening tyrannies it is more than ever the obligation and the privilege of the person to shape himself and to help shape others so that the greatest number possible shall become the proponents and the doers of right action.

I much rejoice in the ideas of the Declaration of Independence, in the conception of the preservation of life, and liberty, and the pursuit of happiness, and in the principles of the French Revolution enshrined in the words, liberty, fraternity, and equality, but I am ever aware that we must constantly be on our guard to see to it that the original meanings of these words are preserved, that they do not become debased and go the way of Gresham's Law, in which the counterfeit displaces the genuine. We must beware of the danger of permitting our idea of liberty to become equated with the concept of economic liberty. An even more insidious danger against which we have to protect ourselves is that the notion of equality must lead to uniformity and the abolition of difference. Unity yes, uniformity no! Equality should imply equality of opportunity for all human beings to develop those likenesses which they possess in common and, equally importantly, to develop those differences which every human being uniquely possesses and which distinguishes him from every other human being in the world. Education should, therefore, consist in the process of drawing out the potentialities of each person for the maximization of his own happiness and that of his fellows. Education will not reduce differences but increase them—to the mutual benefit of everyone involved. Education should be in the theory and practice —that is the science and art—of being human in human relations, in love.

Liberty is too often identified with the freedom to do what we like, but with Lord Acton I hold that true liberty is not the power of doing what we like, but the right of being able to do what we ought. And what ought human beings do in their right as human beings? It is my conclusion as a scientific student of human nature and of human society that the supremest of all values, love, is what human beings ought to hold. They ought to love their fellow human beings as themselves. By love I mean communicating to others by feeling and by conduct a deep involvement in their wellbeing; behaving in such a way toward others that by so doing we contribute to the welfare and assist creatively to enlarge the capacities of others to do likewise to their fellow human beings.

IV

I am asked whether I assume that the supreme values available to moral man, of whatsoever source, are aspects of *one* spiritual reality? I often balk at the word "spiritual," not because it has little meaning for me but because it has so many different meanings to others that I can never be sure of the sense in which it is being used. So let me speak of the sense in which I understand the word. By spirtual I understand those strong desires and emotions which are directed toward the attainment of some ideal object, over and above all selfish objects of desire. In this sense of the meaning of the spiritual I believe, indeed, that there is but one spiritual reality, and that the supreme values available to moral man are but aspects of this one spiritual reality. The essence of what I have defined as spiritual is love. Love, as I have said, is the supremest of all values, and it is from it that the essentially spiritual values flow. All that is good I would equate with love.

The potentialities for love are inherent in the nature of man, and I have written a book which, among other things, is calculated to demonstrate that there is no hostility in man.

In this book, *The Direction of Human Development,*[2] I have shown that all human beings are born not only good but with the desire to love others as well as to be loved by them, and that this, indeed, is the supremest of all the infant's needs. It has now, I think, been demonstrated by numerous investigators that, to the extent to which one departs from satisfying the love needs of the developing human organism in infancy and childhood, to that extent one usually does grievous mental, and sometimes physical, harm to the developing

[2] (New York: Harper & Brothers, 1955).

human being. Such a human being tends to be disoperative, incapable of love, and much given to the responses of rage, despair, fear, and aggression. These are all pathologically induced responses—they are not innately determined reactions; they are, on the other hand, responses to the deprivation of love, to the frustration of the expected satisfaction of love. In short, aggression is love frustrated, and insecurity is the response to the lack of support which the unloved organism experiences. The function of aggression is to secure love.

When we fully understand such facts we perceive that they are in close harmony with many of the basic values which have for generations been taught in the Hebraic-Christian religions (not to mention many others). Thus science, or the findings of some scientists, provide a strong validation for these teachings. This is precisely as it should be, for the experience of thousands of generations of human beings has, in every society, served to precipitate out from the matrix of human experience certain basic principles by which men find that they can most harmonically live. It is not, then, astonishing that these principles should be found by scientific means to be the very principles which men have discovered out of their own and the long continuum of human experience.

All religions of which I have any knowledge as an anthropologist appear to have discovered some of the basic principles which serve to relate their votaries to the harmonies of the cosmic process. These principles are defined by the behaviors which we call altruistic, sacrificial, reverential, pietistic—humility, awe, admiration, and love. By institutionalizing these principles in the practice and ritual of religion human beings have succeeded in harmonizing their conduct with that of their fellow men and with the whole universe. They thus relate themselves not only to the heavens above but to all things whatsoever, hence the great survival value inherent in all religion.

The cosmos, it would seem, is so structured as to permit the development of maximum degrees of order within a completely free universe—completely free in the sense that every unit within it has the power to act independently, though always, of course, within limits. Complete order does not exist within the cosmos—were such complete order to exist there would and could be no change—but there are continuously varying approximations to more or less complete order, and such approximations are achievable only within a universe structured, and so functioning, in the process of freedom. The process of freedom permits of the maximum of error as well as the maximum of harmony—and harmony I equate with truth and beauty —the freedom to be wrong and the freedom to make the necessary corrections, the freedom to learn and to profit from mistakes. Thus, the dynamic values inherent in the processual activity of the cosmos and those inherent in the creative values emerging from man's struggle to build a society of free men in order and in freedom, are really part of the same continuum of cosmic freedom and order.

I do not regard man's efforts to achieve ever higher rankings of order and freedom as anything other than admirable, but at the same time I do not regard man's efforts this way as the highest form of order and of freedom thus far achieved in the cosmos. Such an assumption would be unjustifiable and arrogant, thoroughly unbecoming, but perhaps not uncharacteristic of a creature that names itself *Homo sapiens*. The proper attitude for human beings to maintain is one of profound humility as a member of this wonderful cosmos, in which man is but a brief candle capable of standing erectly and, like a minor sun, throwing light all about him at the cost of his own consumption. The source of that light is love. And love is one of the highest forms of functioning which has yet developed in the cosmos, though not necessarily the highest—though I should not be surprised if this turned out to be the case.

V

Does the concept of "God" serve an essential purpose in my rationale of religion? It does. In the Hebraic-Christian religions God is Love. In my conception of God *Love* is God. Love is an activity, a form of behavior; it is demonstrative, supportive, stimulating, sympathetic, and creative. God is realized in the loving behavior of his creatures. Where there is no love there is no God. Man creates God just as he creates himself, and he creates God in his own image, often as he aspires to be, often as he in reality is.

God being in my understanding Love I consider it necessary for all human beings to acquaint themselves with the nature and meaning of love if they are to realize the best of themselves and of the potentialities of this life for living.

By love I mean the active condition of relatedness, the communication of the feeling to others that we are deeply involved in their welfare and actively interested in contributing to it. Such love is directed to oneself as it is to others. Hence it is necessary to love ourselves if we are effectively to love others. To love ourselves means to make the best of ourselves in the realization that no man is his real self until he is his best self, that in the last analysis man makes himself, that he is as responsible to himself for himself as he is responsible to others.

Perfection for human beings is an unattainable ideal because man is infinitely perfectible—and this is just as it should be, for so men will always strive to attain the unattainable and attain the attainable. Hence, perfect love is the nearest condition to perfection that human beings can attain. But for most it will remain an ideal worth striving to achieve. It is this attainable ideal which I call God.

GARDNER MURPHY

Since 1952 Gardner Murphy has been the director of research at the Menninger Foundation in Topeka, Kansas. A graduate of Yale, Harvard, and Columbia Universities, he taught psychology at Columbia for twenty years. A member of the American Association for the Advancement of Science and the Society for the Psychological Study of Social Issues, a past president of the American Psychological Association, and recipient of the Butler medal at Columbia in 1932, Dr. Murphy has written a number of books including General Psychology *(1933);* Human Nature and Enduring Peace *(1945);* Personality: A Biosocial Approach To Origins and Structure *(1947);* Introduction to Psychology *(1951); and* In the Minds of Men *(1953).*

I

THE BASIC religious values in the Judaeo-Christian tradition are to me two, and they are closely related. The first is the value of love, both given and received, the belief that love is intrinsically satisfying and fulfilling. This would, for example, vary from the idea that love is the expectation of benefit, or that it is a special form of gratitude or appreciation for benefits received. It seems to me, in the light of ethnological, developmental, and psychoanalytic studies, that love turns out to be at least as fundamental as the need for food, air, or water. There is, as David Levy has said, an "affect hunger"; or, as René Spitz has pointed out, children may "die of lack of love." I think that love is an absolutely fundamental central experience rooted in human tissues. Sometimes it seems to need no reciprocation. It is, as in Keats' poem, "unreflecting" love. Ordinarily, and apparently because we identify with those whom we love and conceive them to identify with ourselves, there is a need to be loved while loving.

It is not asserted that the Judaeo-Christian tradition is unique with respect to the development of this belief in the fundamental quality of love as a thing to cherish and magnify. Those who know Moslem life speak of the intense family devotion and the intense in-group devotion which make the followers of the Prophet capable of a supreme and passionate devotion one to another. Buddhism has justly been celebrated for its emphasis upon the therapy of love within the weary or sin-sick soul. The Sikhs, the Parsis, and indeed many other religious groups have discovered the reality to which this tradition points. Rather than making invidious distinctions, I would say simply that to me, reared in the Judaeo-Christian tradition, the central role of love as meaningful experience appears to be supremely worthy of emphasis.

Secondly, and as a counterpart to this first principle, I believe that man finds in other things besides man much that is also profoundly worthy of love. I have in mind sand, sea and stars, snails, robins, and dogs, for example. There is genuine fulfillment in loving the stars, and there is genuine fulfillment in loving dogs, as those who know star lovers and dog lovers can testify. These experiences are profoundly moving and fulfilling and, with certain normal human beings, they may at times be more intense than the love of man. Let the humanitarian hesitate a moment before he condemns those to whom the Milky Way comes first, and those to whom a devoted collie comes first in the order of things excellent in this world. To say that the collie and the Milky Way are in a sense human is permissible. It would be just as well to put it the other way around and say that there is something of a stellar and something of a canine quality in that universality of humanness which the Prophet, who loves man, can define. Love spills over; it does not draw sharp lines. When once it is aroused, it encompasses much which might not in itself draw love into action. I would urge, therefore, that the Judaeo-Christian tradition, with St. Francis preaching to the birds, and with the "Anti-Steel Trap League" trying to put an end to the torture and destruction of the animals of the Arctic tundra, all have their place somehow in a Jesus-like, or Whitman-like, love of all that breathes, or indeed, all that is. Bryant perhaps put it best of all: "To be a brother to the insensible rock."

Such love, however, is not necessarily the love of one plus one plus one. It is not necessarily the serial devotion to one thing after another. It can, in a certain sense, be the love of the all. It was the "intellectual love of God" which dominated Spinoza, the "God-intoxicated" Jewish philosopher of the seventeenth century who found, not in the separate things but in the one which underlay them all, the supreme object worthy of love.

To the intellectualist, this is likely to mean "pantheism." This is, in a sense, a begging of the question, because only a self-confident intellectualist could say what it is that represents the one. In fact, the one may be the abstraction of a scientist who says that the world is one in its lawfulness, or it may be the moving mystical entity with which the human soul has commerce, as in the Neoplatonist philosophy. To the student of comparative religion, it is easy to define this approach as a pantheistic approach.

Pantheism, however, teaches the doctrine that "All is God." What we are saying is that the fulfillment of man is achieved through loving both many individual persons and things and also loving the allness, the totality of the world. To say that such a love forces the individual into the belief that in a certain sense all is God seems to me to be a rather preverse twisting of the immediate empirical realities. To say that a sadist's joy in inflicting pain is God, or an aspect of God, seems to me to achieve no clear purpose. To say that it is an aspect of the all may mean somewhat more. I am at this point, however, developing no religious metaphysics, and I should prefer to avoid the term pantheism, contenting myself simply with the statement that love of the many and love of the all, or the one which embodies all, are good for the spirit of man; and on this I feel reasonably sure that history, anthropology, and psychology will support me. I feel sure that the Judaeo-Christian religions with all their limitations have with consistency and, what is more important, with enormous fire and intensity, cultivated this kind of love; and that the agnostics and the atheists who repudiate the system may nevertheless in their humanitarian intensity keep alive the very principle which is the heart of that which they appear to attack. If one, for example, through love of humanity attacks the pettiness, the hypocrisy, or the self-deception of a dogmatic religious system, this is in no way an attack upon the central values which the religion embodies.

For all these reasons I believe that the cultivation of a free and unlimited attitude of joy and communion with the personal and impersonal processes of this universe, a deep resonance to the world and its beauty and goodness, is the first thing which the Judaeo-Christian religions can offer by way of a value system good for the heart of man.

II

I think there are two distinct reasons for entertaining religious convictions about the lovableness both of individual persons and of the world as a whole. First, I think it is evident that in the evolution of the world and, in particular, the evolution of life within it, there has been an increasingly rich capacity for appreciation, resonance, and love; and I think that this is a trend which the universe is producing not accidentally but by virtue of its very nature. I am not saying that this will inevitably go on forever, and I am not saying that it is "planned" in the sense in which a man doing cabinet work plans the ultimate appearance of a drawer or a shelf. What I am saying is that the universe is doing something which has a capacity for a deep fulfillment of human nature, and that despite all meanness, arbitrariness, and destructiveness, the struggle goes on for a humane and generous social order in which men can love one another with impunity; it continues and perhaps grows stronger.

I would not stake everything on the argument that this looks like something which the universe is fulfilling because it *needs to,* because it is a part of the cosmic process itself. One might well be mistaken about such matters. The world might blow up or deteriorate, and negate any conception of a perpetuating trend. Nevertheless, making the best sense I can out of the picture, I think that there is a lot more in cosmic process than I can find in the accounts of the evolutionary process given by post-Darwinian thinkers, who limit themselves more and more to natural selection as a primary or even a single clue. It seems to me that in inorganic evolution before life emerged in this world, there is much of order, grace, beauty which I do not believe could be read into the world by a nervous system accidentally produced in the course of the struggle for existence. I believe that the world has progressing structure, beauty, and majesty, and that man simply becomes more and more aware of it and capable of responding to it. In the same way, I believe that the discovery of love in the world is a genuine discovery and not a projection by man upon the world.

My second reason for believing that the so-called physical structure —the time, space, mass, energy structure given by physics—is not the only system supplying descriptive and explanatory terms that can be applied to the universe lies in another area of research to which today insufficient scholarly attention has been given. I refer to psychical research, or parapsychology. This type of investigation, which began three-quarters of a century ago, is developing into an organized scientific discipline, representing scores of technically competent research workers from the fields of psychology, psychiatry, biology, physics, anthropology, mathematics, with publications which have now commanded the attention of scholars from William James and Gerald Balfour to Julian Huxley and Evelyn Hutchinson.

These massive materials prove, at the least count, that there are types of intercommunication between human beings over large distances which do not fit our current conceptions of radiant energy; that there are forms of contact with distant objects which can only be called perceptual, though functioning without the use of the known sense organs; that there are forms of cognitive function which reach into the past and into the future in a way which necessitates reconsideration of the meaning of time; and that there are complexities connected with death and with the appearance of phantasms of the dying at great distances to those to whom they have personal meaning, which indicate that the relation of personality to the physico-chemical system is not what nineteenth-century materialism asserted it to be. None of this proves "the immortality of the soul"; indeed, much of it raises the question whether the question of immortality can properly be formulated at this time. The very nature of time, space, matter, and personality represent a forest of interrogation points. Nevertheless, without dogmatism regarding the ultimate meaning of these data, it can be said with some confidence that the interpersonal communion, the reaching out of person to person, the discovery of meanings in the world which are not ultimately reducible to conceptualizations in the manner of physics, force upon one the belief that the Judaeo-Christian conception of the fundamental role of interpersonal relations is a good rock on which to build, and that the intimate relation between interpersonal affection and the outreaching response of man to the universe has some deep psychological sense. From this point of view, the universe is seen to be fulfilling to man, and the data of psychical research support and enrich the data offered by more general biological and psychological considerations. In fact, at some points the reality of interpersonal and man-to-cosmos relationships transcending the time-space-matter category is more strongly stated in the language of psychical research than it can be stated in any other way.

The development of physics as a substantive science, and of physicalism as a philosophy, has tended to create in the last three centuries the naive worldview that man is modeled somehow down to the last detail upon the time, space, matter, energy structure which is evident in the physical world. Quite aside from all questions of what is ultimately meant by matter and energy, there has been the gradual ossification of a world system which assumes, as did Democritus and Lucretius, that tiny material particles in physical interaction constitute the prototype of all reality. It has been hard, indeed, to wrench oneself from the straitjacket of such forms of thought, even though the whole structure of physics has itself recently injected question marks into the scheme. The biological and psychological sciences have more and more tended to encounter realities which poorly subject themselves to such structuring. In particular, parapsychology has more and more explicitly defined, through the investigations of some twenty psychological laboratories, the reality of contact with distant objects, as in the elaborately safeguarded London-to-Antwerp telepathic studies of Soal and Bateman, and in the Pearce-Pratt series at Duke University. Extrasensory communication calls in question the very nature of the time-space structure of consciousness. Time, space, matter, energy appear to be irrelevant concepts when psychological reality is concerned, and we shall need more and more to face the fact that the communication between personalities is not the communication between bits of metal used in modern communication devices.

There is, moreover, much to indicate that the relation of personality to the physical system is complex rather than simple. The moment of death, for example, is in many cases the moment at which hallucinations of the dying are perceived at great distances by those who love them. Such cases, elaborately authenticated, psychologically and statistically analyzed, indicate that there is in reality a connection between paranormal communication and the event, whatever it is, which we call death.

This is no place to expatiate upon the possible ultimate implications of such events or speculations regarding survival or immortality. There is enough here, however, to give an enormous challenge to anyone who would like to see the meaning of science for religion.

For the Judaeo-Christian tradition to ignore psychical research is childish indeed, for here lie the strongest empirical supports which can be obtained. The reasons, of course, are easily to be discovered. If one relies upon sacred texts, which give the final revelation regarding the resurrection of the body and the life everlasting, then contemporary evidence dealing with the nature of death and with the nature of transphysical interpersonal relations will be either pushed aside as "old stuff," or, as is more characteristically the case, will be feared because it represents an empirical rather than a traditional way of solving the question. Fortunately, there are many signs today that the Judaeo-Christian tradition is becoming alerted to the importance, both of general philosophical considerations regarding the evolutionary process, and of the specific implications of psychical research for the understanding of man and his place in the universe.

III

If the term "democratic movement" refers to interpersonal affection, the belief of man in man, and the basic healthiness of cooperative human endeavor rather than cutthroat competition, then emphatically these values are part of my religious faith. The term "democratic movement" is, unfortunately, sometimes used simply to denote a belief in majority rule, regardless of the short-range and often egocentric purposes which individual voters and individual political leaders express. The term "democracy" must be understood in the sense of the belief of the individual man in the long-range capacity of human beings for intelligence and love, as represented, for example, in Gandhi as much as in Lincoln. Realism forces the recognition that human beings are enormously unequal not only in ability, but in sensitivity, capacity to appreciate and respond to one another, and in hundreds of socially significant characteristics. It also necessitates recognition of the enormous amount of cheapness and brutality that are usually found in human beings in the mass. It is the belief in human potentials rather than contemporary actualities that is involved, and it is the love of man, rather than the evaluation of man as he now is, that is most fundamental.

I do not personally find a great deal of value in the traditional or the present conception of "personal moral character." There are two difficulties with this conception. In the first place, simple, warm, strong, goodness to other people and simple objective facing of realities with the kind of self-control that is likely to go with the combination of love and reality-facing, are not likely to get a high place in the hierarchy when terms like "moral character" are used. The term is nearly always defined with rather a large emphasis on negative factors, such as the self-depreciation of one's own needs and capacities, the absence of positive qualities. A person is said to have high moral character if he goes along a well-defined path, showing occasionally the virtue of self-restraint, but all too likely the virtue of self-denial, repression, blockage of his basic humanness. Calvinism, regardless of its origins and original meanings, has stamped on the Western world the conception of moral character as a straitjacket, almost to the point of reminding one of the "Cato the censor" type of negativism in human living. If the term "moral character" is, however, equated with the personal or subjective side of democracy, in the sense of interpersonal warmth—in other words, if moral character is sensitivity, generosity, and warmth to other human beings, with respect for them and the natural refraining from any activity which would injure them—I think it can have an important place in a modern religious faith.

I would be willing to accept the value of such a definition for its immediate and intrinsic results in terms of better human living, and not require any sanction going beyond what can be directly observed. In fact, I should be skeptical of sanctions from an unknown world which seemed to contradict the immediate sanctions of love and generosity in human living. When immediate sanctions are in harmony with what seem to be cosmic sanctions, they seem to me to be all the stronger; but if there is reported to be a conflict between the two systems of sanctions, then I should say I would have more confidence in those which can be empirically supported.

IV

The universe is not big enough, so far as I can see, to contain any ultimate "contradictions." That is, I believe that ultimately, in the time and space canvas which is provided, there is interaction of everything with everything else, and for that reason I believe that ultimately any definition of reality must be unitary. There can be infinite diversity in aspects; but with Spinoza, I would expect to find a oneness in spiritual reality. From this point of view, it makes sense to me to regard the evolutionary process of the cosmos, and of life, and of human society, to be expressive of an ultimate reality in which harmony is in some final sense more real than discord, and love more real than hate. We are here out on the edge of the knowable, and if, like the believers in the Goddess Kali, one believes that creativeness and destruction are two aspects of the same thing, or that love and hate are equally fundamental, all I can say is that I do not feel it this way. Neither do I believe that there is any self-evident or obvious unity in the world to which some flaw in human nature (like man's choice of sin rather than goodness) makes us blind. We move here in a realm of intuitive guesswork, and I am inclined to believe in the ultimate supremacy of love and of unity, without feeling any such confidence as I feel with reference to points one and two above. Belief in the worth of the individual, belief in the worth of affection and human life, belief in the beauty of the universe, are to me somewhat interdependent, but not *self-evidently* related, as in a geometrical type of reasoning. I cannot for that reason believe that a tight value-structure is warranted. I believe rather that there are several values loosely interrelated which can all be pursued by reasonable men. I find myself more at home with agnostics who believe in brotherhood than I do with mystics and theists who reject brotherhood in favor of supposed ultimate cosmic principle which they think makes humanitarianism impractical.

Incidentally, I am not sure whether the term "spiritual reality" is useful except in the sense of the response of man to his fellows and to the universe of which he is a part.

V

It seems to me permissible to use the term "God" to refer to the personal aspects of cosmic structure. Since we know little about cosmic structure and still less as to the ways in which the personal, as contrasted with the impersonal, relates to the structure, I do not believe that the term "God" can be used in a sharply defined fashion. I do not believe, for example, that the concept "God's plan for man," or "the attempt to discover God's will" is likely to be helpful. One's conception of God and of his will and plan depend upon rich cultural and personal contexts. I think it is possible that some may find utility in an unchanging God, others in a self-realizing God, others in a God who develops. It seems to me that science, the arts, and many other human enterprises are literally concerned with the discovery of God, and may also be, to some limited degree, concerned actually with the creation of new human realizations and purposes, and in this way may be fulfilling and extending the nature of God.

I am afraid that there is a good deal of padding put into the term "God," owing to the fact that those who strive to keep some contact with the religious tradition will inevitably use the term in conversation with those who use it in a traditionalistic or dogmatic sense, in order to appear to be intellectually and emotionally close to those with whom they speak. Such a compromise may tide one over many a difficulty, and can probably be justified in short-range terms. Whether it "belongs" in religious philosophy as a stabilizing and creative force is another question. I think the basic problem is to *strive to realize what is now hidden from us,* and that the use of names indicating continuity with the past may at times cause us to lose courage when new definitions begin to emerge.

Those who find value in the term "God" will doubtless find this statement insufficient. They will insist that the basic question is whether a personal force controls the universe, or whether the universe is essentially controlled by impersonal forces. To this, my comment would be that there appear to be personal forces in the universe, but that our experience of things "personal" is based largely upon our knowledge of human beings, and that the term "personal" is all too easily a projection into the skies of something which we observe in ourselves and among one another. To say that the universe is basically controlled by a personal force could easily mean that it is controlled by a quasi-human force. Some have preferred to say that the universe was controlled by a *super*personal force. This is excellent if someone can define what is meant by superpersonal.

Would it not be simpler to say that there is an affinity, so far as we can see, between some of the cosmic forces and some of the forces that we see in ourselves, and that these forces probably belong to some sort of individual or personal entity? The question is, *what sort?*

PAUL ARTHUR SCHILPP

German-born philosopher Paul Arthur Schilpp is a theistic humanist. Professor of philosophy at Northwestern University since 1936, he is the author of Do We Need A New Religion *(1929);* Kant's Pre-Critical Ethics *(1938);* The Quest for Religious Realism *(1938); and* Human Nature and Progress *(1954). Since 1939 he has become increasingly known as the founder and editor of The Library of Living Philosophers, in which series he has already published eight classics on contemporary philosophers. He came to the United States as a boy in 1913. Recent world travels have included a visiting professorship of philosophy at the University of Munich (Germany) in 1948 and lectures in fifteen Indian universities in 1951 under a grant from the Watumull Foundation.*

I

IN VIEW of the fact that the term "religion," in its widest application, includes everything from the most primitive forms of animism, mythology, and superstition, I find it necessary to delimit the term for purposes of this discussion.

Ethical religion I would, for my own part, define in the following two sentences:

Ethical religion is commitment to the highest, noblest, sublimest, and best that I can think, imagine or understand. And, it is a way of life commensurate with the greatness of that to which I have committed myself.

It is, thus, a commitment and a way of life. The commitment aspect makes it something more than a merely intellectual matter; even as the way of life implies conduct, action, behavior, on both the individual and social level.

To any thoughtful person it should be clear that no man *can* commit himself to anything higher than the best he is able to think, to imagine, and to understand.

As I see it, there is nothing in the essential insights of the Judaeo-Christian tradition to disagree with such a definition of ethical religion. "Doing justice, loving mercy, and walking humbly" with both God and my fellowman, certainly is a way of life commensurate with the highest commitment any human being could make. And what else is this but a carrying out of the Nazarene's penultimate principles of love of God and love of one's fellowman—even as one loves himself? Justice tempered by mercy, and both the result of a humanity-encircling-and-including love—this is the essence of Judaism at its highest point as well as of the religion of Jesus.

This love of my fellowman is, moreover, *not* a matter of broad sentimentality or a mere emotional spree. Rather, it is the attitude of good will toward man as such, just because one recognizes in the dignity of the human personality the highest, noblest, and sublimest values yet made manifest to the limited understanding and insight of finite beings.

These highest values are seen not so much as actual achievement—at least not on the part of most men in our age—but as aspects of well-nigh infinite capacity. It is not necessary to deny or even to gloss over any of the lowest depths to which human animals may have sunk in order to see these divine and almost infinite capacities in man. Rather the reverse is the case. The higher man has it in him to rise, the lower he can fall and sink. The evidences of human barbarism and savagery therefore, far from denying man's infinite birthright of intellectual, moral, and spiritual achievements, actually offer one of the best arguments for man's innate capacity for moral and spiritual greatness.

It is, no doubt, true that the world-shaking and heart-rending experiences of the last forty years have made men, even in the Western world, more conscious of human tragedy than we have been for a long time. This explains the present vogue of Neo-Orthodoxy and of the "theologies of crisis." With their one-sided emphasis on the "sinfulness of man" and their running to God and "salvation" for a celestial hiding-place, they certainly fit the contemporary mood. One may readily grant that, more often than not, men do *not* follow their profoundest insights, their deepest convictions, or their highest aspirations and goals. But this is no reason for despairing of or impugning human nature as such. Human nature has, to begin with, infinite possibilities for good as well as for evil. To overlook either possibility is blindness or sheer folly. But it is not human nature as such which produces veritable human devils, but human nurture—as any psychologist or psychiatrist can demonstrate any day.

There is enough reflective reason, moral capacity, and spiritual power in and available to every reasonably normal human being to meet any and all tragedies of life—*provided* he will make use of these powers. It is not fair to blame either God or human nature, if and when anyone is neither willing nor ready to use the powers and capacities available to him all the time.

This insight is contained in any truly ethical religion. It would have been absurd or criminal on the part of Jesus to enjoin men to "love God and our fellowman," if man as such were incapable of this love. If there is any need in this for the so-called "grace of God," this "grace" is found in the way in which the creative process created man and the universe in the first place. It depends no more upon any specific divine intervention than a specific divine intervention is needed to grow the most gorgeous orchids in Hawaii. You need merely provide the right conditions for such growth in the first place. "Peace on earth to men of good will"—and all men can have such good will, if they will but commit themselves to the highest, noblest, sublimest, and best they can think or imagine, and live their lives accordingly.

It is these ethical and spiritual values of religion, therefore—contained as they are not merely in the Judaeo-Christian tradition, but in some other of the world's great religions as well—which still need to be emphasized in contemporary thought and practice. If they were universally emphasized—in place of the emphasis on doctrine, ceremony, and cult (which tend to divide rather than to unite men)—racial discrimination and international suspicion and hatred would dissolve as does snow in the rays of the sun.

Albert Schweitzer has put his (usually incisive) finger on it in these words: "The great question which each religion must be asked is, how far it produces permanent and profound incentives to the inward perfecting of personality and to ethical activity. . . . In religion we try to find an answer to the elementary question with which each one of us is newly confronted every morning, namely, what meaning and what value is to be ascribed to our life."[1]

II

The worldview of modern science is—despite the indeterminacy principle—at least one of order and lawfulness. In fact, in spite of the now almost universal recognition, certainly among scientists, that human knowledge is always and inevitably limited—because finite and relative—it is difficult to see how there could be any science at all without such order and lawfulness. For if science is to achieve its aim of ever-greater generalizations—on the basis of the careful observation, analysis, and measurement of given data of experience—it simply must assume an orderly and lawful universe. Without this assumption the entire edifice of natural science comes toppling down. And if "the proof of the pudding is in the eating," then the proof of the general correctness of that assumption is to be found in the fact of the tremendous success, both theoretical and applied, of science and of the scientific method.

An orderly universe is, moreover, a dependable universe. It is a universe in which like causes tend to have like effects, and which, because of this fact, can be counted upon. It is a universe in which no sane person expects to reap wheat from a planting of potatoes. Does not this basic scientific insight jibe completely with the Biblical assertion that "whatsoever a man soweth, that shall he also reap"? That is to say, in human and even in social behavior, the same orderly and causal lawfulness applies which works in the rest of the order of nature. In a truly orderly universe this would be expected. For man, too, is part of nature, and can never be truly understood until he is placed in the same continuum and evolutionary process with the rest of nature.

[1] In his *Christianity and the Religions of the World*, (New York: The Macmillan Company, 1939), p. 26.

Now it is true, of course, that any concept of strict causality implies determinism of sorts. From this we need not shrink. We need merely recognize that there are all *kinds* of causes, not merely physical and material ones. There are also intellectual causes, moral causes, and—I use the word advisedly—spiritual[2] causes. The concept of human freedom is, after all, not the concept of *in*determinism. This would not be freedom; it would be indescribable chaos, a condition under which no sane man would care to live. Human freedom means, rather, the capacity for rational—moral and spiritual—self-determination, the relative freedom of the reflective human reason to pass upon and control the steps of its own present and future self-determination, always, of course, within limits.[3] It *is* self-determination, but it is not absolute indeterminism or absolute determinism. This, too, fits into the system of an orderly—and therefore *not* irrational—universe.

In this kind of a universe the rational, moral, and spiritual purposes of men are capable of being worked out and of coming to fruition. That is to say, nature is so constituted that, at the human level, rational, moral, and spiritual factors and aspirations—and therefore determinations—have arisen as naturally as have other factors and needs below as well as within the level of man. There is nothing in the nature or orderly working of the universe as such to stop either man's rational, moral, and spiritual (including his religious, as defined under I above) aspirations or his achievements along any of those lines.

In the light of the fact that man himself is a natural product of nature, it seems wholly unwarranted to say that "nature is indifferent to man" or to his interests. Nature is the matrix out of which man himself has come and within which man himself will have to work out his own salvation, if not actually "with fear and trembling," then at any rate with rationally reflective insight, with increasing devotion, and with a determination which refuses to acknowledge defeat even after repeated setbacks.

[2] By "spiritual" I mean the powers and capacities of human self-transcendence, a self-transcendence which seems quite apparent in the temporal and spatial realm as well as in aspiration, in art, in social self-transcendence as well as in what I prefer to call transfinite self-transcendence. *Cf.* Lectures II and III of my Tully Cleon Knoles Lectures in Philosophy, *Human Nature and Progress* (Stockton, Calif., College of the Pacific, 1954).

[3] *Cf.* the writer's article, "On the Nature of the Ethical Problem," *International Journal of Ethics,* Vol. XLVII, No. 1 (October 1936), esp. pp. 66f.

For if this universe has been able to produce Akhnaton, Socrates, Jesus, and St. Francis in the past, and Gandhi, Schweitzer, Einstein, and Kagawa in the present, it is obviously absurd to claim that nature is "hostile" to the production of such human character.

The fact is, the development of human society itself awaits more such characters.

III

At the very heart of any truly ethical religion stand the value and dignity of the human person. The same is true of any democracy worthy of the name. (Even today's Russian and Chinese Communism can maintain its appeal to its masses only by insisting that it is interested in and concerned with bettering the life of the masses—which, in the eye of each individual among those masses, means bettering the life of each individual.)

The personal—rational, moral, spiritual—values are intrinsic, therefore, not merely to my religious faith, but also to my faith in democracy.

I can put my faith in democracy in two sentences, as follows:

Man, being what he is—a rational-moral-spiritual person—can have only one kind of government which is worthy of him, and that is self-government. And the only kind of government of which I have knowledge that even so much as *aims* at self-government—whether or not it has yet ever actually achieved it—is democracy.

Lincoln's famous characterization of democracy as government of, by, and for the people still seems to me the best one-sentence statement of the case for democracy. And this, obviously, is but another way of saying: self-government.

Self-government is the only morally defensible political order—aside from complete anarchy, which latter is both conceivable and desirable only in a state of perfect human beings: a state not to be expected in any foreseeable time, if, indeed, ever—if we grant that the value and dignity of the human person is the highest value which has thus far arisen in the process of evolution.

These same personal values we have already noted in answer to Question I as the highest values to which an ethical religion can aspire and be committed.

It is possible to say, therefore, that as concerns the ultimate and intrinsic values, the aims of ethical religion and of democracy coincide.

I believe this to be so eminently true that I think that, if Jesus had lived in our century instead of nineteen centuries ago, he would have used the "democracy of God" in place of the "Kingdom of God." For even God can, after all, only choose those who first choose him.

Such a view of democracy is no attempt to espouse, let alone to glorify, any self-righteous patriotism or to extol the so-called "American way of life." Rather, the values and aims of democracy, as here developed, are themselves as much an idealized "way of life" as they are the principles of an ideal socio-political order.

If we carefully examine our commitment to democracy and our reasons for this commitment, we shall find that what we are really concerned with and interested in is the preservation and enlargement of human freedom—precisely because we believe in the ultimate value and dignity of the human person. That is to say, only a free man can live a life worthy of being called human; and we find that only ideal democracy aims to secure and maintain this freedom to the human person. In democratic forms and institutions we discover the best means by which freedom can find expression in the socio-political realm.

No freedom on the part of any finite being can, obviously, be thought of as absolute; this is the element of truth in the insistence on determinism, both on the part of the individual and on that of society and of social institutions. Moreover, absolute freedom would be the same as absolute chaos. Even God—if there is a God—cannot possibly be absolutely free without being wholly capricious. God's nature and commitments act as determining factors even in his case.

But without *any* freedom, it is senseless to talk of democracy at all. It is senseless, in fact, to talk even in any meaningful way of man as a rational-moral-spiritual personality if man is wholly determined, if he is entirely the product of blind forces over which he has no control.

In other words, man's ability to reason, to reflect, to draw inferences and conclusions, is itself one of the determining factors in his life, both as an individual and as a member of society.

Here, then, lies one of the foundations not merely for the possibility and meaningfulness of democracy, but for man's being in any significant sense human at all. Here, too, lie the roots of any and all truly ethical religions: in man's being free—within limits—to choose, to decide, to initiate and determine his own life and future individually as well as socially; to be able, on the one hand, to say "no" even to God himself, and on the other, to choose freely to do God's or the universe's will as he is able to see, to fathom, and to comprehend this.

To create a society of free men who use their freedom for personal growth as well as for the increasing benefit of social welfare is the aim of the democratic movement as well as of ethical religion.

In this atomic age such democratic and moral commitment carries implications of a quite specific character for the international scene. Today's problem par excellence is that of world peace. Everyone knows by now that unless this problem can be settled in favor of peace, tomorrow there may no longer be any human problems—because no more humanity. Confronted by this dire emergency, men of good will face an unprecedented challenge. Can today's international anarchy be replaced by an international order which can achieve and maintain peace on a humanity-wide scale?

It should be obvious to any thinking person that, so long as each individual nation claims sovereignty (i.e., being a law unto itself and refusing to recognize any law above itself), international anarchy, and therefore war, are inevitable. Only as ultimate sovereignty is transferred to humanity as a whole can this anarchic condition be ended. Both the religious principle of the brotherhood of all mankind and the democratic ideals of liberty and equality for all demand therefore the construction of a democratic federal world government as the only practicable means of avoiding universal annihilation.

IV

I do not pretend to know whether or not the supreme values available to moral man (of whatsoever source) are aspects of one spiritual reality. What does, however, seem to be the case is that, inasmuch as man himself is a part and product of nature and of its evolutionary and creative processes, it is only natural to assume that this orderly universe is the kind of universe in which the rising, occurrence, and development of rational, of moral, and of spiritual values is as natural as are those of physical, material, and bodily values and experiences.

The age-old quarrel at this point of value-theory between the subjectivist on the one hand, and the objectivists on the other, seems to me to be, for the most part, pointless. Are values—intellectual, aesthetic, moral, spiritual, religious—entirely objective (having an independent existence by themselves), or are they purely subjective (the result, that is to say, merely of subjectively individual or social preference and choice)? This way of stating the problem seems to me to be fallacious. It assumes an absolute dichotomy between subject and object, which overlooks the essentially unitary character of human experience.

What values would be that are not values to someone capable of evaluating, I confess I am unable to conceive. To this extent it seems to me not merely necessary but self-evident that values are subjective —that is, they do depend upon subjective evaluators.

But if—as I maintain—all intellectual, aesthetic, moral, spiritual and religious values are rooted in the existential nature of man as a being innately capable of having, experiencing, creating, and appreciating such values, then obviously these values can *not* be put down as *merely* subjective. For, in this case, they are objectively rooted in the very nature and being of man and, inasmuch as man himself is part of the order of the universe, in the nature and being of the universe itself.

True, they are values to and for man. But they are this because of man being what he essentially is—a rational-moral-spiritual person, at least in potential capacity, regardless of the degree to which any *specific* man may realize or actualize these potential capacities. All values are thus objectively grounded in the very nature of man and thus of the universe, even though they can become values for man only to the extent or degree to which he, as an evaluating subject, experiences and appreciates them, either positively or negatively.

Inasmuch as these values are thus objectively rooted in the existential nature of man, it is clear that the values of science, the values of a society of free men (democracy), as well as the values of ethical religion are not merely accidentally or fitfully superimposed by man, but are rooted in the very nature of man as a potential rational-moral-spiritual person. This explains their survival-value.

Nor, in the light of these considerations, does it seem to make sense that there could ever be any real, imaginary, or surreptitious conflict between the values in these various areas. If science is concerned with the discovery of truth (of the ascertainable facts) in any of the areas where it legitimately operates with any and all of the tools at its command, it becomes inconceivable that it could ever come into any except a purely *apparent* conflict with the values of democracy or with those of ethical religion.

If democracy, on its part, is concerned with the creation, development, and enhancement of a society of free men, how could it ever be blind to the truthful—within the limits of the possibilities of human, and therefore finite and relative—knowledge, discoveries, and revelations of science, on the one hand, or find itself at variance with the moral and spiritual demands and challenges of ethical religion, on the other?

And, if ethical religion is commitment to the noblest and best man can think or imagine, and a way of life commensurate with the greatness and magnificence of that noblest and best, how could it possibly close its eyes to the truthful revelations of science any more than to the values which arise from and accrue to the creation of a society of free men (democracy)?

Both truth and goodness are human needs and values, without the appreciation and realization of which man would not at all be what we know him to be in our own and in everyone else's experience. Neither truth nor goodness could have any meaningful content without the possibility of their opposites, falsehood, error, and evil. (If there were any angels and it were asserted that, by definition, they could neither make a mistake nor do wrong, then they could in no meaningful sense be said to be moral beings at all.) It is only by darkness (the relative absence of light) that man can become aware of light at all. The same holds for the values of truth and goodness. It is only in this sense that it may be said that evil, so far from being a "problem" at all, is actually a blessing.

Any man who, never having eaten from the tree of the knowledge of good and evil, not merely could do no wrong but could not even make any distinctions between good and evil, would not only *not* be in paradise, if paradise were thought of as a desirable place, but would be just plain ignorant and incapable of being called a moral being at all.

V

The concept "God" is for me, in the first instance, not so much a requirement of my religion as it is a requirement of my rational account for and interpretation of the universe. Not being able to account for even the silliest and most meaningless newspaper without assuming that some purposive agent intended it, I confess that I find it inconceivable to account for this universe of magnificent and inexhaustible order without assuming some—purposive—agent who meant to and creatively has been at work producing it down through the practically endless aeons of universal evolution. Nor can I see any conflict whatever between divine creation and natural evolution. To me, evolution is simply the natural method the divine creator has been employing in creating (i.e., evolving) a universe.

I readily admit (as, indeed, the above used analogy clearly shows) that this is, obviously, an anthropomorphic point of view. But I fail to see what *other* point of view man—being, after all, an *anthropos*—could possibly employ. Every human conception—of no matter what—must inevitably be anthropomorphic. The charge of anthropomorphism, if it is meant to be a valid criticism, becomes meaningless therefore, because it applies to every human idea and is, moreover, unavoidable in any case. The question which should legitimately be asked of any human concept is not: Is it anthropomorphic? but: Is it first, factual, and second, reasonable?

Here a second admission becomes necessary. The question of "God" is not capable of being answered at the factual level either. If God be God at all, he must by initial hypothesis be infinitely beyond man—and therefore beyond man's finite comprehension. As such he is also, obviously, beyond proof as well as beyond disproof. (In my humble judgment, no rational mind acquainted with the work of Immanuel Kant has at this point attempted to "prove" the existence of God since 1781.) At the factual level, therefore, God can ever be only a matter of hypothesis or of faith, never a matter of demonstration or proof.

From the standpoint of religion, this is a service rather than a disservice. A God who would be capable of human and therefore finite and relative demonstration or proof would, as such, have to come within the circumscribed realm of finite demonstrability and thereby lose for man precisely that aspect of his nature as the transcending and transcendent deity by virtue of which claim it is that he is God. After all, man can truly worship only that which is quite transcendently beyond himself. A proved God would become religiously almost irrevelant.

The other—and only remaining—question to be applied to the God-concept—Is it reasonable?—is capable of a meaningful reply. To this writer "God" is not merely a reasonable hypothesis, but is to me—in the light of all presently given data and available facts—the *only* reasonable hypothesis. However, I would not wish to impugn either the motives or the rationale of anyone who would arrive at an opposite conclusion.

Having asserted that God is the most reasonable hypothesis to account for our universe of marvelous order, let me make another admission. I do not claim to be able, with my puny, finite mind, to comprehend the transcending (as well as immanent) deity—any more than a marvelously existing microbe in my body could be expected to be able to comprehend and understand my nature as a human being. I am, after all, as infinitely beyond the comprehensibility of that microbe as God is infinitely beyond mine.

Nor can any so-called and supposed divine self-revelation of God alter this basic fact of my inability to comprehend God. For, no matter what I as a human being might undertake to make my nature and my purposes comprehensible to that microbe within my own system, I would still be bound to fail in such intentions, however good, not because of my own failure of self-disclosure, but simply because of the microbe's own lack of capacity of comprehension. This is why every so-called self-revelation of the deity, in most major religions that have a God-concept at all, has found it not merely expedient but necessary to clothe itself in human form—for example, Buddha, Krishna, Jesus. The only "God" my microbe could really grasp would simply be a "bigger and better" microbe. At the same time, it would obviously be not merely silly but plainly false for the microbe within me to assume that there was no other being beyond itself!

Nevertheless, it makes sense to me to assume that the universe is the work of rational, orderly, purposive Mind. Granted that this can only be a reasonable hypothesis—a rational faith, and an anthropomorphic one at that—it still seems more reasonable than any other possible hypothesis. That by sheer accident of completely blind and wholly meaningless collocation of atoms, first a perfectly marvelous universe of order should have evolved, which itself then finally produced—equally blindly and unintentionally—a being capable of rational reflection, of moral judgment, and of spiritual self-transcendence, is to me such a preposterous assumption that even the most credulous kind of credulity would seem to me to have to balk at it.

I insist, therefore, that—aside from any religious reasons—"God" is for me a rational necessity, a philosophically required hypothesis.

It is only natural, therefore, that I should find the roots of man's rational intelligence, moral judgment, and spiritual values firmly rooted in the nature and being of God: In the same sort of fashion in which I find that the electricity within my own body is part and parcel of the electricity in the universe at large. Nor can I see any good reason why the rationality, moral judgment, and spiritual self-transcendence of my own nature should not be capable of tapping the rational, moral, and spiritual resources both within as well as beyond me, any more than I can see why this should not be possible in the realm of electricity.

Mere analogy? Analogy, true. But I can see no valid arguments against the analogy, though I readily admit that analogy is no proof. But I admitted the impossibility of proof in this area at the beginning.

While God—like electricity—is thus always available, I do believe that the contact has to be decided upon and made by man himself taking the initiative. This is why under Question III I stated that God can choose only those who first freely choose him. And what men choose to see in God will obviously depend upon the point any specific individual has reached in his own rational, moral, and spiritual development. This being the case, it is only natural that there should be almost as many concepts of God as there are human beings holding such a concept. This fact is nothing either against God or against men; it is inevitable in view of the tautological self-evidence of the fact that any man can only comprehend that which he is able to comprehend. To ask more of him would itself be unreasonable.

PITIRIM A. SOROKIN

Pitirim A. Sorokin was born in Russia, educated and later a teacher of sociology at the University of St. Petersburg, a leader in the founding of the Soviet Republic, then condemned to death and finally banished by the Communist Government in 1922. He has been a professor of sociology and law at the Universities of St. Petersburg and Minnesota; since 1930 the founder and chairman of the Department of Sociology; and since 1949 the director of the Research Center in Creative Altruism at Harvard. A member of the American Academy of Arts and Sciences and the American Sociological Society, and an honorary member of various European academies and institutes, Dr. Sorokin has been a prolific writer of scholarly books. Among his publications are Social Mobility *(1927);* Contemporary Sociological Theories *(1928);* Social and Cultural Dynamics *(1937); and* Ways and Power of Love *(1954). His books have been translated into many major languages.*

INTRODUCTION

I AGREE with the true mystics and great logicians of all great cultures that our language cannot define adequately the ultimate reality or/and the supreme value. All our words, concepts, and definitions, and all our signs and symbols have evolved for indication, denotation, description, and definition of only the finite, the limited, the specific differentiations of the all-embracing, undifferentiated, and quantitatively-qualitatively infinite ultimate reality or the *summum bonum*. They are fit for designation of the finite, differentiated subjects, objects, and phenomena, and they are unfit for definition or conception of the total reality in its infinite manifoldedness.

By our words and symbols we can define any of the bounded, specific ripples of an infinite ocean of reality, and we cannot adequately describe the ocean itself: it contains all the ripples and at the same time it is not identical to any and all of them. The same is true of the supreme value or the *summum bonum*. Even the most general categories of our thought, like substance, quantity, quality, relation, time, space, state, subject-object, cause-effect, being-becoming, are fit for identifying the ripples only and are inadequate for definition of the total cosmic reality. J. S. Erigena's "God Himself does not know *what* He is because God is not *what*" well expresses the idea of inapplicability of the categories of our thought to the ultimate reality or/and the supreme value. God, or the ultimate reality, is not identical with either substance or non-substance; with being or becoming, with subject or object, with quantity or quality, with cause or effect. God is neither temporal and spatial nor timeless and spaceless; neither matter nor spirit, neither personal nor impersonal; God is neither He nor She nor It; neither this nor that of these "ripples" or differentiations. At the same time God contains all these ripples; they are "God's ripples," God's aspects, God's parts and parcels. God transcends any and all of its differentiations and ripples.

In this sense the ultimate reality-value is the *mysterium tremendum et fascinosum,* the veritable *coincidentia oppositorum,* transcending all our concepts and categories, all our logical laws, including the laws of identity, contradiction, and others. For this reason the total true reality is undescribable by any words and undefinable by any rational concepts. This explains why many a mystic called it "the Unutterable," "the Unexpressible," "the Divine Nothing," into which fade all things and differentiations.

Omnia exeunt in mysterium of this reality, as St. Thomas said about it. Only symbolically can it be designated by a word or name or sign like: God, Tao, Chit, Jen, Brahman, Atman, Nirvana, the Oversoul, the Cosmic Mind, the True Self, the Supraessence, the Pure Intelligence, the All-Pervading, the Creator, and so on. These names and the visible symbols of the mainly invisible ultimate reality or of the supreme value are but a mere "finger pointing at it," in no way identical with it. Nor can any of these names or symbols claim monopolistic privilege of being the only true name or symbol of the true reality-value. Any of these human words and signs beginning with "God" (Deus, Gott, Bog, Dieu, etc.), and ending with Brahma, Indra, Vishu, Osiris, Ammon, Ra, Ahura-Mazda, Jehovah, Zeus, Jupiter, Allah, and so on, are not God's own names but our human terms, superimposed upon the ultimate reality, each term coined in accordance with the linguistic, social, cultural, and personal properties of a respective social group or person.

Being the infinitude of infinitudes, the ultimate reality contains in itself all and any of "the ripples" with which the believers of various religions identify it. It can have, for instance, the personal and the superpersonal aspects, "the spiritual" and "the material" ripples, "the never-changing" and "the ever-changing" differentiations. It may be thought of as "the God-Father" or as "the Divine Mother," as "the Holy Trinity" or as "One in Many," and so on. Each of these and many other ideas of God (the ultimate reality) is partly correct because all these aspects are God's differentiations. At the same time, none of the credos defines God adequately in the inexhaustible plenitude of his infinite aspects.

This means that all the existing theologies and philosophies, including the materialistic, agnostic, and atheistic ones, contain an element of truth, each stressing some of the infinite aspects of the *mysterium tremendum*. The material, the unknowable, the superpersonal aspects are also "the ripples" of the true reality, though not necessarily the important ones. On the other hand, none of these beliefs contains the whole truth and nothing but the truth about the total true reality. Insofar, there is no serious reason for religious rivalry and intolerance, even for claiming a monopolistic superiority for one's own conception of "God's ripples" and for a condemnation of other religious conceptions as false.

My conception of God's aspects does not hinder me at all from admiring religious beliefs different from my own. Just as an admiration of Bach's music does not hinder at all an equal admiration of Mozart's or Beethoven's music, similarly my brand of religious ideas and experiences does not exclude a sincere appreciation of other religious conceptions and experiences. By stressing different "ripples" of the infinite ocean they enrich my conception of the ultimate reality and value.

The above implies that by our definite mind we cannot fully understand the infinite *mysterium tremendum et fascinosum*. On the other hand, being ourselves one of its "ripples," we can grasp roughly some of the important aspects of it. Its sensory aspects we can perceive through our sense-organs (reinforced by microscopes, telescopes, and other extensions of these organs). Its rational aspects, exemplified by the cosmic order and laws of the universe, and, in the human universe, by the phenomena of science, rational philosophy, and fine arts, by rational conduct of human beings and rational order and laws of human societies—this rational aspect of the ultimate reality we can roughly understand through our rational thought, through mathematical, dialectic, syllogistic, inductive, and deductive logic. Finally, we can have some notions of the suprasensory and suprarational aspects of the *mysterium tremendum* through our suprarational and suprasensory "intuition," "direct vision," "mystic experience," with which, in a small degree, almost all human beings are potentially endowed.

Unfortunately, most of us cultivate little this suprarational creative grace and develop little this "line of communication" with the highest forms of ultimate reality. Only rarely and for a short moment we experience the grace of this supraconscious "enlightenment." Often we even fool ourselves by taking mistakingly a bizarre, subrational and irrational experience for this suprarational intuition and direct identification with the ultimate reality and value.

Fortunately, these limitations in our comprehension of the suprarational aspects of the *mysterium tremendum* are greatly alleviated by a fuller and more frequent supraconscious enlightenment experienced by a few "chosen and anointed": by the founders and great religious and moral leaders, by the true seers, sages, and prophets on the one hand, and on the other by the creative geniuses in all fields of culture: by great scientists, philosophers, artists, poets, musicians, and other constructive creators of the greatest masterpieces or values of the human universe. Moses, Buddha, Zoroaster, Confucius, Lao-Tze, Jesus, Mohammed; Plato, Aristotle, Shankara, Al Ghazzali; Plotinus, St. Thomas Aquinas, Kant; Mo-Tze, St. Francis of Assisi, Gandhi; Galileo, Isaac Newton; Pheidias; Bach, Mozart, Beethoven; Homer and Shakespeare; Praxiteles, Rafael, Michelangelo; these creative giants are the examples of these chosen and anointed. Graced and moved by the highest suprarational genius, they reveal to us by their discoveries and creations (any discovery is a creation and any creation is a discovery) several suprasensory and suprarational aspects of the ultimate reality-value which otherwise would remain hidden from all of us who are not endowed by the suprarational genius. Through the "revelations" of these great discoverers and creators we are enriched in our knowledge of the suprarational forms of being of the ultimate reality-value.

Integrating these three channels of cognition of this reality—the sensory, the rational, and the suprasensory-suprarational—we grasp an understanding of the three important aspects of the Infinite Manifold: its sensory, rational, and suprarational modes of being.

Through the same integral method we become aware of a sort of gradation of the ultimate reality into its higher and lower forms of being, beginning with its supreme form of being or its *summum bonum,* and ending with its least important, or even what appears to us negative or evil form, of being. It is likely that this "hierarchization" of modes of being of the *mysterium tremendum* is largely subjective evaluation of our finite "mind," which superimposes its puny gradations upon something that infinitely transcends our understanding and intelligence. Some aspects of the true reality remain incomprehensible to us: "The ways of Providence are inscrutable and unfathomable." Especially incomprehensible is the eternal problem of evil—of the evil mode of being of either one ultimate reality or of two primeval and primordial cosmic ultimate realities—the good and the evil, God and Satan, Ahura-Mazda and Angra-Mainyu.

For this and other reasons, our hierarchization of the forms of being of the ultimate reality with the ensuing scale of our values can, at best, only roughly reflect the true gradation of the forms of being of the reality itself. On the other hand, the rough correspondence between our hierarchization and objective gradation of the ultimate reality itself seems to be probable. Inevitably suffering from a puny anthropomorphization, imperfection of our language, and limitations of human intelligence, the hierarchical differentiation of the forms of being of the *mysterium tremendum* can be roughly depicted as follows.

1. Its supreme form consists of the concentrated highest creative forces of the total ultimate reality. All great religions express this idea

in viewing God, first of all and most of all, as the Creator. "I am the Way, the Truth, and the Life" is another formula of the supreme creative focus of this reality. Whether we conceive this highest form of being of the ultimate reality as a personal or superpersonal agent (and it has been stressed above, both conceptions are equally correct or inadequate), the creativity of the ultimate reality infinitely transcends any human creativity. Even the highest creativity of the greatest human genius is a mere drop in comparison with the creativity of the infinite ocean of the *mysterium tremendum et fascinosum*. Though human creativity is also one of the *mysterium*'s creativity ripples, we do not have any basis for claiming that human creativity is the zenith reached by this cosmic creativity (or by God the Creator). In the infinite universe of the ultimate reality there probably are a legion of conceivable empirical agencies far exceeding the creativity of man, and a host of creative forces that are beyond our present comprehension.

The lowest modes of being of the ultimate reality consist of all the inert, uncreative, lifeless forms of being serving the role of a material for creative activity of the supreme forms of the *mysterium tremendum*.

Still lower modes of being of the true reality are possibly what appear to us as the evil forms of being, though their evilness may be due to our incomprehension and misinterpretation of these seemingly evil phenomena. Perhaps from the superhuman standpoint these evil forms of being are not evil at all, and play a constructive role in "the infinite household of the cosmic reality."

2. When our limited mind tries to differentiate the supreme modes of the undifferentiated *mysterium,* we grasp, at least, its three main differentiations: *creative truth, creative goodness-love, and creative beauty*. Like the Christian Trinity of God-Father, God-Son, and the Holy Ghost, each of these aspects of the supreme forms of the ultimate reality is distinctly different from the other two; at the same time, like the Trinity, each of these aspects is inseparable from, and is transformable into, one another: genuine truth is always good and beautiful; real goodness-love is always true and beautiful; and pure beauty is always true and good.

On the human level, the supreme form of being of a person or a group differentiates itself also into the form of living in and creating an ever-fuller truth, ever-nobler love, and ever-sublimer beauty in the human universe. The low forms of being of a human person or a group consist in living in an uncreative ignorance, in destroying truth, in doing evil, and in cultivating ugliness in the human universe.

Partly explicitly, partly implicitly, the outlined metaphysics above contain the answers to the five questions of this inquiry. However, let us work at each of them separately.

I

In the Judaean and Christian[1] as well as in any other genuine religion three things have to be emphasized at the present time: (1) the ultimate reality in its supreme modes of being; (2) being and living in truth, love, and beauty; and (3) realization and practice of creative, unselfish love especially.

Comments to point 1: The ultimate reality can be experienced and thought of by various religious persons in the form which is most suited and most appealing to each person according to his vital, mental, and moral equipment. For a majority of believers the personified forms of the *mysterium tremendum* are the most suited, while for others, its superpersonal forms are more congenial. Finally, many persons experience it now as personified, now as superpersonal reality. There is no reason to quarrel about the diverse modes of experiencing and conceiving the concrete forms of the *mysterium*. All the images and concrete conceptions of it are largely anthropomorphic, and partly inadequate. The main thing is a clear realization of the verity that the ultimate reality and value are not exhausted by the sensory empirical phenomena and values, and that this sensory aspect is only one—and not necessarily the main—aspect of the infinitude of infinitudes.

[1] The expression "the Judaeo-Christian religions" appears to me ambiguous and misleading so far as it suggests Christianity as a continuation and development of Judaism and Judaism as the only source of Christianity. In their character these two religions are as different as Christianity and Manicheanism or Hinduism or Buddhism. Likewise, besides Judaism, Christianity had several other sources: Neo-Platonism, Neo-Pythagoreanism, Stoicism, Manicheanism, the cult of Mitra, of Isis, Osiris, Hinduism, and Buddhism (brought in through Plotinus and some of the early Church Fathers, like Clement of Alexandria) and others.

Comments to points 2 and 3: The paramount task of a genuine religion at the present time consists in mental, moral, and behavioral transfiguration of human beings and groups, in making them more aware of the *mysterium* spiritually, more intelligent mentally, nobler morally, purer aesthetically, and more creative in their total life. This transformation must be *total,* involving not only ideology and vocal utterances of a person but his total being, and especially his overt behavior. The "converted" or transfigured individuals must practice the noble precepts and verities they preach. *Fides sine operibus mortua est.* At the present time there exists a deep chasm between what most of us preach and what we practice. There is no scarcity in "highfatulin" mottoes and preachings; there is a great poverty of deeds and actions that practice these preachings. A mere performance of a prescribed ritual, more frequent vocal or silent prayers, a mere "conversion to Jesus" after an hour of eloquent sermon, are not enough for the total transfiguration discussed. Our study of seventy-three "hour-converts" in Boston shows that, with the exception of one person, such an "exhibitionistic conversion" did not change anything in the behavior and even in the mentality of these "momentary converts." Objectively such conversions are mainly an easy and cheap self-gratification of neurotic and selfish persons.

A striking discrepancy between noblest preachings and ignoble practices has increasingly marked the Western Christian world for the last few centuries. Professing in their speech-reactions the noblest precepts of the Sermon on the Mount, the Western Christian world has shown itself in its overt behavior to be the most belligerent, the most aggressive, and the most power-drunk part of humanity. During the last few centuries it has been the Western Christendom that invaded all the other continents, robbed, subjugated, exploited, and exterminated the native populations of Asia, Africa, the Americas, and other regions. During the same centuries the conduct of Christians towards one another has also been murderous. Often in the name of God and Jesus, the Christians of diverse denominations and nations liberally engaged in numerous religious, civil, and international wars, in the savage persecution and extermination of "the heretics" and the nonconformists, and in all sorts of iniquities perpetrated by one Christian faction in regard to the other Christian denominations. In their overt behavior the Christians of these centuries have been the most un-Christian.

This deep chasm between the noble preachings and ignoble practices continues to exist at the present time. Perhaps even more cynically than before, the name of Jesus and his eternal precepts are sacrilegiously misused now for promotion of commercial and material interests, and for justification of the hate-laden and murderous policies of various "Christian" nations. No wonder that this sham Christianity has utterly failed to realize the vision of "Glory to God in the highest, and on earth, peace, good will toward men." Instead of this peace, the nominally Christian world has given us the twentieth century as the most inhuman, most ungodly, and the bloodiest century of all the twenty-five preceding centuries. At the present moment, some of these sham Christians even openly preach, in the name of God and Jesus, "crusades against disbelievers and atheists" in which the Gospel of Christian Love is to be proved by the argument of thermonuclear bombs and missiles. One can hardly imagine a more sacrilegious perversion and a more devilish falsification of the Gospel of Jesus!

The same discrepancy between the noble preachings and the ignoble practices permeates the much advertised religious revival and the moral rearmament movement of our days. So far revival and rearmament have shown themselves mainly in "the exhibitionistic momentary conversions," in a slight increase of pious speech-reactions and ritualistic religiosity, in political conventions of "the moral rearmament party," and in a great deal of publicity used for a commercial exploitation of rearmanent and revival. So far both movements have hardly totally transfigured many persons and groups. Side by side with the superficial and pale fruits of the rearmament and revival of religiosity, they generated two dangerous falsifications of religion itself and of religious transfiguration.

The falsification of religion in these movements has consisted in an increasing degradation of religion to a sort of magical, effective, utilitarian art of how to secure easily and cheaply: health, pleasure, peace of mind, lasting happiness, and a comfortable place "for keeps" in the Kingdom of Heaven. The Gospel of God or Jesus is often replaced in these movements by the libidinal gospel of Freud and by the utilitarian gospel of a businessman. A true prophet or religious creator tends to be supplanted by the highly successful managers of "religious business." Religious community tends to be turned into an effectively organized "religious corporation" efficiently managed according to the latest techniques of management of the General Motors or Du Pont corporations. Religious education and transfiguration are increasingly reduced to "the conditioning" in reflexological performance of ritualistic actions, in automatic verbal utterances of the prefabricated prayers and magic words; and in the consumption of various "spiritual pills" that, with "double money back guarantee," promise to the believers "a song in your heart," "peace in your mind," "a joy in your life," and "prosperity in your business." In brief, the value and the *raison d'être* of religion in these movements tend to be debased to material utility and hedonistic pleasures.

The falsification of religious transfiguration and the religious life in these movements consists also of a preached substitution of utterly primitive, largely magical, hedonistic and materialistic conceptions and practices for certain extremely difficult achievements. According to these preachings, as soon as a person verbally declares he or she "enlists in the army of God," and begins to attend church services, says his or her prayers, contributes to the church finances, and especially enters a monastery (often for publicity purposes), such an individual is considered to be "converted" and transformed religiously. Such believers are assured that now they are fulfilling all religious duties and are saved from damnation. It is needless to add that such conversions are utterly superficial. The religious leaders must hammer into the believers the point that until they begin to live their religious and moral precepts in their daily life and in all their deeds, they remain untransfigured and as "pagan" as any "atheist" or religiously indifferent person. Even more, when such "speech-reactional converts" or self-advertising "believers in God" boast with their religiosity, claim an exclusive superiority of their brand of religion, damn "the atheists," and start bloody "crusades" against the "disbelievers," such "believers" are possibly more atheistic than the open atheists and religiously indifferent persons.

Especially important is this point in regard to the moral transformation of persons and groups. If a Christian, zealously professing his religious devotion, does not practice as much as one can the precepts of the Sermon on the Mount in one's relationships with all human beings, with all living creatures, and with the Cosmos itself, such a Christian remains as "pagan" as any open disbeliever.

In our age of hate, living and practicing sublime unselfish love, so beautifully defined by Jesus and unanimously taught by the ethics of all genuine religions, becomes the paramount need of humanity. Only a notable altruization of persons and groups along the precepts of the Sermon on the Mount can save mankind from the pending catastrophes. Only growth of the unselfish and creative love can decrease the raging interhuman strife and can help in establishing a lasting peace in the human universe. Such are the main tasks of Christian and other religions at the present time. The more they concentrate at their realization, the more fruitful and significant their creative labors are going to be. The more they dodge these assignments, the more ossified and moribund are they bound to be.

II

According to the outlined integral conception of the true reality and value and of the integral theory of the cognition of these, as stated in the introduction to this paper, there is no conflict between the scientific (predominantly sensory), the philosophic (predominantly rational) and the suprarational (predominantly religious and aesthetic) cognition and conception of the ultimate reality. Sensory perception and observation are fit for the cognition of the sensory aspects of the true reality and value; rational (logico-mathematical) thought is particularly fit for the cognition of the rational aspect of the *mysterium tremendum*; and genuine suprarational and suprasensory intuition gives us the "enlightenment" concerning the suprarational aspect of the true reality-value. All three ways of cognition mutually check the correctness of cognition of each other and, when integrally used, deliver to us a fuller, richer, and more adequate cognition of the ultimate reality than any single way can give. This shows that the integral conception of the true reality-value and of its cognition radically eliminates any conflict between a genuine science and genuine religion, and unites into one integral system of reality-value-cognition all three—sensory, rational, and suprarational—conception, cognition, experience, and evaluation of the true reality and value.

As to whether "the cosmic reality cares for man's well-being," my notions about this difficult problem can be put as follows. Endowed with a considerable creative-sensory, rational, and suprarational potential, man is one of the creative agencies in this reality. His status in the cosmic universe is that of a grown-up person rather than that of a baby or of a helpless creature. As a grown-up person he is largely set on his own and granted a large margin of freedom to make of his life either a marvelous epic of living in truth, love, and beauty, or a wretched failure. As a creator he has at his disposal a considerable amount of forces and material to use for satisfaction of his needs and for a desirable recreation of the human universe, as well as of the nonhuman cosmic environment in which he lives and acts. If the human race acts wisely and fully uses its creative potential, it can take good care of itself and of its creative mission on this planet. If human beings fail either to use their creative endowment wisely or do not use it at all, like an irresponsible and straying grown-up person freely wrecking his life, such human beings have to bear the disastrous consequences of their foolishness and demoralization.

To sum up: man is set in the cosmic universe not as a baby to be cared for and rigidly controlled by its parents, but as a grown-up person, well endowed with creative potential and given a large margin of freedom to make his life and the life of mankind either a creative masterpiece or a miserable failure with an unglorious death at the end of man's history. Well endowed with all the means for making its life creative, and for making itself a worthy participant in the total creativity of the true reality, mankind is set free to either faithfully discharge its mission in the total cosmos and to grow to the ever higher levels of creativity, or to misuse and abuse its potentials and eventually pass into oblivion. This state of man makes his "condition and history" particularly significant and fascinating.

This general attitude of the superhuman centers of creativity in the cosmic reality toward man is possibly changed in the cases when man or a group or the whole of mankind are attacked, without any fault on their part, by the overwhelming constellation of the human and the non-human inimical forces threatening their existence and their creative work. It is possible, though not certain, that in such situations the superhuman creative "agencies" of the true reality once in a while directly interfere by helping the guiltless man, group, and mankind to extricate themselves out of the desperate and undeserved situation.

Considering, however, an enormous legion of innocent individuals and groups that have not received such help and have unjustly suffered and perished, these empirical facts do not allow the conclusion that the superhuman creative centers invariably come to the rescue of all the innocent persons, groups, and mankind itself from the unjustified attacks of the inimical forces. Such facts of "the inscrutability of Providence," of "the cosmic injustice," or of "the vindictiveness and jealousy of gods," as the Greeks call them and as Sophocles so splendidly set this problem in his *Antigone, Oedipus Rex,* and *Oedipus at Colonus,* have been differently explained away: now by the theory of man's expendability in the infinite cosmic reality in which he is but a negligible and expendable speck; now by the assumption that man's measuring stick of justice-injustice, of innocence-guilt may be false and, anyhow, quite different from that of the higher centers of creativity. Therefore, what appears to us as an injustice and innocence may not be such from the standpoint of the superhuman creative agencies.

Finally, many have tried to explain away this problem by after-death retribution, by compensations and rewards in the Kingdom of Heaven for innocent sufferers, and by penalties and damnations in the inferno for the men of iniquity. This interpretation has been offered in a wide variety of forms, such as: transmigration and reincarnation of the souls according to the merits and demerits of their preceding ways of life; eternal or temporary paradise for the virtuous innocents and eternal or temporary purgatory and inferno for the sinners; and so on. Whichever of these explanations is accepted, all of them remain but mere beliefs neither proved nor disproved by empirical and rational evidence. The ugly empirical facts testify that from the standpoint of the moral standards of practically all religions a vast legion of virtuous and guiltless children, women, and men have unjustly suffered and perished without receiving any tangible help from the superhuman creative centers of the cosmic reality. Exactly these facts of the "cosmic injustice," or of the inscrutability of the ways of Providence, daily rendered to innocent children—tortured, mutilated, harmed, and murdered—evoked the rebellion of Ivan Karamazov (Dostoievsky) against the justification of this injustice by the justice of "the last judgment" and by the future, eternal harmony of the kingdom of Heaven.

All the religions of the world are built on this longing [and belief]. I am a believer. But then there are the children [guiltlessly tortured and murdered] and what am I to do about them? That is a question I cannot answer. . . . Listen! If all must suffer to pay for the eternal harmony, what have children to do with it, tell me, please? It is beyond all comprehension why they should suffer, and why they should pay for the harmony. Why should they, too, be turned into manure to enrich the soil for the harmony of the future? . . . And if it is really true that they must share responsibility for all their fathers' crimes, such a truth is not of this world and is beyond my comprehension. Some jester will say, perhaps, that the child would have grown up and have sinned, but you see he did not grow up; he was torn to pieces by the dog [as was described before by Ivan Karamazov]. . . . I am not blaspheming. I understand, of course, what an upheaval of the universe it will be, when everything in heaven and earth blends in one hymn of praise and everything that lives and has lived cries aloud: "Thou art just, O Lord, for Thy ways are revealed." When the mother embraces the fiend who threw her child to the dogs, and all three cry aloud with tears, "Thou are just, O Lord!" . . . But what pulls me here is that I can't accept that harmony. . . . And so I renounce the higher harmony altogether. It's not worth the tears of that one tortured child who beat itself on the breast with its little fist and prayed in its stinking outhouse, with its unexpiated tears to "dear, kind God!" It's not worth it, because those tears are unatoned for. They must be atoned for, or there can be no harmony. But how? Is it possible? By their being avenged? But what do I care for avenging them? What do I care for a hell for oppressors? What good can hell do, since those children have already been tortured? And what becomes of harmony, if there is hell? . . . I want to forgive. . . . I don't want more suffering. And if the sufferings of children go to swell the sum of sufferings which was necessary to pay for truth, then I protest that the truth is not worth such a price. . . . Too high a price is asked for harmony; it's beyond our means to pay so much to enter on it. And so I hasten to give back my entrance ticket into the Kingdom of God, and if I am an honest man, I am bound to give it back as soon as possible. And that I am doing. It's not God that I don't accept. . . . I only most respectfully return Him the ticket. . . . Imagine that you are creating a fabric of human destiny with the object of making men happy in the end, giving them peace and rest at last, but that it is essential and inevitable to torture to death only one tiny creature—that baby beating its breast with its fist, for instance—and to found that edifice on its unatoned tears, would you consent to be the architect on those conditions? Tell me, and tell the truth". . . . "No, I wouldn't consent," said Alyosha softly. "And can you admit the idea that men would agree to accept their happiness on the foundation of the unexpiated blood of a little victim? And accepting it would remain happy forever?" . . . "No, I can't admit it," said Alyosha.

This "rebellion" of Ivan Karamazov-Dostoievsky most poignantly sums up this great mystery of the "cosmic injustice" or of the inscrutability of the ways of Providence. With my finite mind I can neither solve this mystery nor brush it aside as something unimportant. It only reinforces my outlined notions about the free and grown-up position of man in the universe, about the noninterference of the superhuman creative centers into an autonomous man's management of mankind's life and destiny, and, at best, only a sporadic interference of the "Providential" forces into the human affairs.

III - IV - V

The preceding statements contain my answers to these three questions. Yes, my religious faith consists of the outlined conception of the ultimate reality in its differentiated aspects of truth, love, and beauty; and my notion of a truly religious life consists of a maximally-possible life for each individual and group, creative realization of these primordial values in the thoughts, words, and especially in the overt deeds in the total life of the persons and collectivities. Without such a realization of especially the goodness of an unselfish love, preached and practiced in regard to *all human beings*, and toward the ultimate reality itself, no religiosity is possible. If persons and groups are not animated by the values of truth, love, and beauty, and do not practice them at all, such individuals and collectivities are irreligious, no matter how regularly they perform religious rituals, how frequently they utter sacramental formulae, and how intensely they profess their religiosity.

Likewise, without these values no real democracy and no real freedom are possible, even when the nations have an elective system of government and various bills of inalienable rights. The highest formulae of the sublimest democracy are given in the Sermon on the Mount, and the best articles of the truly democratic constitution are formulated in the precepts of this Sermon and the Beatitudes. If a nation is not animated by creative living in truth, love, and beauty, and does not try to realize these values in its collective behavior, institutions, and culture, such a nation or group remains in a pre-barbaric state, having little in common with a true democracy. In such a sham democracy the inalienable rights of its members will be incessantly alienated, their freedom continuously violated, and each citizen will be a mere means, not the end-value for the other citizens and their government. In brief, such a nation, living in the darkness of pseudo-truth, hypocritical selfishness, and "polished ugliness," always is bound to be a sham democracy.

Such, in a rough outline, is my "integral religion." I realize its inadequacy. I do not claim any superiority for it over any and all the other religions. I do not even have any missionary zeal to convert to it followers. At the same time, it is the result of my humble observations, thoughts, experiences, and actions carried on for many years of my life. As such, this integral religion fairly well satisfies my needs, quests, and inquiries concerning the *mysterium tremendum and fascinosum*.

MARK STARR

As a boy Mark Starr was an English coal miner and became active in the British Labour Movement. In 1928 he entered the United States and taught at Brookwood Labour College. Since January 1935 he has been educational director of the International Ladies' Garment Workers' Union. A labor consultant of the Office of War Information in Britain (1943) and of SCAP in Japan (1946), a delegate to the UNESCO Conferences in London (1945) and in Denmark (1949), Mr. Starr has been a member of the executive board of the American Labor Education Committee and a vice-president of the American Federation of Teachers. Among his publications are: A Worker Looks at History *(1917);* Trade-Unionism, Past and Future *(1923);* Labor Looks at Education *(1946);* Labor and the American Way *(1952),* and *(co-author)* Labor in America *(1955).*

I

THE Judaeo-Christian religion, and particularly its ethics, has a tremendous value to men and women living in the twentieth century because it embodies the wisdom of the past centuries. However, in my own mind, the dogmas and doctrines are another matter. It is another case of whether the letter of the law does not kill the spirit. It would be foolish to ignore the changing content of past religions. The application of ethics must vary according to their economic context. Take for example the first ideas about usury and money lending as compared to their later adaptation; or the position of organized religion on chattel slavery.

At times, religion has been merely a reinforcement of the status quo, to the extent that it has jeopardized and delayed necessary social changes. The Judaeo-Christian ethic makes a necessary emphasis upon the integrity of the individual, but I think that this needs correlation with the unavoidable necessity of group activity and group responsibility in modern times. Of course this has been done, particularly in the Middle Ages, and it should not be forgotten in these days when collectivism in the hands of Hitler and Stalin discredited group action.

However, I think that it would be wrong to think that all ethical standards must come from the Judaeo-Christian source. I think that secularism can develop a very real and important code of ethics without any supernatural rewards or punishments. The Golden Rule is to be found in Confucius' teachings as well as in Western writers. If we knew Oriental cultures better we should probably find other similarities.

II

It seems to me that the only purpose which exists in regard to Nature is the purpose that human beings read into evolution. Human beings, as far as we know, are the only part of the universe in which such a purpose can become conscious of itself. G. G. Simpson defines man as "the most highly endowed organization of matter that has yet appeared on earth," with no reason to believe that the universe holds any higher. He had faith in the capacities of men and women to respond to good treatment, but he was no superficial Utopian.

Edmund Ware Sinnott's view of man is challenging:

. . . not as a sinful and degraded being, fallen from his previous high estate and needing to be redeemed, but as a noble animal who has struggled up the long evolutionary pathway to that exalted biological level where he can accumulate the experience of the past and thus become the heir of all the ages, moving on to heights of which he now hardly dreams. Science he sees as the bright sword of the mind, cleaving through ancient irrationalities, taboos, and dogmas that hinder the free sweep of his powers toward that more abundant life where the immense possibilities of man will come to full fruition.

Man develops a purpose and then applies science to the control of nature, which apparently can only be mastered if natural laws are understood. Of course, the process of understanding Nature is itself an infinite one, and no one can possibly foresee an absolute finish to the process of learning or investigation. The difficulty is that the power of science can be misused and perverted even to the extent of self-destruction, but one cannot have the possibilities of great power without the dangers of a corresponding greater misuse and abuse of such knowledge.

III

I think that many of us are not associated with the organized religions and their rival dogmas because we have found them unacceptable in an examination of history. We are outside such organizations, in many instances, after a conscientious attempt to reconcile ourselves to what proved to be illogical and irrational conclusions.

IV

It seems to me that the only spiritual reality is that created by men and women. I think that the evolutionary humanism that Julian Huxley has developed has a survival value because it creates faith in the possibilities of future progress. If men and women learn to cooperate with each other, that surely is the only way in which cosmic suicide can be avoided and the human race can go on to improve its methods. I think we can build up standards of progress without resort to what is usually called religion, in the sense of dependence upon some outside supernatural aid. Evolutionary humanism is a dynamic philosophy which makes possible conscious change.

We have to take this world as we find it and discover a middle way between Utopianism and despair. Indeed, if we did not smile in understanding pity at the frailities of ourselves and our fellow citizens, our hearts would break.

We must realistically accept the world as it is, and resolve to improve it. We must believe that there are great ideals in the mind of man beneath the current corrosions. The yellow crocus will emerge from beneath the ice and snow of winter. The seed of goodness will yet grow out of the deep mud, the encrustation of the ages.

Our working faith in humanity, moreover, will have to grow without authoritarian dogma or static creed; and without the support of a totalitarian authority, physical, or metaphysical. We shall have to cherish hope without illusions and develop love and affection among human beings without the promise of reward or of punishment from the old-time anthropomorphic gods in the old-time hell or heaven. "We need must love the highest when we see it." By thought and will, we rise "out of the earthy dust to finer things." Against the subway rush and the panic-stricken mob we can place the heroic sacrifice made in the mine disaster and the shipwreck. The mother, the nurse, and the doctor, with their devotion, run counter to the accepted normal laws of self-interest. When a Kathie Fiscus falls into a disused oil-well, men slave for days, regardless of expense, to rescue her.

V

The idea of an anthropomorphic God creates insuperable difficulties as a basis for belief. If you spell it *Good,* and in that generalization place all the endeavors and aspirations of human beings to apply the Golden Rule, then it has an essential purpose. The mind generalizes Good from many individual goods just as it conceives the One out of the Many. But both exist only in relation to each other and there is no need to separate them, and all the time there is growth and change arising from new experiences. This concept gives one a faith in the possibilities of improved existence based upon mutual aid and cooperation between men and women of good will throughout the world.

ORDWAY TEAD*

➤➤➤◄◄◄

Since 1925 Ordway Tead has been the editor of social and economic books published by Harper & Brothers. A graduate and Fellow of Amherst College, he became an industrial consultant, was in charge of war emergency employment management courses of the War Department at Columbia University (1916-18), and since 1920 has been lecturer and adjunct professor of personnel administration in that institution. For thirteen years Mr. Tead was chairman of the Board of Higher Education, New York City; he has been a member of the executive committee of the Institute of International Education, and a member of the National Commission for UNESCO. Mr. Tead's books include among others: Instincts in Industry *(1918);* Personnel Administration: Its Principles and Practice *(1920);* Human Nature and Management *(1929);* The Art of Leadership *(1935);* The Case for Democracy *(1937);* College Teaching and College Learning *(1949);* The Art of Administration *(1951);* Character Building and Higher Education *(1953).*

I

THE knowledge, the beliefs, and the insights of men about nature, themselves, and God are slowly but surely cumulative in history. There is a continuing spiritual tradition in the record of man.

* The structure of this paper, the sequence of its topics, the specific questions posed—all these are supplied in the editor's instructions. I have therefore confined myself within this prescribed frame. In order to achieve the desired brevity, I have made no attempt at documentation or citation or at quotation from numerous authorities whose knowledge and opinion are far more valuable than my own. What follows is in almost outline form a distillation of my own layman's expression of conviction and belief, deriving from a lifetime of unsystematized philosophical inquiry and genuine religious concern.

We in Western society think and feel, we love, aspire, and worship, on the shoulders of the past. Progressively greater depth and greater breadth of human insight into the beyond-human are acknowledged realities.

In my own sense of what are religious values, there can today be no denial of the essential spiritual and ethical truths embodied in the Hellenic-Judaeo-Christian religious and moral traditions. These values can be ignored and people can fail to be guided by them. But the great majority do not repudiate them; they seek to secure for them wider and deeper understanding and to achieve for them more adequate fulfillment.

How these values are stated and defined, how they may be deemed applicable to present personal and social problems, what wider and deeper reaches of meaning and ethical impact they may currently be found to have—all these are matters for study and action. The light of scientific knowledge, the progressively richer insights or "revelations" of prophets and seers, the social experience with more complex civilizations—all will help us to relate the perennial truths to the improvement of the contemporary scene. For related they have to be in some effectual way if religious motives are to be kept influential in elevating the life of man toward God.

The historic values of this tradition are quickly recited in abstract words, however difficult the interpretation of those words into today's significance may prove to be.

We of Western civilization still hold as of the highest order of human value the roles of love, friendship, fellowship, brotherly kindliness, human compassion, and mercy. We continue to place high value upon rational truth-seeking—as in natural science and in human relations. We cherish all efforts to appreciate and to create beauty. We hold justice high, and prize truthfulness, honor, and honesty. We believe that in and through productive work of all kinds, rationally and affectionally interpreted, there can come about the significant creative social contribution of each person.

All this means also that religiously, no less than socially, we have to place a high importance upon each individual's sense of personal responsibility, both for his own best fulfillment and for his maximum social contribution.

We find high value in the importance of occasional withdrawal, in periods of meditation, contemplation, and worship.

We believe that in the moral choices of life requiring us to select paths of action where conflicts will normally arise among our values and aspirations, there has to be, as a religious value, a sense of proportion, of balance, of humor, and of basic *joie de vivre,* as a guide to choices in individual experience.

The religious tradition also calls for a belief in "God." This is not deemed to be "provable"; rather it may be reverently held in faith. It has to be recognized, of course, that human expressions of the nature of God and of the relation of God to man and nature are manifold. They have changed, grown, and deepened in the historic unfolding of human insights.

All of the above outlooks are to be achieved in naturalist terms. They can be apprehended within the frame of a world interpreted in terms of natural laws and processes. This leads to a consideration of what meaning one gives to such a phrase as "natural laws and processes" and leads thus, too, to a consideration of whether such a phrase as "cosmic reality" has human meaning and validity.

II

I have an unqualified sense of being confronted with mystery, awe, and wonder in any effort to view or to speak sincerely about "cosmic reality."

I take the view that there is a defensible balance between rational evidence and something acknowledged and deeply felt beyond reason, that one is explicitly prepared to accept as the result of "the leap of faith." By this is meant the readiness (not irrational) to make certain affirmations beyond objectively provable evidence. Here, too, the individual may feel some experience of inner assurance and confidence that his faith makes sense and reassures him in some inexplicable and ineffable way in his relation to the cosmos.

I believe we have every right to read a progressively richer and fuller meaning into the historic phrase, "natural law." "Natural law" relates beyond "nature" to all that we seek to discern in our understanding of man and of his cosmic world. The documentation here in the writings of the wisest scientists and scholars in recent years is tremendously impressive.

By the phrase "natural law," I mean to suggest the assumption of an orderliness and uniformity of process and outcome. It has, also, purposive intention and direction in its own essence as law. It comprises a recognition of forces at work, of directions of emerging human tendency, of creative implications, all of which seem fraught with a significance and power beyond themselves, looking to results, or culminations and justifications beyond their own processes.

The more we understand of nature and of man, the more we are willing to reinterpret with richer and contemporary discernment Kant's phrase as to the wonders of the starry firmament above and of the moral law within.

There is evidence, progressively discernible, that whether it be the stars, the atoms, or human beings, their conduct is to be understood in terms of orderliness and lawfulness, which assume order, organic unity, and uniformity in the nature of things.

A science of man as part of such assumed lawfulness is of course as yet only fragmentary. But the assumption seems rationally justifiable that the conduct of the "objective" world and of the "subjective" world is eventually to be comprehended in terms of expressed and tested natural laws. Indeed, such language as to two kinds of world and experience is a crude expression of a duality which is unreal. Rather the law of wholesome and happy human conduct is infinitely more difficult to discern and apply. And in this situation while the laws of nature's process are descriptive from one angle, they become also definitive of desirable and necessary standards for human behavior.

One of the mandates upon human beings is surely the continuing study, scientifically and by every other avenue of discernment, of man and nature or cosmic reality looking toward a fuller and more truthful statement of the laws under which this interrelated world operates.

With our innately required effort toward fuller understanding and fuller obedience to natural law, our problems of ethics and indeed of the acknowledgment of God imply that the Law itself, its making, and its meaning, partake of the processes of God. They seem to me to imply a *God-ordered* cosmic and human reality.

If something like this is true, the problems that may be humanly interpreted as the "indifference of nature" are, in all humility, aspects of a situation set in motion by a Divine ordering of affairs which human beings can only dimly understand and are not rationally required to justify or even necessarily comprehend in our own human terms.

The natural law as it applies to our understanding of men comprises by definition the reality of freedom of choice, of creative manipulation by man of all his experience toward more helpful and more happy ways. All this seems also to be descriptive of what we actually experience in the world.

Cause and effect in the unfolding of human conduct may thus be viewed in one of two ways. They may be used to explain what *has* happened; or they may be more dynamically and organically viewed as the grasp of an intrinsic quality in the natural law toward form, toward order, direction, and purposiveness, all of which are integral influences toward the limited freedom we enjoy.

Human freedom has obviously to be understood and accepted as a *limited* one—limited in various ways by factors of heredity, environment, education, and the like. But whether human beings act more or less lawfully, this is to some degree a choice they are truly free to make. It seems to be that kind of a world in which the effort to bring conduct into line with what we can dimly but progressively sense as God's purpose and law can only be realized as man chooses to collaborate in the process. It is an unfinished world. God and man are still creating and being created. The "perfection of God" (whatever that may mean) is not to be attained without the creative effort and participation of men. God and man work together toward the transcendence of the human toward the divine intention.

III

The ways and means by which men associate themselves and order their lives to assure greater happiness of selves in communities would desirably be such as would enable the largest possible number of human beings to grow, mature, express, and realize themselves in fullest harmony with their natures.

What would seem required of human beings for their own best good and for their own highest satisfaction is thus becoming known. It is required that as selves they be creative, be individually responsible in all necessary social relationships; be to some degree individually autonomous, be generously loving and compassionate, and structure their organized life in its institutional phases in order to help all these valuable personal attributes to become progressively supported and reinforced by the total environment.

If this is what the fulfillment of the nature of man implies and entails in psychological idiom, it means in a *political* idiom that men have to build their relations together in government, work, play, home, and worship, in self-determined ways that help to assure this self-fulfillment. These ways and methods are what we call *democratic* ways and methods. Historically, democratic ways seek the cultivation of precisely those personal qualities and social relations which assure the finest selfhood as psychologically and spiritually corroborated and defined. Democratic methods are by definition those which provide responsible, shared, and equal participation of people in ordering their lives in such ways as to yield maximum individual and common satisfactions of a quality that transcends the trivial and selfish.

A science of man is increasingly trying to say that the conditions of a good life for man are those which are at the same time democratically organized and controlled in the broad direction and pattern that our own American society strives to realize. All we know about the fulfillment of the nature of men seems to offer support to the view that democratic methods of conducting human affairs are those which are morally defensible ones.

The mandate to strive to achieve personality or socially effective selfhood under lawful processes seems to me absolute. The democratic processes and relationships looking to this end require, however, continuing rational inventiveness and intuitive creative ingenuity. There is no absolute pattern of *method* here, only an absolute purpose and required experimental attitude. All individuals, groups, and societies have progressively to find out how democratic relationships can best further the absolute search for that combination of selfhood and selflessness (or self-transcendence) which a science of man indicates to be our destiny.

Indeed, in one sense, human history can be interpreted as the record of the extension in society of the actualizing in ever-widening circles of democratic institutions designed to foster better selves for all.

The facts of autocracies, denials of democratic ideas, of mistakes and back-slidings—all these are inevitable aspects of the slow growth of humanity toward a natural, democratic self-awareness and governance. Tyranny has in the long historic look been self-defeating. Yet democratic structuring to the end of fulfilling the natural law as it relates to personality will require, as it always has, "eternal vigilance" as the price of the noblest freedom.

There has also in history been found to be an explicit causal relationship between the possible realization of democratic values and the economic and cultural background of any given community. In brief, democracy requires for its best nurture an institutional setting of economic adequacy. There has to be the persistent effort to remove such obstacles as poverty, landlordism, corruption, illiteracy, and religious authoritarianism.

In this important sense the mundane values essential in the realizing of democracy are organically related to an understanding of the unity of spiritual reality.

IV

It is thus my belief that "the supreme values available to moral man, of whatever source" (see editor's memorandum) are indeed aspects of *one* spiritual reality.

In the profound and permeative sense in which I accept the idea of natural law as at once descriptive and value-defining, it would seem that the religious effort becomes one effort toward understanding and conforming to natural law. There has to be a persistent effort of discovery and disclosure of truth and law in which the fraternal ordering of human affairs is one-half the purpose, and the other half is the progressive mastery of so-called material nature.

Both of these efforts are supremely important, valuable, and imperative. They are two aspects of the *same* organic process. Within himself, within his societies, and in relation to the natural world, man is trying in a unified way to obey the Law. He is trying to understand and implement the Divine. He is striving to attain his noblest selfhood with its paradoxical and transcendent selflessness. He is trying to sanctify himself. He is trying to make himself holy. He is trying to become a co-worker with God in the improved conduct of that small segment of an unfinished universe of which he has experience and within which he has creative power.

In this human career and exploration toward Lawfulness and Love, seen as two aspects of one reality and accepted in faith by virtue of man's extraordinary boldness of imagination, confidence, and courage, it goes without saying that man does not possess (indeed is never likely to possess) all the answers. Humans are fatuous indeed if they expect to attain to any fullness of knowledge of the nature of God. Yet affirmation of a *faith* in God becomes a defensible, a rationally acceptable, and a daring effort and aspiration of humanity, despite every recognition of tragedy and sin. For men become aware of enough knowledge to be heartened and to be led on to more. Somehow there comes reality of corroborative meaning for sensitive souls in the phrase "The Spirit beareth witness with our spirits."

In a variety of ways toward understanding, it seems to me we are truly able to say, "Center and soul of every sphere, yet to each loving heart how near."

We are brought thus to the final question about the idea or ideas of God.

V

I realize my presumption in undertaking on this point any formulation whatever. I do it with humility, while also realizing the historic inevitability of the human effort to attempt some expression on this score. I should perhaps start, therefore, with the statement of the unknowability of God. "I am that I am." Yet certain deeply-sensed things seem true and in conformity to a reality which we dimly but truly sense.

This which we dimly sense seems to have its own dialectic in which opposing truths are embraced and in which paradoxes have inevitably to be accepted. One is here in an area which transcends man's traditional logic—even though it does not require that he abandon his inherent and passionate desire and mandate to be rational. He finds that different aspects of what seems to him as true *complement* each other, even though the one seems logically to negate the other. There is the deeper truth of what one philosopher has called "the fecundity of contradictions."

For example, God would seem to be Law. And God works through Law, and God is a Law Creator.

God would seem to be in some insights impersonal, the Ground of our being, the mysterious Force animating the processes of nature and human life. Yet there is no reason (in a divine logic) why this idea cannot be held, while in some other mood one speaks of God and strives to approach Him in personal terms, and is confident of the possibility of a personal relation of human beings to a loving God as his "children." The great historic expression of the "Fatherhood of God" gives voice to this aspect, this yearning, and presumably this truth.

In our tradition we are familiar with such phrases as a just God, a righteous God, a merciful God, and a loving God. These and others are all feeble attempts at attributing qualities admired by human beings to the "I am" in the universe that humans, without provable knowledge, are willing to hold as truth through the "will to believe" plus some effort to interpret history and nature.

Again, in another sense, God is to be understood as a Creative Process, needing and requiring the moral and spiritual effort of mankind to actuate Him. Thus, paradoxically, God is to us at once complete and incomplete. And man's career is toward his own and God's actualization.

The aspect of incompleteness calls into focus the importance of seeing certain historic ideas in this frame of reference. Hence we find in the historic religions such ideas as those of incarnation, revelation, sin, salvation, redemption, atonement, and immortality. The realities of the human spirit's real concern as suggested by these words (as well as others in the traditional Judaeo-Christian theologies) require to be redefined in their contemporary orientation.

My own idea of God thus sees Him as working in and through the processes of nature (animate and inanimate) and the aspiring conduct of human persons as a part thereof. The working of forces which we may metaphorically speak of as *upward* is thus the working of forces active or immanent in the world, that are struggling to emerge and transcend the sheer "material" process toward the fulfillment of the Divine. In actuality, the two are conjoined as two ways of looking at the unified, ongoing process.

If the whole process of human living is thus deemed to be the mysterious will of God, then it is in this frame that we find the rationale of our religion. And all of this, necessarily, helps to illuminate the nature of each man's moral and ethical responsibility. It helps also to make clear and helpful a feeling for and relation to ultimate and unified spiritual reality which can give an encouraging sense of support to the human aspiration. Also it can be regarded by men as the *seat of authority* for the human effort to fulfill God's purposes.

One would like to be as clear as possible on how man may get support from beyond himself and some guidance on behalf of the enterprise of living.

Guidance *is* possible toward wisdom and loving relations—in short, toward God. This guidance derives from the experience of disinterested love, from scientific knowledge, from experiment, progressive discernment and insight, from the corroborative shared feeling of like-spirited individuals that some specific experience of values has been good. All these can bring the feeling of a supporting morale as it derives from others of like mind and heart and includes, also, all that is to be learned through history from scientists, prophets, saviors, and artist-creators in all the great expressions of human aspiration in all religions and all cultures.

The heartening sense of being upheld in good purpose from God to man is further found in man's feeling of resonance within his own spirit, in a certain impulsion and subtle awareness that in and through the processes of living, learning, and aspiring there does in all honesty come to the individual the sense that creative effort has a real creative result; and that as one labors upon human problems in fact and in faith, the total experience is buttressed by a heartening corroborative aura of being undergirded.

In this relationship and aspiration a contemporary understanding of *prayer* is found. Prayer becomes the expressed and conscious affirmation of desire to know and to do the will of God—to be experientially "at one."

Several further insights about the human self or spirit are here implicit. They serve, for example, to suggest the relation of the religious life in its purity to the educational effort at its noblest. For these two are fundamentally inseparable.

The human self is comprised of *more* than factual knowledge ever reveals as to its nature and promise.

The human spirit is rallied toward its highest selfhood by realization not only of its inherently social and fraternal nature, but also of its potential relation to an all-encompassing Self in which it somehow shares—in which it lives and moves and has its being.

There is in this relationship an "unconditional imperative" (Jaspers) upon each human self to realize through his own creativity and his own loving relations with his fellows the best in conduct and in an internal "reverential serenity," which it may share. This "best in conduct" is discerned, as I have said, through progressive human search and understanding of the laws of our being and of the cosmos. The role of education is crucial and integral here; and ignorance partakes of vice and stultification, as Whitehead has repeatedly affirmed.

The good, the valuable, and the holy are thus discoverable in human experience through the continuing interplay of reason, reverent obedience to lawfulness, intelligently guided expressions of love, and the adventure of faith. And all this is possible because the nature of man as organically related to life—his deepest needs, desires, and satisfactions—come to be more fully, if never completely, comprehended.

The human self has—within acknowledged limits—its own freedom as to its choices in life. But as a part of this sufficient freedom goes an intrinsically *absolute summons* to choose freely the good and the valuable as fully as each self can discover and pursue these.

To inform and reinforce this crucial human freedom and to give rational and enlightened undergirding of emotive and rational support to that absolute summons—these become imperatives upon education as well as upon religion.

Basically, a good education and a high and purified religion are united in their purpose and effort to release the self from ignorance and to guide the self to achieve its actualization at that highest level which will hopefully mean an inspiriting relation with a divine Self. These two—religion and education—have complementary roles in their guidance and support to the God-committed life.

A qualifying word, however, is needed. The simple heart and humble mind may in their measure have, equally or even more, obeyed the injunction implied in "unless ye become as little children" in respect to their way of life. Nevertheless, in contemporary Western society today the values of simplicity have of necessity to be reinforced by the now more urgent value of a scientifically motivated and sophisticated awareness of realities interpreted by love. To live in our civilization is, in short, a *difficult* emotional and deliberative experience.

The seat of authority for man's categorical imperative, as well as the vivid awareness of a sense of being upheld from sources of power beyond himself—these cannot derive from natural and mundane man as *materially* viewed. Rather they are to be apprehended from our knowledge of the *nature* of man and our awareness of the quality and character of his selfhood as it strives to partake of the divine. For his selfhood is organically composite of his natural and his transcendent or suprahuman self comprising all the forces intrinsic to his nature driving toward creative achievement and toward integrating more harmoniously the natural and the spiritual. It is this conjunction which appears to be what is ordained in the onward process of that Being beyond the human who has ordained that life should be.

Not man, the evidence seems clear, but a God of law, order, and love ordains and rules the world. And He asks and requires for man's fulfillment that man freely take up his cross (in symbolic language) and follow Him.

To do justice, to love mercy, to walk humbly with our God—this ancient counsel has to be redeemed to contemporary significance and relevance.

For man does not live of, for, or by man alone.

In conclusion, my text does not intend to be a statement to arouse disagreement; it is not one of denial but of fulfillment. It is an effort to reconcile a great tradition with a still greater spiritual unfolding which impends.

I have tried to make an honest statement of intellectual and spiritual conviction. Yet there obtrudes the disturbing thought: can one expect others to be helped and supported toward moral and spiritual affirmation by such an utterance as this—necessarily abstract and lacking in persuasive appeal as it may sound?

My answer has to be this: one listens to the voice which one hears.

One takes the direction of the logic of thought, feeling, and experience which the years have brought. I have thus to make my own affirmation, my own "yea saying."

One would hope to be counted among the "so great a cloud of witnesses," while believing it necessary to join with those others who seek always greater coherence of expression through an approach and a language consonant with contemporary outlooks upon Process and Reality, upon Being and Becoming.

ROBERT ULICH*

Robert Ulich was born in Germany and educated at the universities of Freiburg, Neufchatel, Munich, Berlin, and Leipzig. He became counselor in the Saxon Ministry of Education (1921-23) and was in charge of Saxon universities for the next ten years, as well as an honorary professor of philosophy at the Dresden Institute of Technology. He entered the United States in 1934 and since then has been a professor of education at Harvard University. Dr. Ulich holds membership in the American Academy of Arts and Sciences, the Mediaeval Academy of America, and the Conference on Science, Philosophy and Religion. He has written a number of books including Fundamentals of Democratic Education *(1940);* History of Educational Thought *(1945); and* The Human Career: A Philosophy of Self-Transcendence *(1955).*

I

IT WAS and still is the underlying philosophy of our "liberal" or "humanist" education, or the French *"culture générale,"* or the German *"Allgemeinbildung,"* that a person becomes the richer the more he assimilates the intellectual and moral values which have emerged in the history of our civilization. As it does physically, so also mentally the growth of the individual should reflect the historical development of the race. As a living and constantly self-molding art work, the educated man should have the depth of tradition in order to view with a mature mind the tasks of the future.

Since the Renaissance this humanist ideal has formed our best

* The reader will note that the subdivisions of Mr. Ulich's essay do not follow the five questions proposed in the inquiry.

minds. Aristocratic in nature, and unattainable to the majority of toiling men, it has nevertheless provided the vision of greatness. Amidst the increase of mass standards it still prevents us from complacently sinking down into the bog of mediocrity. Thus, even from a pragmatic point of view it has worked well. Yet, though our modern civilization has freed an increasing number of people from exhausting labor and provided unheard of chances for learning, the humanist concept of education has lost in attraction, even among the intellectually capable. We still profess it in our colleges, we create ever new institutions and devices to strengthen it, but the tautness of the effort reveals the inner weakness. The faith that motivated earlier generations, the banner that led them into the battlefields of spiritual, intellectual, and social progress, the sense of hierarchy that lifted the cultured man's aspirations above the crowd all seem to be lowered. The liberal ideal is on the defensive, and in many of our humanist departments there is a hospital atmosphere, with teachers behaving like physicians around an important patient, constantly concerned, never really assured of victory.

This, however, is not merely an academic affair but of immense practicality, for—paradoxical though it may sound in our mass culture —the humanist ideal of the unique worth of the person and his obligation to strive for ever higher forms of self-realization is one of the constituent elements of modern democracy. The two are bound together in life and death. And in the tendency of humanism to extend the values of a good life toward ever-wider groups of mankind lies also the origin of modern public education. *La combinaison de l'humanisme et du christianisme*—so says André Maurois in his *Histoire de la France* (p. 133)—*constituera la civilisation occidentale.*

II

Where then, we may ask, are the causes of humanism's decline? They have been explained in too many books to need more than quick mention.

1. The technological temper likes to measure things in money and quantity rather than in quality. It looks for quick results; the investment must soon pay off. But the humanist ideal, like good wine, demands patience.

2. The cruelties and sacrifices of two world wars have eventually left every nation in a state of defeat. One of our modern catchwords is "anxiety," whereas the liberal-humanist concept of man is essentially optimistic. Hence anti-humanist, anti-democratic, and obscurantist tendencies emerge everywhere, even under the cloak of liberty and patriotism.

3. All great nations have handled cynically the most fundamental principles of justice on which the self-respect of man depends—in spite of the increase in what Dean James A. Pike has called "official piety." After criticizing the willingness of military groups in our country to bargain the American heritage of religious freedom for air bases in Spain, he refers to the recent vote in the United Nations General Assembly on a resolution for the continuance of a commission to study apartheid (race separation) policies of the Government of the Union of South Africa and continues:

The Christian principles at stake were defended by votes of the Communistic countries and of the Moslem countries, while not one leading Christian country was found to support the resolution. . . . We leave it to atheistic materialists and to Moslems to sustain the Christian principle of the equality of all men regardless of race or color, whereas we —with all our burgeoning religiosity—do all we can to impede the proclamation of this principle, presumably because of some short-range advantage in our diplomatic relations with the Union of South Africa.[1]

4. Modern mass education increases the distribution of knowledge over ever-larger parts of the population, many of which are not interested in its depth and responsibility, but merely in its usefulness. It also increases the indulgence in criticism without increasing the appreciation for the struggles and difficulties in real creativeness.

5. The relativization of the values on which the older humanistic tradition was built has been fostered also by the impact of scientific and historical methods on the discussion of human problems. Science has changed our picture of nature and its laws, history our picture of man and his values; the human universe has started wobbling and we do not know where it will land—in a new world or in disaster.

Yet, some of the factors which we blame for the crisis of humane

[1] Taken from *The New York Times,* Monday, Dec. 27, 1954.

values could also have been promoters of civilization. When used in the right spirit, they actually have been so.

Technology has increased our health and welfare beyond all previous standards. Whatever one may think about the political game of the first World War, the second, at least, has freed mankind from a devilish offender of human rights; and our international politics, vacillating though it is, nevertheless struggles desperately for peace. Modern mass education has liberated men from serfdom and peonage and opened to them unimagined vistas of experience. Finally, the one-sided use of science should not deceive us over the fact that it has delivered and will still deliver us not only from physical ills but also from old fears and superstitions. False hopes in the omnipotence of science have already undergone a self-corrective process to which —in contrast to theological dogmatism—true science always feels obligated.

If the humanist tradition had been strong enough, it could have used all these ambivalent factors for its own advantage. Hence, we must not always look for external enemies, but search for the enemy within. And the enemy within, or the weakness which does not allow the humanist-liberal tradition to meet the challenge of our time, lies in its lack of commitment, or its superficiality. It has forgotten its own dual roots and the eternal challenge that lies in this duality.

III

As a boy who received a classical-humanist education in the schools of Europe, I was only dimly aware of the discrepancy in our religious and our classical, or as it was called, "humanist," education. Somehow we all realized that the teachers of religion lived in the lesser suburbs of the academic city, respectfully tolerated but nevertheless peripheral. We suspected that some of them had escaped the strain of speaking from the pulpit only to fall into the hands of juvenile rascals eager to compensate for the strength of school discipline by maltreating their weaker teachers. When they were older, we also felt that some of them preferred to teach in a secular institution rather than to profess religion in a sacred profession; they no longer believed in the Christian dogma. And these, of course, we respected highly. With its whole air of superiority the humanist spirit expressed itself when, before reading the Letters of St. Paul in the original, we were warned not to imitate his language. St. Paul did not live up to the standards of classical Greek, as St. Augustine offended the classical rules of Latin grammar. His *City of God* was never mentioned.

Later on I discovered that the situation in the schools signified a deep split in our Western civilization. With few glorious exceptions, it never has taken Christianity seriously—at least not among those who were destined to rule and not simply to obey. Nor did our civilization take Greek-Roman Antiquity seriously. The English gentlemen of the seventeenth and eighteenth centuries rarely, if ever, mentioned Christ in their educational writings (see Chesterfield and Shaftesbury) and though they were perhaps more Roman than anyone else, they called the ancient studies merely "ornamental." Either one, Christianity or Antiquity, was used to take the sharp edges off the other. In the schools of the young aristocrats Plato's dialogues and Cicero's philosophical writings were read with the same devotion as Christ's Sermon on the Mount, though the two do not belong together. And while one memorized large parts of the Letters of St. Paul, Plutarch's *Parallel Lives* offered the real examples of great living and effective ruling. Philosophically, the compromise between Christian transcendentalism and pagan worldliness began early; it was the requisite for the Emperor Constantine's peace with the Church in the fourth century. And, if Christ came back and read the canonic work of Catholic theology, the *Summa* of Thomas Aquinas, he would shake his head in amazement—after all, he did not study the Greeks and thus knew nothing about Aristotle, whom Thomas calls "the teacher." Nor would He understand our modern theologians, Protestant and Catholic.

But perhaps Christ might understand Nietzsche, for in the latter the conflict between the two contrasting cultures, the Greek-Roman and the Judaeo-Christian, erupted in utter violence.

Much more than the professors who happily preach to their students ancient philosophy and at the same time want them to be nice and untroubled Christians, Nietzsche has fathomed the profound contest that the Gospel has brought into our history. Since then, Western man has had a restless conscience. He admires the founders of the great empires of might and mind; he would like to have lived in the

Renaissance of the Medici; and he hates surrender, perhaps even to God. But he would also like to be with Christ's disciples, or with St. Francis of Assisi.

Yet, despite all contrast, the spirit of Greece and Rome and the spirit of Israel cannot drive each other out of the life of mankind. Both signify the desire of human nature to express its final depth and destiny, though aiming toward contrasting goals: one toward self-assertion and the autonomy of human reason, the other toward humility and love.

IV

Thus, the humanist ideal and our whole liberal civilization and education live in tension. The present crisis is not that there are so many seeds of conflict (human existence is always conflictful, or it is sterile) but that we have forgotten about it. More and more we have lost contact with the roots from which our specific form of civilization arose. We play around with pagan Antiquity, as we play around with Christianity. We have even no longer a feeling of compromise (which, if not too complacent, leaves a sense of the unattained and thus serves as a challenge to conscience). Rather we have convention that eats on itself and consequently is in danger of withering away. There is too much knowledge, and too little excitement.

One learns Latin in school because it is still required; the Greek originals stand dusty on the shelves of our libraries. The ancients no longer inspire in us a mode of living. And something similar happens in our religious classes, our Bible departments, and even our Divinity Schools. Antiquarian research spreads toward all sides. One excavates forgotten cities (almost the only historical activity which besides the atom bomb "gets the headlines") and one unearths so many unknown treasures of art that a Michelangelo or a Johann Joachim Winckelmann would tremble in excitement. But the momentum comes more from the self-expanding nature of scholarship than from the soul's search for sources of old wisdom and beauty.

V

Yet, since man cannot stop being interested in himself, a new way of investigation has now been opened. It no longer remains within the orbit of the old "humanities" or "humaniora," but prefers to acquire respectability as another form of "science." Thus we have now a new territory on our intellectual map, called "The Social Sciences." No doubt it attracts our students much more than the old liberal studies. These students not only believe that by attending classes in clinical psychology, sociology, statistics, and anthropology, they find better "jobs," for intellectual preferences are contingent upon the chance for occupation; they also believe that the new disciplines of thought explain man, his nature, and his society better than philosophy, history, philology, and theology. There are now even philosophy departments which, a bit ashamed of their old dwellings, scramble desperately for a minor place of farmland along the new frontiers.

But if we view with distress the neglect of the older humanities, let us not blame our youth. They are still looking for that which once they looked for in the humanities: explanations for the great actions and decisions of man, his ways of conduct, his virtues and vices, his profound conflicts, and his rare victories. Often they found nothing but smugness, even snobbishness, or a thick crust of learned words too hard for the untrained mind to pierce. So, they go somewhere else.

Yet I do not believe that the salvation lies in the new sciences. There are exceptional men in them with a fine sense for the connection of the actual with its unseen background. But especially the younger writers reveal a kind of agoraphobia in regard to any philosophical speculation, even if needed for the explanation of the premises and results of their own investigation. To be sure, in recent times the problem of "values" has attracted more and more interest (probably as reflection of the general anxiety that we may be torn off our moral anchorage), but the discussion is circular. On the one hand, one emphasizes the necessity of values for the survival of a civilization; on the other hand, one explains them merely as "environmental," as results of "conditioning," as "patterns," or as "habits," in other words as phenomena of merely horizontal nature. But if they are nothing but that, they may just as well be respected or disrespected, preserved or changed, sanctioned or smilingly tolerated as "myths": they no longer serve as permanent criteria. Men may then change their loyalties according to the direction of the wind (as they mostly do anyhow), or wait for the dictator or the "social engineer" to tell them what to do.[2]

Because the time has been too short to observe the results, it has not yet been recognized that the new, so-called "empirical" and "environmental" approach to the problems of man—despite its claim to be progressive—carries with it the danger of stagnation. For in explaining man's intuitions and aspirations as dependent upon the environment, it makes the environment the master of man instead of making man the master within his environment. The whole doctrine is much more fitting to a totalitarian state and its practices than to a democracy. May the irrational hysteria which mingles into our defense against communism be due to the loss of vitality in our own traditions and convictions? If the humanities have failed, so also neither the natural nor the social sciences can pull us out of the predicament, but only a comprehensive faith. Unless we somehow acquire it, we may, as already has been said by great historians, be in a situation similar to that of the decline of Antiquity, with the great emperors Marcus Aurelius and Julianus trying in vain to save the old tradition. But the emerging new would certainly not be Christianity, but the loss of individualism in a mechanized culture.

VI

At this juncture in our thinking we may dare a conclusion which will put into proper proportion all that we have said so far. I believe that the comparison of our time with the end of Rome is false. We do not suffer from a lack of new ideas as did the ancient world. Our problem is not one of dearth, but of bewildering wealth that needs to be put into proper order. We are not the *old* rich like the Roman aristocrats, but the *nouveau riche* or *parvenu*—and we behave accordingly.

We could not push aside the new experimental sciences of man and his society even if we wished to do so. Juvenile though they may sometimes be, they have arisen from our desire to come to grips with our personal and social problems. But they cannot live on their own

[2] See the excellent analysis of the psychology of the "conditioned reflex" in the recent book by J. W. Krutch, *The Measure of Man* (Indianapolis: Bobbs-Merrill Company, Inc., 1954).

soil; it is too thin to provide the theoretical basis for cultural survival. If we delude ourselves about this, severe harm may be done. It has already.

For their own self-understanding the social sciences need the long tradition of the humanities, including theology. On the other hand, the humanities need the refreshing stimulus of the social sciences to answer more effectively the questions of modern man.

But where, then, can be found the meeting ground between the two? If things go on as they have so far, the fence of separation will grow. At the same time the departmental cleavages to which our youth are already exposed will become increasingly forbidding. Yet there can be an understanding between the various camps, provided they do not cling to the extremes of dogmatism. The hope lies in the fact that both the older humaniora as well as the new social sciences represent, in essence, the same interest, namely the study of the human being. Though the thread is bent, it is not broken, and one can still wander from one end to the other, if one interprets man as an ever self-transcending being, reaching in thought and action horizontally along his natural environment and his contemporary society (the social sciences), and vertically into his history and the deeper grounds of all existence (the humanities).

This concept of self-transcendence has nothing mystical about it. It must not be confused with transcendentalism. Not even the most rabid empirical scientist would deny that man does not live on himself, but on an embracing and permeating force that he may call "Energy" or "Life" or "The Cosmos." The surgeon knows that his knowledge and his hands are helpless when this mysterious force refuses to re-enter into an anesthetized body. There is no piece of so-called matter that could be explained only in relation to itself. Birth, growth, sickness, age, and death are witness of the greater order. On the other hand, also, the true humanist's data are witness of man's self-transcendence: "mind" and "soul" (whatever these symbolic terms may indicate), tendencies and systems of thought, heroic deeds, and dismal failures. The more developed the individual and the more advanced the culture the larger also is the span of self-transcendence, from the life in the primitive tribe to the life of scholars and explorers in a modern university.

In every important act man transcends himself. In disciplined thinking he reaches into a world he may never fully understand (for how can he know that human reason is capable of comprehending the nature of reality?). But he may well assume that the inner order, which is the characteristic of sound logic, somehow reflects an underlying Logos, and that every forward step in systematic search opens a further door to Truth (though the last door may never yield). The greater the artist, the farther wanders his forming imagination into the heights and abysses of nature and man. The greater the ethical act a person performs, the more he leaves behind himself habit and convention and all similar categories of the social scientist, in order to achieve unity between his self and the commandment that speaks through his conscience. The better a man's education, the less adequate become such concepts as "training" and "instruction." There may even be relatively little instruction. That which counts is a person's ability to grow with the tasks and responsibilities he has set for himself.

In the religious experience man's self-transcendence achieves its highest stage in the reverential recognition of his "being within" a spending Order, the gifts of which he should not wilfully destroy, but acknowledge through devoted and grateful living. The more man advances in these diverse modes, the more he acquires freedom; freedom to be interpreted as the victory over the narrow and fortuitous and the gradual self-identification with the universal. Freedom is the opportunity to be greater than one's ego; it is the soul's dialogue with its better future. If creeping self-love is on the negative end of the scale, man's communion with the ideal is on the other. The result of this outgoing living is the certainty of the interconnection of all things living, not only because they are causally related to each other in space and time but because they all come from the same ground of reality. What I do I do not only unto me but I do unto all.

Under this aspect one acquires not merely "tolerance" for that which is different. There may even be situations where tolerance is not a virtue but a vice. Rather one acquires an appreciation of hierarchy, or of the difference between the essential and the unessential, the important and the unimportant.

VII

To return, then, to the beginning of our discussion, I would call a humanist, or liberal, education one which awakens in a person the desire of continual self-transcendence—even if he has never heard of the term—or, simply speaking, the desire never to get stuck where he is "anyhow," but to make his own the great impulses in the intellectual, ethical, and aesthetic unfolding of mankind's experience. Everything, then, becomes transparent to a deeper reality. There is always the metaphysical behind the physical, and a further commitment behind every action. The old perturbing difference between the "relative" and the "absolute" disappears. For everything that man does and knows is relative because of his inborn limitations, but it is relative within and toward an embracing ultimate, and though finiteness is everywhere, there is also the infinite. The great religions, which so far have often divided humanity, can become bonds, because the differences fall into proper order, while the inner unity appears like sunlight behind dawn. One can be a Jew or a Christian and believe that God reveals himself in the Torah or in Christ; yet, one can also understand a Buddhist to whom God speaks through the language of Buddha. The different rituals will not carelessly be pushed aside, for they represent the forms by which members of a group communicate with each other under the roof of the divine. But the differences in cult and language cannot overshadow the unity in aspiration. And there will always be a continuous struggle between the worship that leads the community of men above, and the superstition that holds them down in the arrogance of magical exclusiveness.

Also, the diverse academic "schools of thought"—let us call them "Isms"—will lose their false pretensions. It is for example, a dismal picture to see, in the field of psychology, analytical and empirical, introspective and behaviorist doctrines as well as different learning theories fight within and against each other when, with more perspective, each of them could learn from the other approach. We have philosophy departments that almost appear intended to destroy themselves from within by setting the diversity of schools above the philosophical spirit. In the meantime, the schools of education seem to collect at random the good and bad fruits from all adjacent fields and to neglect in the process the building up of criteria as to what to accept and what to refuse. What we need in our schools of education is not a dominating or all-uniting philosophy which—in our pluralistic society—would only create an unreal uniformity. The one-sided acceptance and interpretation of Dewey's pragmatism has done enough harm and should not be replaced by another dogmatism, even if it claims divine sanction. More perhaps than anywhere else, we need in the preparation of our future teachers a profound interpretation of man. We may use experiments with rats for whatever can be learned from them. But whatever the similarity between animals and men, there remains the essential difference that with an animal, however intelligent, I cannot discuss concepts, I cannot evaluate its past and its future; in other words, I cannot live with him in a universe of discourse. If this difference is forgotten, animal experiments will not help to understand man, they will only blur the picture.

VIII

The tendency toward universality, inherent in true liberal education, leads on to our last problem. In our public controversies, especially in the discussion of the relation between our national school system and religion, the concepts "secular" versus "nonsecular" are often used. "Secularism" means for many the same as "naturalism" or "materialism" (whatever these words mean), and "nonsecular" generally connotes the emphasis on a particular religious section, or the whole body of ideas which explain man not only as a "self-transcending" being but make him and his education contingent upon "transcendental" or "supernatural" forces, suggesting at the same time that without the awareness of these forces there can be no real morality and civilization.

Now, if I may use the pragmatic test (inadequate indeed if confined to a single person's experience) I cannot honestly say that the so-called "secular" type of man is morally or culturally inferior to the nonsecular. Many of my scientist friends—indifferent or suspicious though they often are in regard to all metaphysics—seem to derive from their scholarly self-discipline (accuracy, patience, self-correctiveness, seeing things in context, etc.) a general ethics. This general ethics has nothing ecstatic and self-concerned, as we often find it in the religious tradition, yet harmonizes perfectly with the best rules of human decency.

However, I often ask myself whether these scientists, perhaps because of their original upbringing, may still live on an essentially religious tradition without ever thinking of renewing it. This assumption is difficult to verify. It may be wrong. The deeper reason for the adequateness of the secular ethics of the scientist lies in the fact that, actually, he is not secular in the sense of the crude "materialist." I often suspect that the equation of secularism = naturalism = materialism = atheism = lack of moral standards is one of the confusions intentionally spread by certain groups which have a vested interest in discrediting the other fellow. In recent times these groups have also intimated that they alone can save the world from communism. But, though often averse to what he falsely considers the religious interpretations of man and the universe in reality, often superstitious interpretations, a productive scientist lives in a profoundly self-transcendent mood, aware of the interconnection of all life, trying to come closer to its inner laws, and standing in reverence before its mysterious creativeness. If this is "secularism" or "naturalism" in contrast to "supernaturalism," let it be so. In this attitude, I am convinced, millions of our fellowmen wander over our earth, suspicious of "big phrases," troubled or untroubled agnostics, afraid of emotionalism, yet kind and decent. And if you would point at the crimes committed by "faithless" people and peoples, remember that, unfortunately, crime, persecution, the burning of heretics, treachery, and the violation of human fellowship grow out of the dark abysses in the nature of man, his fears, his passions, and his greed for power and are, consequently, to be found everywhere, also in the history of churches. The dividing line between the constructive and the destructive is whether or not a person or a system of thought or an institution permits and helps man to transcend his ego toward higher forms of existence and achievement, to respect human dignity and "the inalienable rights of man," and to admire the depth and beauty of the creation of which he is a part.

All education that in a young person creates the desire to live according to these values is liberal and humane in the deepest sense of the word, irrespective of whether this education is provided by a simple home and a village school or by a university with a glorious name, by a humanist who reads Plato or an astronomer who reads the stars, by a theologian who discusses the nature of God or an artisan who teaches his apprentice respect for material and excellence in work.

In the subtropical parts of this country one can see gigantic old banyan trees with evergreen leaves and of beautiful shape. Not only are their trunks anchored in the earth as for eternity, but they send from their spreading crown aerial roots down into the soil to provide ever new support and nourishment. A native with whom I spoke called these trees "splendid engineers." To me they have always appeared as a magnificent symbol, not only of the wonders of nature, but also of the wonder that is in all great men and cultures. The more they grow and spread, the more anxious they are always to find their way back to the native soil.

This is the contrast between uprooted and self-isolating intellectualism, which creates sickness, and responsible living, which creates health. The first tries to thrive on itself and thus becomes barren. The latter always reminds man of his dependence on a greater creation to which he should be grateful in view of what he receives. If we live in this spirit, which I call piety, it makes no difference whether we are humanists, or scientists, supernaturalists or naturalists, and whether we find our vocation in a learned profession or a simple craft. The essential criterion is that we know that man always stands on the edge of the great mystery, and that we find the *aliquid sanctum* in whatever we meet.

HENRY NELSON WIEMAN

Since 1926, when he published Religious Experience and Scientific Method, *Henry Nelson Wieman has been a provocative student and teacher in the field of the philosophy of religion. A graduate of Park College and Harvard, he taught philosophy for ten years at Occidental College and the philosophy of religion for twenty years as the University of Chicago. He has delivered such lectureships at those of Nathaniel William Taylor at Yale, Mendenhall at DePauw, Carew at Hartford Seminary Foundation, and Ayer at Colgate-Rochester Theological Seminary. A member of the American Philosophy Association and the American Theological Society, his publications include* The Wrestle of Religion with Truth *(1929); (co-author)* American Philosophies of Religion *(1936);* The Source of Human Good *(1946); and* The Directive of History *(1949).*

I

DISTINGUISHING what is important in the Christian tradition requires a standard. The standard, I take it, is the adequacy of its answer to the universal religious question arising out of the nature of man. This question might be stated thus: What has such character and power in human life that it can transform man as he cannot transform himself to save from the worst and lead to the best on condition that man accept it as his ruling devotion?

The nature of man which makes this question imperative is his capacity to be transformed to the depths of misery and evil and to the heights of blessedness and nobility. Human beings are capable of more variation while still retaining the essential characteristics of humanity than any other species.[1] The variation here considered is in character, organization of personality, interpersonal relations, social institutions, habits, and customs. This enormous range of variation through which human beings can pass generates the most important problem confronting human existence. It is the problem indicated by the first question in this inquiry. It is the question which all the great religions try to answer. Broken down into its component parts it appears as the following: What is the direction of the best? What is the direction of the worst? What transforms the human being away from the worst and toward the best? What conditions must be present for this transforming power to operate effectively?

This question cannot be answered by consulting our likes and dislikes, our moral standards and religious convictions, nor by appealing to the special tradition which we happen to inherit, whether it be the Judeao-Christian or the Hindu or some other. It cannot be answered by these because these are precisely what must be transformed. We can see this clearly in Nazis and Communists and all who follow ways of life alien to our own. But to assume that our own highest ideals and religious convictions need no transformation, when all others do, is indefensible. The arrogance and folly of this assumption become increasingly obvious as all peoples are drawn together into a single society where members of each tradition must live in mutual support with all others or else frustrate and antagonize all others.

This drives us back to the question about man's transformation, by what agency and in what direction. Obviously no simple appeal to Christianity can give us the answer. It cannot partly because the answer given by Christianity is not one but many, and these many answers contradict one another. Protestant and Catholic, Southern Baptist and Unitarian, Augustine and Aquinas, Calvin and Servetus cannot all be reconciled along with many others. Also it cannot be found by simple appeal to the Christian tradition because the right answer must be demonstrated by evidence other than the authority of one tradition held in opposition to all others. The answer must be

[1] Julian Huxley, "The Uniqueness of Man," published with other essays under title, *Man in the Modern World* (New York: Mentor Books, 1948), p. 11.

found by searching the nature of man which underlies all traditions and all diversities.

What distinguishes man from everything else is the ability of individuals to learn from one another by the use of language and other symbols. This learning is not merely of knowledge; we also acquire appreciative understanding of the subjectivity of the other person— his sorrows and joys, hopes and fears, regrets and anticipations, appreciations and antipathies, and all that myriad of felt qualities, impulses, and actions which make up the mind of a human being. Our appreciative understanding of all this in another person is of course meager and imperfect; but the miracle and glory of man is to develop such a subjectivity and to recognize it in others by the use of language and other symbols.

This peculiar nature of man developed by symbolic interchange between individuals generates a body of shared experience which is transmitted through many generations and is called a tradition or culture. In this way occurs the creative transformation of the human mind that under favorable conditions can increase beyond any known limit what man can know, feel, and control. This creates the greatness of man and marks out the course of his destiny.

Everything can be called evil which hinders this creative enrichment and expansion of the mind by interchange between individuals. Many kinds of interchange hinder it, such as the deceptive kind of interchange, the manipulative, the reiterative, the muddle-headed, the malicious, and the adoption of false fronts to win social approval. But in contrast to all of these is the one kind of interchange which creates the human mind progressively when conditions permit. To distinguish it from the others let us call it creative interchange.

Creative interchange widens and deepens appreciative understanding between individuals and peoples; it can enrich beyond any known limit the body of experience which individuals can share in community; it can increase indefinitely the mutual control exercised by individuals and peoples dealing with one another, thus reducing the need for authoritarian control; it can increase freedom when freedom in social relations is mutual control over against authoritarian control and freedom in the mind of the individual is the ability to control and shape to his own ends the consequences of any cause acting upon him.

All this results from the kind of interchange here called creative; it does not result from the other kinds of interchange going on between individuals and peoples. Rather, these other kinds often obstruct it, when they do not bring on fear, hate, suspicion, conflict, mutual frustration, and mutual destruction. The moral and religious problem of human life is to bring creative interchange to dominance over the other kinds.

Love variously interpreted has been one theme running through the Judeao-Christian tradition. It is also found in other traditions. All too frequently it has been interpreted and practiced as though it were a kind of feeling for other people or a kind of doing or both. Certainly creative interchange includes a kind of feeling and a kind of doing, but it is much more. It is the creative transformation of the human mind and of human society toward the best that man can ever attain. It is the creativity in human history and carries the promise of the Kingdom of God.

If "love" in the Christian tradition can be identified in some of its interpretations with creative interchange, then this is the value in this tradition to be emphasized above all else.

II

Science and the worldview which issues from science are themselves the products of the creative interchange described in answer to Question I. One scientist learns from others, adds something to what he has learned, and communicates this to other scientists. Thus does science arise and expand into a theory about the physical universe.

But science and the scientific view of reality are only one segment of life. Every scientist along with every human being engages in interchange with others from infancy, and this creates in him some appreciation of beauty, some experience of love and friendship, some moral ideals, some hate and fear, some sense of justice and injustice, some political understanding and political responsibility, some beliefs about human destiny. Science is one part of this totality which we call the human mind and its world. All of it, including science, issues from the same source, namely, creative interchange.

The scientific picture of cosmic reality changes from day to day. Einstein's representation of it is very different from Newton's and Newton's from Aristotle's. Cosmic reality as known to science a thousand or million years from now will doubtless be so different from what we know it to be that similarities will be hard to find.

The most important thing created by interchange between individuals is not science and scientific knowledge. The most important thing is the human mind itself—a mind able to use a language and other symbols, thereby learning from others and undergoing creative transformation beyond any known limit. Far more important than the transitory scientific picture of cosmic reality is the ability of the individual to recognize in every other human being a subjectivity in the form of hopes and fears, joys and sorrows, memories and dreams, sensitivities and outreachings. Without this science itself could not arise, because scientists must learn from one another by discovering what is in the mind of the other scientist when he makes a mark like the mathematical symbol used by Einstein to represent cosmic reality. Without this kind of interchange love and friendship could not occur, nor could art and culture. Without this we would treat one another as we do sticks and stones, oblivious of any thought or feeling in the mind of the other, without respect or concern for the sensitivity of any human being.

When a child learns to talk he is reproducing and perpetuating the meanings put into the language by millions of human beings through thousands of years. These meanings have been put into these sounds by the suffering and doing, failing and succeeding, and all the multiform content of human experience undergone by these millions of human beings. This is the creativity of history. It creates the human mind with all its distinctive powers and all the resources of human culture. This creative interchange should command the ultimate commitment of faith because it is the only way to attain the highest destiny of man's peculiar capacity.

No matter what the ultimate nature of physical reality may be we can come to know it and deal constructively with it only by committing ourselves in religious faith to the kind of creative interchange that expands indefinitely what man can know, feel, and control; that deepens the appreciative understanding between individuals and peoples; that enriches the life of each and multiplies the resources for human living; and that creates science itself.

The physical sciences predict a time when life on this earth will cease. That prediction is based upon physical data only, and cannot include in its calculations the creativity which rears the human mind from infancy and accumulates through many generations the resources for mastering the physical processes. Whether this creativity will ever develop human resources to the point where we can guard against this final doom no one can say. But to assume from the start that this can never occur because of a calculation which excludes from consideration the very creativity which might develop such resources would seem to be foolish. In any case we have everything to gain and nothing to lose by committing ourselves in religious faith to this creativity.

The ultimate nature of reality for the human mind is this creativity because it creates all we can ever know, including the knowledge we gain of this creativity itself. Thus it reveals itself to man by creating the knowledge by which we know it. If anything can be called divine revelation this is it. Also it is ultimate for the human mind because the mind can never know anything beyond the creativity which enables it to know, feel, control, and appreciate whatever it comes to know, feel, control, and appreciate. Beyond this there can be nothing of any concern for the human mind.

III

Political democracy is a way of making the decisions which determine social policy. Democratic government is always a matter of degree, but a government is democratic to the measure that all the citizens exercise effective influence in making the important decisions which are announced and executed by the government. This influence is exerted in many ways besides the vote although voting seems to be one of the indispensable instruments to this end.

Social democracy is often distinguished from the political. It refers to the way other institutions and social relations are administered besides the government. It is sometimes put in economic terms and is interpreted to mean the widest possible distribution of economic opportunity and economic well-being. It is true that economic well-being is an indispensable condition for the development of capacity in all members of a society to understand the decisions under consideration by the government. Without this opportunity, combined with leisure and education to study and understand these social problems, there can be no effective influence upon the government by the people who make up the society. No matter how democratic may be the mechanisms of government, there can be no political democracy if the entire society is not so ordered as to permit and incite the people to exert effective influence upon the government when it decides important issues.

But when social democracy is defined purely in economic terms it does not cover what is needed throughout society to make possible a democratic government. Economic abundance widely distributed will not automatically enable people to understand the needs common to all that are of such character that they can be satisfied by political action and are also of such character that they will not frustrate other needs equally significant when they are promoted by political action. It is possible that a wide distribution of economic wealth easily acquired by all might prevent that development of the mind by which the human person comes to know the needs of his own person and those of his fellow men sufficiently to exercise intelligent influence upon decisions of the government.

Understanding the needs of human life is not merely an economic and political problem. Individuals cannot discover their common needs without expressing themselves to one another freely and fully. This in turn cannot occur unless they find appreciative response when they express themselves in this way. This requires that people try first of all to understand the other person and only thereafter pronounce agreement or disagreement. It requires also that even when they disagree and disapprove they shall seek above all to learn from the other, because error and evil can be as instructive as, often more instructive than, the true statement and the good motive or action. But this kind of interaction between individuals is precisely what is here called creative interchange.

So we conclude that political democracy is possible only if society is so ordered that people can express themselves to one another freely and fully and truly and find appreciative response from others

THIS IS MY FAITH

when they do so. This is necessary because people cannot discover their own needs nor the needs of others nor their common needs nor the needs which can be served by decisions of government unless this kind of interchange occurs. Not only is this kind of society required in order to have political democracy; it is the first responsibility of political government to sustain, protect, and build up this kind of social order in all walks of life so far as government is able to do this. Of course many other agencies are required for this besides government, such as education, industry, home, neighborhood, and religion—all organized to achieve this end.

From all this the answer to the third question which is here under consideration would seem to be obvious. Democracy in the sense of political and social organization should never be a religion. But the democratic organization and action of government and other social agencies to the end of providing conditions most favorable for the creative transformation of the mind through history is demanded by religious commitment. The creativity itself, and it only, commands religious faith; but such a commitment leads one to struggle for political and social order which is democratic in the sense indicated.

I think my answer to the fourth question has become apparent. I affirm one spiritual reality but its relation to the Christian religion calls for further explanation.

The one spiritual reality is creative interchange. It may have risen to dominance in the fellowship which formed around Jesus. Whether it did or not must be determined by historical research. If it did rise to dominance, thereby transforming the lives of the persons concerned, these persons would have had unique power to bring about like transformation in the lives of others with whom they communicated. This follows because this kind of interchange has great transforming power.

If this transformation did occur in the fellowship of Jesus, bringing creative interchange to dominance in the lives of the disciples and their followers, the experience of undergoing this transformation must have been interpreted by these people as the presence in their lives of the resurrected Christ. They must have visualized the man Jesus as the source of this transforming and saving power in their lives. If all this did occur, then in a sense it can be said that in Christ is the revelation of God, and the saving power of God.

If all this did occur, it transpired under social, psychological, and historical conditions of such sort as to establish a continuing fellowship able to transmit this transformed way of life to subsequent generations. When the transformed life was not itself transmitted, the fellowship seems to have perpetuated a tradition commemorating this kind of transformation by myth and symbol, ceremony and sacrament.

While this can be called revelation and salvation, *the revelation and salvation as here interpreted must be identified with the transformation occurring in the lives of men.* The revelation is *not* any set of doctrines or other propositions *about the transformation.* Salvation has nothing particularly to do with accepting any set of doctrines about the transformation. The transformation itself, bringing creative interchange and the creativity of history to dominance over other kinds of interchange between men, this and this only is the way of salvation.

The persons who underwent the transformation could not have understood it and therefore could not have laid down any true doctrines about it. They could not, because no words then existing could have the meanings fit to state what happened. Words are mere sounds which have only the meanings attached to them by the people who use them. If the transformation occurred as described above, and if it was truly a revelation in the sense that it was not a common occurrence in the lives of men prior to the revelatory events, there could not have been any words in existence fit to state what happened. This must have been the case because language and forms of thought can only arise concerning matters sufficiently common for people to think about them and talk about them. Therefore if revelation did occur in Jesus and his fellowship, this revelation cannot be identified with any teaching or other propositions issuing from that source.

Another misunderstanding must be removed. If the revelation is the transformation of the human person and not any set of teachings about it, then the revelation cannot reach me unless I myself undergo the transformation. Mere knowledge about the past events and mere belief in the truth of statements about them cannot possibly bring to me either the revelation or the salvation contained in the trans-formation.

Furthermore, if this transformation of the human person occurs in any other tradition or in any other religion or culture, it is the same identical revelation and salvation regardless of whether it can be traced in any way to Jesus and his fellowship. There is every reason to believe that it has occurred many times to persons in all the tradi-tions and cultures of the world. Perhaps in none has it occurred under such psychological, social, and historical conditions which prevailed when Christianity originated. Possibly in none has it formed an en-during fellowship with the transforming power expressed in the Chris-tian tradition. But this is speculative. I do not think we can claim any such unique transforming power for the Christian tradition until we know more about the history of all other peoples, cultures, and re-ligions, and achieve a more profound and appreciative understanding of them than we now have.

In the world-society now emerging, the Judeao-Christian tradition will lose whatever saving power it may once have had unless it is purged of its arrogance and its claim to possess in some superior form the way of life which all men must follow. There is a truth and a way of life which all men must follow, but it is not confined to any one tradition, either Christian or any other. It underlies all traditions and has created them all. Today this way of life by which we can be saved demands the most profound appreciative understanding between diverse traditions, persons, and cultures. It further commands that we oppose and condemn in every tradition, person, culture, and way of life whatever prevents the creation of this most profound appreciative understanding of diversities. On this ground we must condemn and oppose the prevailing tone of the Christian tradition because it dis-plays a moral and spiritual arrogance beyond most others. On the other hand, beneath this arrogance and all the other evils of this tra-dition, I believe the one spiritual reality of greatest value for all men can be found in this tradition as well as in the other great traditions of humanity.

The dynamic values inherent in the activity of the cosmos I do not think I can discuss because we do not know enough about the cosmos, unless one wishes to identify these dynamic values with the creativity which has been central throughout this discussion.

I think I have already made sufficiently plain the relation of this one spiritual reality to the creative values emerging in man's struggle to build a society of free men.

V

The saving power in human life must be found by each individual amid the inner conflict and confusion at the deeper levels of his own consciousness. These contrary demands and drives, which cannot be made to fit the established order of life, are often hidden by more superficial preoccupations. The anxiety, the sense of need, and the suffering generated by them cannot be appeased, although they can be concealed. But all this can be accepted fully and openly into consciousness when it is seen to be an essential part of man's greatest glory. This condition of man, which appears when nothing is hidden and nothing is covered over, is a necessary part of creative transformation. This condition of the total self is the condition of one whose organization of personality must be continuously reconstructed; whose loves and loyalties must be continuously reconstructed; whose ideals must be cast off and other ideals accepted; whose society must be constantly exposed to reordering, sometimes with great suffering; whose sojourn in any dear and homey place is always brief because man is a pilgrim on his way to ends he cannot know; all this the human being must undergo if he is to be transformed creatively to comprehend a richer abundance of quality and wider scope of knowledge and control, and if he is to have a love that grows in depth and range of appreciation beyond any known limit.

The corruption and degradation that enter human life when creativity is not allowed to dominate the mind reveal that man is made for this creativity. Self-destructive propensities arise in human life when men refuse to commit themselves to the sovereign control of creative interchange. As the shriveling of a plant when water is lacking shows that the plant is made for water, so the decay of man's humanity when creativity is lacking shows that man is made for creativity. With this interpretation the horrors of history testify to the potential greatness of man and manifest by their destructive character the transcendent outreach of the divine imperative in human nature.

At each higher level of transformation man becomes more self-conscious and this makes him more fully aware of the perplexities of his existence, the dangers within himself and the dangers in his society and in the movements of history. The higher levels multiply the problems and aggravate difficulties. If all this is called evil, then evil increases with every advance in the creative transformation of man. But if all this is accepted as essential to man's high destiny, and if the individual commits himself completely and ultimately to the creativity which endows him with this destiny, and if he accepts without evasion or concealment these perplexities, these problems, these dangers, these corruptions, and these sufferings as essential to the glory of his existence, then he can live in the midst of it all with a peace and joy undiminished by the perplexity and the suffering. This statement is not a contradiction in terms because the perplexity and suffering on the one hand, the peace and joy on the other, refer to different levels of being.

Creativity can be found at the depths of corruption because, as said before, a creature capable of undergoing creative transformation is a creature capable of being corrupt. Corruption is what occurs when conditions do not permit this creativity to exercise its saving and transforming power. These conditions are social and historical as well as psychological and individually personal. This corruption is the negative sign of the presence of creativity; it is a characteristic distinguishing one capable of undergoing creative transformation. Furthermore, under some conditions the individual at the depths of corruption can recognize this creativity in his life and may be more free and ready to give himself over to its transforming power than one who finds satisfaction in his noble virtues. Satisfaction in the good already attained may cause one to resist the demands of creative transformation.

Thus a door is open to creativity, salvation and transformation at the depths of suffering, corruption, and frustration, even when it is closed at the heights of moral and spiritual achievement. All too frequently satisfaction in present attainment deafens the ear to the call of creativity. This applies to Western culture and the Christian tradition at the present time.

Periods in history when great troubles arise caused by the accumulated consequences of evil practiced through several generations are often times when men are better able to recognize the saving power of the creativity in history and their need for transformation than they are in times of well-being. The reason for this has already been stated. But the door which opens to saving power in time of troubles may not be entered; frequently it is not. A deceiver always arises in such a time of trouble, leading men away from the open door. This deceiver is the body of traditional beliefs to which men turn when trouble assails. These traditional beliefs may once, in the form of myths, have led some to find the way to salvation. But a myth which guides where knowledge cannot lead derives its functional significance from the social-psychological conditions in which it is developed. When these conditions are changed, it can no longer point the way. When troubles are due to radical changes in the psychological-social conditions, as is the case with us, the old myths lead astray.

Men today, because they are bewildered and aware of great danger, are turning to the old mythical beliefs. But today we must have knowledge to guide us. The greatest danger threatening us, the danger most likely to be our doom, is this turning away from the open door of salvation to follow traditional beliefs which lead nowhere except into the night.

I have tried to answer the question about God by describing the place of creativity in human life. I think that there is no other word in the English language fit to designate the religious significance of creativity except the word "God." But proper use of a word for any person is determined by the meaning which his own mind can attach to it. Many minds may not be able to find for this word any meaning relevant to what, in truth, does transform man as he cannot transform himself, thus saving him from his own self-destructive propensities and leading him to the richest fulfillment of his creative potentialities, on condition that he accept it as his ruling devotion.

QUINCY WRIGHT

Quincy Wright has been a distinguished interpreter of international law for many years. A graduate of Lombard College and the University of Illinois, he has taught international law and political science at Harvard, Minnesota and Chicago (1923-54). At various times he has served as a consultant to the U. S. Navy Department, the Department of State, the International Military Tribunal at Nuremberg, UNESCO, and the U. S. High Commissioner of Germany. A former president of the American Association of University Professors, the American Political Science Association, and the International Political Science Association, he is a fellow of the American Academy of Arts and Sciences and the Conference on Science, Philosophy and Religion. His publications include Enforcement for International Law Through Municipal Law in the United States *(1916);* Mandates Under the League of Nations *(1930);* The Causes of War and the Conditions of Peace *(1935);* A Study of War *(1942); and* Study of International Relations *(1955).*

INTRODUCTION

MR. STEWART G. COLE's contribution to the eleventh symposium of the Conference on Science, Philosophy and Religion contrasts secular with religious points of view concerning human goals and values. The problem discussed seems to me essentially that of determining the roles of scientific method and of religious method in human action. The problem is a large one and I speak with hesitancy because I know little of scientific method and less of religious method. From the little I know, however, I would say that science rests basically upon confidence in observation and reason, whereas religion rests upon confidence in introspection and tradition. The latter is found in

272

historical, inspirational, and dogmatic writings, disclosing the insight of spiritual leaders.

If this distinction is acceptable, it seems to me that scientific systems can be objective in the sense that they can mean the same to every reader who understands the definitions of the terms used and the rules of reason, logical or mathematical, by which inferences are made. Science attempts to define terms operationally, that is by pointing to an experiment or observation. The meaning of the term can then be ascertained through making the experiment or observation. These operations generally refer to measurements or observations dependent upon the sense of sight, often in modern science upon observation of the movement of dials. The objectivity of the term therefore, depends upon the assumption that to all human beings the reading of the same dial, or the observation of an image at the same moment in a telescope or a microscope, will be identical. It is also assumed that all sane individuals agree on the validity of simple processes of addition, subtraction, multiplication, the demonstrations of Euclid, and other logical systems which, with varying degrees of elaboration, provide the inferences by which scientific conclusions are demonstrated. Thus, while scientific systems may be difficult for many people to understand, the ultimate verification of their generalizations depends upon identities of vision and inference which everyone accepts. It is in this sense that scientific systems are objective.

Religious systems, on the other hand, depend, as I understand it, upon the individual's reflection concerning cultural traditions and his own experience with values. Since individuals differ greatly in cultural tradition, in individual experience, and in inferences from them, it might seem that there would be as many religions as there are persons. In this sense, religion is subjective. Even persons brought up in the same culture and religious tradition and familiar with the same religious writings will interpret them differently, because the terms used are not operationally defined but refer to complicated experiences and insights, and will therefore inevitably be interpreted by everyone in accord with his personal experiences. Religious writings may teach, but the content of the teaching is bound to be greatly influenced by the pecularities of the individual in a way which is not true of scientific expositions.

Because of the objectivity of science, it constitutes not only a method of discovery but also a growing system of propositions by which human observations and experiments are stored and made increasingly available to predict and control the future. In proportion as human beings have become interested in guiding their action by knowledge of the probable consequences of the alternative choices which circumstances and imagination suggest, science and secularism have gained in prestige. It is often said, however, that while science can throw light on the probable consequences of actions, and consequently upon the choices and decisions which are most likely to bring about desired consequences, science cannot throw light on the consequences which *ought* to be desired; it can not solve the problem of values.

There have, it is true, been efforts to deal with this problem by scientific method. It is possible to compare the numerous value systems which have been established by different religions, different cultures, and different societies, and from this comparison to reach conclusions about which values have produced the most generally satisfactory societies and persons. This method, however, neglects the possible interrelation of values and scientific knowledge. The character of a society or of a personality may depend not only on its values but also on its science. Particular values may produce very different social and personal results among the scientifically ignorant and the scientifically wise. The religion most suitable to a person or society may, therefore, be relative to other aspects of culture and personality.

This comparative method also leaves open the question of what is the best society and what is the best person. Efforts have been made to answer these questions in terms of the theory of organic evolution (the best is that most capable of surviving) or in terms of psychology (the best society is that which best serves the biologic and psychic needs of the individual) or of sociology (the best person is he who best fulfills the requirements of society). There are, however, many types of society that can survive, and the needs of individuals and societies are flexible and interdependent. It may be doubted whether "the best" or even the "better" can be satisfactorily determined by biology, psychology, or sociology.

The function of science is to facilitate prediction and control. Can it tell whether what is probable is valuable, and to what ends control should be exerted? Some believe that a science of ethics can eventually deal with these problems but many scientists believe that methods other than those of science are necessary to deal with the problem of values, that man must seek guidance from those of superior spiritual insight, and seek, difficult as it may be, to understand what this superior insight has sought to convey concerning the nature of the good act, the good man, and the good society. If knowledge is to assure virtue, it must include knowledge not only of science but also of values.

The social sciences differ from the natural sciences in their relation to values. The natural scientist, as scientist, can ignore values but the social scientist can not. This is because beliefs concerning values exert major influence upon human behavior. A social science capable of predicting behavior in a society, therefore, has to assume that existing values will continue to be accepted and acted upon within the society or to consider the effects of their change upon behavior within that society. The value system, together with the institutions maintaining it, must be treated as a condition, as a parameter, or as a variable of the social science.

A social scientist, seeking to predict or control human behavior, therefore, has to understand the values of the people with whose behavior he is concerned. But if he has adequately related his predictions to existing values, and those predictions prove unpalatable to the people, the effect of his writing may be to change the attitudes of the people toward those values. The science "feeds back" upon its subject matter in a way not true of natural science, the subject matter of which does not read. The social scientist, therefore, has to ask himself, even in his "scientific" writing: What will be the consequences of publication of my conclusions upon the applicability of my predictions?

As a good citizen, he has to ask himself also: Do I want to influence values in the direction likely if my writings are read? The natural scientist as a citizen is faced by a similar problem. The atomic physicist may for example ask: Should I give the human race the means of self destruction when I am aware of the imperfections of statesmanship? The problem of human responsibility is the same for both, though it exists in greater degree for the social scientist, but the latter alone is faced by the influence of the publication of "scientific" conclusions upon their own applicability. Social scientists must, therefore, both as scientists and as citizens, give attention to the question: What is the social effect of acceptance of particular value systems? Which of available value systems, judged by its consequences, is the better? By what method can these questions be answered?

These questions are, I take it, the primary concern of the religious mind. But most religious minds answer them in terms of a particular religion, and such an answer is likely to be unconvincing to persons brought up in a different religious tradition. The result of this situation has been many religious wars and persecutions to induce acceptance of the "true" religion, leading to widespread conviction, during the last three centuries, that politics ought to be divorced from religion so that men and societies can tolerate all religions and coexist peacefully. This conviction evolved from the religious controversies of seventeenth-century England and is formulated in the first amendment of the United States Constitution. It was recently expressed by Prime Minister Jawaharlal Nehru of India with reference to the extensive forced migrations and massacres, among the worst in history, which attended the separation of India and Pakistan in 1947, motivated by the religious difference between Moslems and Hindus. In 1948 he remarked: "We must have it clearly in our minds and in the mind of the country that the alliance of religion and politics in the shape of communalism is a most dangerous alliance, it yields the most abnormal kind of illegitimate brood."[1]

European statesmen had reached the same conclusion after the Thirty Years War of the seventeenth century between Catholicism and Protestantism. Their conclusion was registered in the Treaty of Westphalia (1648) which asserted that international relations should be based upon the sovereignty of territorial states and that every prince should deal with religious and ideological problems internally. *Cuius regio, eieus religio.* The same idea has terminated the thousand years of strife between Islam and Christendom. It is expressed in the United Nations Charter as the principles of the sovereign equality of states, the self-determination of peoples, and respect for the human

[1] "Dangerous Alliance of Religion and Politics," in *Independence and After* (New York: John Day Co., 1950), p. 47.

rights of individuals irrespective of religion. Politics and law are to confine themselves to secular ends guided by a sound science developed from observation and reason indicating the probable consequences of policies proposed to achieve these ends.

But this secular reaction from religious wars has not entirely answered the questions. Separation of church and state meant that assumptions had to be made concerning secular ends. It was assumed that each government would guide its policy by a dominant interest in the security of the state and the prosperity of the people. It has, however, always been true that some governments have in fact had other interests, such as expansion of a particular ideology or religion or the universal protection of particular "human rights." Furthermore, a particular state's security and prosperity might seem to require injury or even elimination of another state, often leading to wars for "reason of state." *Political* wars in the twentieth century proved as bad as the *religious* wars of the seventeenth. The secularization of political values by calling them "national interests" did not do away with the problem of values. The decision of Westphalia, which let each state deal with conflicts of values among its own people, has proved progressively less sufficient as the world has shrunk under the impact of inventions, as people in one state have been shocked by the values pursued in others, as war has become intolerably destructive, and as opportunities have increased to promote general welfare by international cooperation.

The United Nations Charter has tried to meet the problem by asserting in its preamble and first article certain secular values which all its members formally accept. It is assumed that all states exercising their sovereign equality, all self-determining peoples, and all persons enjoying their human rights will observe these values. But are these relative values—that peace is preferable to war, that national self-determination is preferable to imperial control, that respect for human rights is preferable to absolute state sovereignty, that cooperation for human welfare is preferable to freedom in the pursuit of national interests—really better than others that could be imagined?

It may be that no definition of the better values for politics and law can be made other than that implied by the Charter, that they are the values which are most widely accepted at a given time. It may be that while truth in regard to scientific problems of prediction and control, especially in the nonhuman field, is independent of human belief, truth in the field of social values depends in no small measure upon its capacity to engender belief. It may be that in this field propositions become true in proportion as they are believed—*vox populi, vox dei.* Therefore the arts of education and propaganda may be creative of the truth about social values. If this is the case, propositions must be formulated and asserted as truth before they are tested. That is what I understand by faith. In the field of values, individuals must believe without sufficient evidence, and that faith may subsequently develop evidence by encouraging general acceptance.

In this sense the religious attitude might be defined as confidence that the best values are those that can be made universal and that the discovery of such values will be continuous, approaching a value system perfectly adapted to the nature of man and to the nature of the world. This, as I understand it, is the essence of Kant's categorical imperative, and also of the scriptural prescription concerning the brotherhood of man and the fatherhood of God. Both assume that men are morally equal and that the best values are those acceptable and apprehensible to all. In this sense the will of God can be defined as the perfect value system which the evolution of human values approaches as a limit, but never completely achieves.

There is an objective world of event, probabilities, and possibilities organized into physical, biological, psychological, sociological, and other scientific systems. There is also a subjective world of feelings, desires, and values organized into religious, moral, legal, political, and other normative systems. Both of these worlds are evolving. There is tension between them. The objective world is never quite as one wishes it. The subjective world is never quite realized. The social sciences deal with this tension from the scientific point of view. The normative disciplines deal with it from the evaluative point of view. Religion deals with it metaphorically. It identifies the will of God with the subjective world if it were in harmony with the objective world, and it identifies the knowledge of God with the objective world if it were in harmony with the subjective world. God is the synthesis of the two worlds.

Man makes God in his own image. But his image changes as he

becomes aware of himself, of his neighbors, of his society, of his world, and of his universe. As the "wish principle" is influenced by the "reality principle," religion adjusts itself to science. The gods become less numerous, less different, and perhaps less hostile to one another as they converge toward one God, understanding of and obedience to whom would maximize the satisfaction of all human needs and aspirations. That God, who is approached but never reached, can be said to seek to realize himself by making man in his own image. A man-made God seeks to become realized in a God-made man. A human concept of reality and values seeks to become realized in the universe. Man-made syntheses of realities and values strive to become so objective, through the progress of science, and so adequate, through the progress of religion, that they can feed back on men, making them wise and virtuous. Thus men continually seek to interpret the pluralism and pragmatism of values which they accept in the world into a monism and rationalism, unifying all the scientific and normative systems, toward which each of them aspires. The moral evolution of man may be asymptotic to the will of God.

Some secularists and humanists may accept faith in God in this sense and say that it is exemplified in the democratic faith in the people. In the market place of free opinion, according to that faith, the better will eventually prevail. This point of view, which denies the value of political absolutism, raises doubts as to the value of dogmatic religions and ideologies. While such skeptics may readily agree that institutionalized religions and doctrines can assist many people in understanding and accepting superior values, they may fear that the method of dogmatic assertion of the "best" values sets a limit to moral evolution, and that the efforts to justify dogmatism through historical mythologies or revelations stultifies the progress of science. It is perhaps significant in this connection that the recent statistical study by R. H. Knapp and H. E. Goodrich on the *Origins of American Men of Science*[2] finds that an atmosphere of dogmatic religion has been stultifying to the production of scientists in American colleges and universities. The problem seems to be whether inquiry concerning values, and persuasion to accept the values that at a given moment of history appear to be superior, can be conducted in a way which will

[2] (Chicago: University of Chicago Press, 1952.)

be effective in advancing knowledge and virtue without stultifying progress in either science or religion. In the political field, the west has accepted the processes of freedom of opinion, public education, and democratic elections as the answer.

With these general comments, I will try to answer the five specific questions which Mr. Cole asked.

I

I should say that human brotherhood and reciprocity, and faith in the continuous progress of values toward the most perfect adaptation to conditions are the primary religious values. Such an adaptation may be called "the will of God." It seems to me a stimulus to moral behavior and a contribution to continuous moral progress to accept the equality of man in moral dignity, to regard moral insight as susceptible of continuous improvement, and to consider steps in moral evolution as a convergent series which approaches but never reaches a state of society which will maximize human satisfactions.

II

On the matter of science I think I would go along with Albert Schweitzer, who recently wrote that the ethical conception of the world "attributes to the universal will, qualities and intentions which give satisfaction to its own way of feeling and of judging. But in the course of the nineteenth century the research which allowed itself to be guided solely by concern for truth was bound to surrender to the evidence that ethics can expect nothing from a true knowledge of the world."[3] It seems clear that the cosmos is morally neutral; ethical systems and values are man-made. It may be that some are better adapted to the nature of the world and of society than others. If this is the case, there is perhaps a process of continuous selection toward moral beliefs that are better adapted to survive. On the other hand a considerable variety of value systems seem to manifest viability. Perhaps, as I have indicated, the faith that, on the whole, the selective process will make for evolution of values toward the "better" is itself a contribution toward that result. I think morals as well as science will gain if the cosmos is not thought of as man-centered or as value-

[3] *Saturday Review,* June 13, 1953, p. 48.

centered. Value systems must adapt themselves to the cosmos and not the reverse. God can be conceived as a synthesis of the impersonal cosmos and the personal value system most perfectly adapted to it in each situation.

III

As I have indicated, I think religion is primarily subjective and has to do with personal behavior. As groups become large, their values become objective and therefore susceptible to investigation by scientific methods. They come into the realm of law and politics, rather than religion. I think the realm of personal values manifested through religion and morals, and the realm of group values manifested through law and politics, should be kept distinct. The interaction of individuals with their personal religions creates objective social values but these social values can progress toward more perfect adaptation to changing conditions only if the opportunity exists for interaction among varied personal religions. If large political groups become committed to a particular religion or ideology, they become unprogressive, belligerent, and dangerous to the world. The ideal state of values involves diversity as well as unity. It is a dynamic equilibrium or a progressing field of competing values, some universal and some local, not a logical system or an organized hierarchy.

IV

I think that variety is as important as unity in the moral realm. It is only through a variety of faiths that spiritual progress is possible. Because there is this variety we can assume that spiritual values are continually evolving. For the individual, spiritual conviction flows from personal experience and reflection, but for the group it flows from the interaction of many different points of view, thus developing systems of law and politics which, however, are pragmatic and susceptible to continuous change, permitting each individual to hope that his particular values will eventually play a larger role. We may assume that the evolution of values is manifested by the development of larger and larger human societies giving an opportunity for synthesis of a greater variety of moral opinions. The development of a world community, all the varied sections of which continually communicate with one another, makes possible, although it does not guarantee, great advances in spiritual and moral values. The development of a more comprehensive human society, facilitating the peaceful competition of a wider variety of independent value systems, facilitates more rapid and perfect adaptation of human values and behavior to social and material conditions.

V

As I have said, I think the term "God" can best be used to signify the source of the system of moral and spiritual values which, if universally adopted, would best satisfy human needs under existing conditions. Such a value system can be called "the will of God." Faith in God can then be interpreted as confidence that mankind will develop toward an acceptance of such a value system. It may be that some existing religions and value systems approach this limit more nearly than others, though we should not assume that any is perfect and it is likely that the continuous interaction of all will make for progress.

It is to be expected that science and technology will continue to advance and to change the conditions of human life, and that new values will be essential to adapt man to these new conditions. Human values must be dynamic, and if the will of God is conceived as permanent it can only be a limit which may be approached but never be wholly known. Perhaps it would be better to think of God himself as dynamic and creative. His will changes conformably to changes in the cosmos and in man's knowledge of the cosmos and of himself, which together constitute his knowledge of God.

An eschatology that assumes that there is an end to evolution, and that somebody knows that end, seems to me stultifying to progress and productive of violence and deterioration. Does not the book of Job have something to say about the unwisdom of assuming that we know what the best value system is, or, in the terminology of religion, that we know what is the will of God? I seem to find the same idea in the Baghavadgita.

III

EPILOGUE

EPILOGUE

This book opens with an inescapable question confronting every person who aspires to develop a reasonable framework for living the good, full life: Where can man turn to discover those spiritual values which experience has shown contribute most to human well-being?

The sharpness of this challenge is heightened by the fact that we are living in the midst of a social upheaval of global proportions affecting every aspect of traditional insight, thought, and value. What reflective individual is there who, in his candid moments, is not faced with profound personal problems and doubts, and is not reaching for a more rational faith to sustain his unfolding life? The more sensitive and courageous he is, the less opinionated and arbitrary he becomes, for he is ever seeking clearer mandates to meet the overwhelming responsibilities facing man in our time. The values he does succeed in distilling, and upon which he is betting his life, are monuments to his fearlessness in facing reality and to his integrity in attempting to resolve the enigma of human existence.

In these pages twenty-five representative men of our generation offer their considered replies to five questions designed to clarify their basic religious beliefs.* They have assumed that the Judaeo-Christian tradition, experimental science, and social democracy provide essential materials for this purpose. The first three questions in order center upon these areas of universal human interest. The fourth question subjects them to critical review to determine whether there is a common strand of spiritual meaning running through all of them, and, if so, what that strand is. The last question invites the contributor

* The questions are listed on page 8.

to indicate what content, in the light of the foregoing conclusions, he ascribes to the concept, "God."

The viewpoints of the contributors are many, but their spirit is one. If they have arrived at varying conclusions, it could scarcely be otherwise. Every intrepid soul must face reality from his own angle of confirmed perception and look at it through his own prism of structured experience. The convictions he holds point to the particular values which he has hammered out in the process of living in a baffling world.

The spirit that unites these men is their common allegiance to the search for the truth that sets men free. They are one in such a like-minded dedication and, therefore, in a high social trust. They share a profound kinship with every person who is similarly committed. Furthermore, they believe that the frontiers of faith are not impregnable, that they do yield to him who perseveres.

Such a cooperative study as this places in bold relief certain fundamental issues facing every serious-minded individual. It may serve a purpose to point out a few of them and to list them in order of deepening significance. They are, first, the age-old problem of the one and the many as it pertains to religious beliefs; second, the issue of the relative significance of belief and of faith; and third, what, after all, is religion, and who is a religious person. Let us look briefly at each of them.

We have mentioned the fact of the diversity and unity characterizing these essays. The reader will recall that the contrasts are not so striking in the realm of human attitudes and values as they are in the context in which these are interpreted. For instance, certain of the statements are conceived in a man-centered or humanistic framework, while others are construed in a God-focused or theistic frame. In the second place, and among the latter, there are those who conceive of God as dwelling "beyond" the cosmos and operating through it to reach spiritually handicapped human beings, and those who identify the activity of God with the value aspects of the natural world including man.

The humanist believes that man is solely responsible for his own moral and spiritual fate. Every person has therefore the ability to wrest out of his mundane habitat the values he requires to live the good, full life. As for the cosmos that environs him, it affords certain physical and psychological advantages to human beings, but it is indifferent to their quest for moral and religious undergirding. Values reside as potentials within the human stream of life and are achieved as men learn how to cultivate the bonds of mutual understanding, cooperative endeavor, and world brotherhood. Humanism presents a rugged, homocentric faith such as is inherent in a vibrant democracy.

The proponents of a theistic faith regard the humanist as being remiss at one focal point in his philosophy of life. He rejects belief in a divine reality transcending the plane of mankind, and thereby disregards man's primary mainstay of inspiration and help. From the viewpoint of the theist, the human spirit is akin to this reality, and the latter is available through the instrumentality of faith to every individual, and remains the source and fulfillment of all human values. It is referred to as "God," who has produced man, sustains him, and cooperates with him in overcoming evil and doing good. The theist conceives of faith in a socio-cosmic range of reference outdistancing the frame of the humanist.

There is also a sharp cleavage between the viewpoints of the theists who contribute to this symposium. They disagree chiefly as to their beliefs about the nature of ultimate spiritual reality and the manner of its communication with man. Some of them hew to the line of traditional Judaism and Christianity, affirming that God is concealed to "natural" man because of man's spiritual incompetence. Although He dwells beyond the time-space-energy compass of the natural world in an eternal order, He does take the initiative in seeking out his wayward children and making available to them the resources of a redemptive faith. This process of salvation is assumed to act primarily through the revelatory channel of religious institutions, although its consequences are supposed to affect the motivations of redeemed persons in all their human associations.

Another type of theist is also represented. He is a positivist, sharing with the humanist the conviction that man possesses the intrinsic capabilities to rise in the moral and spiritual scale. He is a naturalist in his approach to religious faith, believing that the dynamic cosmos including creative man is the locus of divine activity and the medium through which man discovers the ultimate meaning and purpose of human life. He is an immanentist in his philosophy of values. That is, he believes that they emerge in the course of everyday human experience as powerful assets of the inner life, insofar as the individual pursues the true, the good, and the beautiful in fellowship with other people and the "mysterious" universe, which undergirds them and him. The *summum bonum* in the hierarchy of potential values is God. God, who is man's peerless Other, transcends the understanding of man in two senses: His providential activity may operate in the widest ranges of superhuman reality (the cosmos) and it may focus in the individual or society in ways that exceed man's capacity to comprehend it. Finally, and like the scientist, this religious man is an empiricist. He assumes that all truth, including his convictions about human values, is subject to constant testing and restatement in the school of life. As any of his convictions are proved unfounded, or become inadequate, they are discarded in favor of beliefs that conform more consistently to the processes of clear thinking.

In the face of the divergence of religious viewpoints included in this anthology, an appropriate question is, What are the prospects for unity within this diversity? I think it can be affirmed that on the level of a formal statement of human faith there is no possibility of a unification of the points of view. The claims of the spokesmen and their assumptions are too scattered, and some are contradictory. However, this question in its present setting requires a second thought. If a wayfarer in life assumes for a moment that his spiritual convictions represent *the* truth which only is worthy of man's highest loyalty, then he is in danger of becoming a bigot and resorting to the censorship of those views which disagree with his position. He is disregarding the potent fact that the highway to reality is not a well-paved, royal road but comprises a multitude of tortuous paths emanating from divergent points and converging on remote mountain peaks of truth, goodness, and beauty. Human achievement is marked by progress in prehension throughout the scaling venture, rather than by easy pronouncements about religious finality. When an individual allows his attention to become monopolized by the discoveries that he is making, he not only fails to discern the grandeur and the majesty of the prospects ahead, but he is prone to consider the testimony of other pilgrims as inconsequential and perhaps as heretical.[1]

This observation leads directly to the second issue mentioned above: the relative significance of belief and of faith in man's religion. A few reflections upon this question will throw further light on the problem of the one and the many.

The criteria of belief are ideas and linguistic symbols which convey human thought. If any ideology or system of beliefs is made the final arbiter of faith, then men become hopelessly confused in their deliberations. The history of religion is strewn with a plethora of competitive systems of thought and divisive social institutions defending them. While a person's beliefs are meaningful for him and should be socially esteemed, at their best they still remain symbols and guideposts. They point to something more basic in human experience: attitudes and values which are the primary evidences of religious faith. They are the personal attitudes which an individual has learned to cherish toward values intrinsic in himself, society, and the universe. He commits himself to them as the priceless qualities of spiritual reality. For example, modern man has discovered the significance of the attitudes of reverence, love, fair play, and humility, and of the values of human dignity, good will among men, and God.

While persons may and do express beliefs about these realities and exchange ideas with respect to them, at their best moments they also engage in "a conversation of attitudes" with their fellows concerning the imponderable and imperishable values of human faith. This art of communication is maintained on the subverbal level. It taps immediately the wellsprings of the heart and the mind. True lovers are expert in this discipline with respect to each other; abiding friendships are nourished by the same process; and high religion, with its fellowship of kindred hearts dedicated cooperatively to the pursuit of the good life, also maintains this distinction. Here is a level of human intercourse transcending in importance that depending upon the instrumentality of formal language and the exchange of religious beliefs. This intercourse involves a vital enlistment of faith and reflects its first fruits. Thus the basic attitudes and values of

[1] Stewart G. Cole and Bernard Heller, "A Preface to Religious Pluralism," *Christendom,* Winter Number, 1944, pp. 69-76.

faith may, and often do, unite men of diverse ideologies in the bonds of a common life.

Here, then, lies the hope of high-minded men for religious unity within diversity. It is an achievement which many of us share occasionally. We can approach it more consistently as we learn to put first things first in our loyalty to goodness and truth. Edwin Markham captured the impulse when he wrote:

> He drew a circle that shut me out—
> Heretic, rebel, a thing to flout.
> But love and I had the wit to win:
> We drew a circle that took him in!
> —"OUTWITTED"[2]

The third issue raised above follows as a direct consequence of these reflections: What, after all, is religion and who is a religious person? Is he not the man who directs his developing life by the headlight of faith? He does not commit his course in human society and in the face of the mysterious universe by any specificity of beliefs, however profound and purposeful they may be. In the final analysis such beliefs are too rigid, arbitrary, and exclusive; they short-change the meaning and worth of life. The truly religious person interprets his finest ideas as he does other works of art. They are rough-hewn vehicles of reference. In their most refined form they serve to signalize spiritual realities transcending in worth and meaning every claim of social symbolism. Religion, for him, is the constellation of volitional attitudes he cherishes toward what he considers to be the most important values in life.

This man's primary "language" of religion consists of particular attitudes and corresponding values. The attitudes include such elements as those of human sensitivity, insight, and dedication to the pursuit of the highest and the best that is inherent in society and the universe. The values toward which these attitudes are directed point to such real, though intangible, forces as the innate human impulse to love, the immeasurable drive of human society to improve itself,

[2] From *The Shoes of Happiness and Other Poems* (New York: Doubleday Doran & Co., 1930). By permission of Virgil Markham.

and the potentialities of the cosmos available to man to meet every reasonable expectation of life.

Some of us believe that these fundamental values inherent in man, society, and the universe are aspects of the life and activity of God. We should recognize, however, that this is a belief subject to the limitations of linguistic symbolism. Certain of the essayists included in this study are unable to affirm such a conviction. That does not necessarily invalidate their sensitivity to the qualities of human enlistment which we regard as religious. Skepticism is a normal attitude of every devout person, active in his unfolding faith and with respect to a variety of subtle problems. It becomes a negating force, cutting at the very taproot of a man's religion, only when it shifts to a pattern of dogmatism, whether denying or affirming the reality of God and his providence in human life. Then this man substitutes the dead hand of dogma for the flickering light of a nascent faith. The trail of religion described in these pages is a hazardous highway. When a person lives religiously, he directs his life by the delicate instruments of an attitude-value structure of faith. However, the path is beautiful and inspiring, for is it not the road that God enlightens and the way to man's fulfillment of his heart's desire?

This book will accomplish its purpose if it succeeds in stimulating the reader to grapple with the same issues which have engaged its contributors. We hope that it inspires him to persevere everlastingly in the quest for the sinews of a viable faith. Verily, the person who keeps his mind and heart turned toward the eternal light shall see and understand. "For everyone that asketh receiveth; and he that seeketh findeth; and to him that knocketh it shall be opened."

S. G. C.